Soviet Communes

SOVIET
COMMUNES

Robert G. Wesson

Rutgers University Press · New Brunswick, New Jersey

This book was manufactured with the assistance
of a grant from the Ford Foundation

Acknowledgment

If this book has merit, much is owed to various members of the Russian Institute of Columbia University, especially Professor John N. Hazard, for numerous suggestions and comments at various stages of its development.

Contents

Soviet Communes

1 Introduction

In November, 1917, the Bolshevik Party, which a few months before had been a handful of conspirators and agitators, seized power in Russia. Lenin and his followers were so impractically extremist that the whole world was sure they could not long wield the power of the Tsars; in days or weeks they must be toppled, like the Paris Commune of 1871, bloodily liquidated as soon as the forces of order could take action.

The Bolsheviks were as radical as they had promised. A decree immediately abolished private ownership of land; thereafter, industry was gradually nationalized, and the government proclaimed, though ineffectively, the socialization of all commerce. Wages were nearly equalized and were paid mostly in rations. There was talk of abolishing money in preparation for the extinction of the state itself. There was an unprecedented attack on religion and "bourgeois" morals. But the acme of the Revolution was the commune, wherein "All belongs to all," in the words of an official enactment. In it, as nowhere else, the ideals of the Revolution were incarnated: brotherly living and working together in equality, and sharing all things freely without greed or envy, as in the communal societies dreamed by utopians of all times.

The Soviet State has grown strong under the rule of a Party calling itself "Communist," but the communes, symbols of communist ideals, have long since passed away. Very few were ever established in cities, and their numbers in the countryside remained far below the ardent hopes of their supporters. It soon became clear that these "seeds of communism" were not taking root and spreading, and they never attained economic importance. Within a few years they began to decline and were outnumbered by less communal associations. Only a thousand or so managed to survive the period of strategic retreat beginning in 1921 after the end of the civil war. In the first years of Stalinist mass collectivization, 1928 to 1930, the communes enjoyed a resurgence, but Stalin decided in 1930 that they were a form for the distant future, not the socialist present. Even those communes which had long been held up as models were degraded into the less fully collectivized form which has remained the rule for Soviet agriculture. As years passed by, the communes were slowly forgotten. Only recently, when the Chinese "People's Communes" revived the name and some of the features of the long defunct Soviet communes, have they been brought back to mind.

Why were communes established and then discarded? It is easy to assume that they were simply a Bolshevik notion which proved unworkable. But this is hardly correct. Communes were not on the Bolshevik agenda before the Revolution, and the top leadership never had great love for them. If they were merely impractical, it should not have required fifteen years to discover this. The story is much more complicated and cannot, with the evidence at hand, be fully clarified. However, even partial unravelling of it casts light upon the inner springs of the Bolshevik Revolution and the Soviet State.

The word *kommuna* came to Russian from French socialism. Free cities in the Middle Ages were called "Communes," and the term thus early acquired a popular-libertarian connotation. In the French Revolution, the local parishes were converted into communes with elected governing boards; many of these formed revolutionary committees. More important, the legal government of Paris was displaced in 1792 by an insurrectional commune, which led the movement to abolish the monarchy. For some months, relations between this radical body and the National Assembly were somewhat like those between the Petrograd Soviet and the Russian Provisional Government in 1917. But with the fall of Robespierre, the more conservative elements were victorious, the Commune was overcome, and many of its leaders were beheaded. In the nineteenth century, the term *commune* was used by French socialists, Proudhon, Cabet and others, to designate the unit cells of their ideal societies; it thereby acquired a utopian significance. In 1871 another Paris Commune established a short-lived socialist government which Lenin held up as the prototype of the Soviet State. Suppressed after a few weeks with much bitterness and many executions, it added greatly to the revolutionary aura of the word *commune,* which bespoke the height of fiery radicalism in Russian as well as in French socialist circles. Consequently, it was very popular in the first militant years of the Bolshevik Revolution. *Pravda,* the chief Party mouthpiece, often compared the Paris Commune with the Soviet State, and sometimes called the latter the "Russian Commune." It even wrote optimistically of the future "World Commune." (1) Young Communists (Party members) were frequently called "communards." On March 14, 1918, Petrograd was officially made the "Petrograd Workers' Commune," as *Pravda* expressed it, "proclaiming the unity, brotherhood and community of all peoples." But this was not a reorganization, only the flaunting of a name. Lenin, before the Revolution, also spoke loosely of communes as cells of the future order: "The socialist society of the future can rise only as a network of producer-consumer communes, conscientiously accounting for their production and consumption . . ." (2) But such communes or local governments had little to do with the communes of total sharing which later arose.

The Russian word *kommuna* thus had a range of significance from revolutionary local government to utopian community. On the other hand, it is necessary to distinguish clearly between two communes in Russian history. One was the commune of the Revolution, which, aside from largely rhetorical use in the first years, meant primarily a group which farmed and lived with more or less common property. This is the subject of the present study. The other was the old "village commune." Confusion arises in large part from the weakness of the English language, which has only a single translation for *kommuna* and *obshchina* as the village commune was usually called. In some ways, the village commune pointed to the Soviet commune, as discussed in Chapter III, but the institutions were quite distinct. The village commune for centuries had included practically all Russian peasants; it was usually just the old village as a corporate body. It continued to hold the bulk of Russian peasants until they were collectivized after 1929, and until then likewise most Soviet agricultural production was furnished by the peasants of the village communes. But only a fraction of one per cent of Russian peasants ever joined Soviet communes (and the number leaving the village communes to join other forms of collective farms was not over one or two per cent as long as they were quite voluntary).

There was also a great difference of kind between village communes and Soviet communes. The latter were far more equalitarian and collectivist. The village commune, although it usually divided the land, left its members relatively free to farm for themselves. Comparatively rich peasants, or kulaks, like others belonged to village communes. Moreover, the patriarchal, tradition-bound spirit of the village commune was a far cry from the utopianism of the Soviet communes; true radicals despised the one and exalted the other.

Despite these clear differences, Russian usage did not always distinguish clearly between *kommuna* and *obshchina*. The word *obshchina* also meant community and was applied to utopian socialist communities before the Revolution. At the time of the Revolution, anarchists and religious groups commonly called their societies *obshchiny* rather than *kommuny*, though they were very communistic in sharing. Even Soviet communards referred at times to their own societies as *obshchiny*, thus referring back to the old Russian village commune. It is a sign of their relatively Western orientation that the Bolsheviks preferred the foreign word *kommuna*.

The Soviet communes cannot be satisfactorily defined, as they were far from uniform. Frequently, they had a utopian purpose of instituting an order without property; generally, they were marked by a strong spirit of equality and collectivism. The significantly brief article of Vol. 22 of the *Great Soviet Encyclopedia* (1953) has the following to say about "Agricultural Commune":

"A form of agricultural producers' cooperative, one of the forms of collective farm, cooperative peasant producers' enterprise of socialist type. In contrast to the agricultural artel, all means of production without exception are collectivized: buildings, tools, cattle, fields, etc. Members of the commune do not carry on individual production. Their consumption and daily needs are fully cared for by the collective.

"In the first years of Soviet rule, the communes were the dominant form of collective farm. They were organized chiefly on former estate and monastery lands. They also received from the proletarian government without charge living quarters, farm buildings and equipment, as well as other forms of assistance. The first communes were largely composed of city workers returning to the country, Red partisan fighters, and leading elements of the most proletarianized poor peasants and farm laborers. Later, other forms of collective farms came to occupy a dominant role. In 1921, communes were about 15 per cent of all collective farms. As the collective farm movement developed, it appeared that, in conditions of technical backwardness and limited production, the commune was a less viable form than the agricultural artel; consequently, the communes changed into artels."

To what extent this is an adequate account of the communes may be judged from subsequent chapters. It is useful, in any case, to contrast the communes with the less fully collectivized artels which eventually replaced them and became the sole form of Soviet collective farm or kolkhoz. The general distinction was that the commune was more radical, antiproperty, and in favor of collective living. The commune wanted to supersede the individual households. An artel should hold the principal means of production—plowland, horses, and major tools—and its members farmed jointly; but they maintained their individual households. There was also another form which for a time outnumbered both artels and communes. This was called the "fellowship for joint cultivation" or "fellowship for collective working of the land"; from the initials of its title in Russian (*tovarishchestvo po obshchestvennoi obrabotke zemli*) it was labelled "toz". (Although this designation appeared only late in its career, it is here used for convenience throughout.) The tozes were still less collective than artels, perhaps carrying out cooperatively only the main field tasks and having little common property.

Commune, artel, and toz thus formed a series in descending order of collectivism or, as it was long considered, in descending order of socialist perfection and political desirability. The commune most fully absorbed the life of its members and the toz least. But the division was not clearcut; especially in the first years, the categories merged and overlapped.

Commune, artel, and toz were all called collective farms or kolkhozes. Associations of peasants, they were in theory always self-governing and voluntary and in practice were so until the government applied stronger and stronger pressures for collectivization toward the end of the 1920's. Their harvest (after exactions) was their own, to be divided among the members. With them may be contrasted the state farms or sovkhozes. These were formally government agencies, with appointed managers and hired workers, like industrial enterprises. Most important from the point of view of the peasant, they paid regular wages. Generally, the sovkhozes were quite as distinct from kolkhozes in practice as they were in theory.

The significance of the communes lay in their social radicalism. The ideal commune was dedicated to the joys of sharing: members worked together without pay, ate at a common table, and lived in a dormitory. They had no use for money; everything but clothing, and sometimes even that, was collective property. According to an early pamphlet, "In the commune, everybody works and is expected to contribute according to his capacities, and everybody receives according to his needs and requirements, that is, equally, since all are equal and are in equal conditions of life and labor." (3) The much repeated motto was, "Brotherhood and equality." Of course, most communes fell far short of perfection. In the first years of civil war and economic breakdown, it was difficult to set up the material arrangements. Later, the communes tended to lapse under the pressures of human nature, of a market economy around them, and, subsequently, of Soviet policy. But they always stressed collectivism and equality.

From first to last, the communes were extremely varied in their degree of communism, in their size, wealth, organization, and even their politics. However, one might imagine the history of a hypothetical commune about as follows: In 1919 a dozen peasants without sufficient stock to benefit from the division of estates and an equal number of workers driven by hunger and unemployment from the city made themselves at home on what remained of the local manor, moved into old buildings, and called themselves the Proletarian Way Commune. The local soviet loaned them a hundred rubles and provided a few head of confiscated livestock; with these, they began farming, living on government rations, like city workers, until the first harvest.

The Proletarian Way led a rough existence indeed for the first years. Everything was badly organized and crops were poor. Several times anti-Soviet peasants or White bands attacked the commune before 1923. Leaders were drafted for military or other Soviet or Party duty. All produce over the barest subsistence needs was requisitioned by the government. There was a huge turnover of membership, communards withdrawing in large numbers especially before the busy season. There were endless dissensions; one even led to the dissolution and subsequent reorganization of the Proletarian Way.

When the civil war ended, the Soviet leadership felt driven to strategic retreat. Trade, especially in agricultural products, was largely set free and considerable free enterprise was permitted in the economy. The communes gained more freedom to sell their grain and manage their own affairs; but now the communards found themselves no longer so highly regarded as élite pioneers of the new order. Morale fell. Some said the whole idea was a mistake and returned to individual farming. The ex-workers drifted back to the city as slowly reviving industry promised jobs. What little assistance the Soviet authorities had once given was replaced by indifference. Still, with reduced membership, the Proletarian Way crept along, gradually gained experience and some stability. With a few fair harvests, the economy improved enough for the communards to shed some of their rags and acquire such luxuries as plates in the dining room and iron cribs in the nursery.

After 1925, Soviet officials again became attentive, bestowing small loans and other favors. In 1926, the commune even acquired a Fordson tractor. Life seemed to be getting better, but prosperity was diluted by an influx of indigent peasants. Meanwhile, the commune was becoming less communal. Years earlier the communards had ceased trying to provide everyone with all the clothing he needed, and instead they gave allowances from which members paid for clothes and other minor needs. They also instituted cash prizes for outstanding work. At length, the commune, while feeding and housing all alike and taking full care of non-workers, was even paying small wages with which members could buy what they pleased.

Talk of collective agriculture grew louder after 1927, and the communes again found themselves, as in 1918-19, in the ideological vanguard. Collective farms were given more advantages, and peasants were ever more insistently pressed to join. The Proletarian Way was soon bursting at the seams, and swollen with new applicants, until, for lack of space, it had to shut its doors. More and more peasant parties were herded through to inspect its fields and crop rotations, its barns and machinery, and its strange living arrangements. Communards were called to organize new collective farms, and, as the Party drove for full collectivization in late 1929 and early 1930, the Proletarian Way found itself surrounded by many junior communes and artels. Many of these artels were virtually communes, as peasants were required upon joining to give up their household plots and all livestock, including chickens. Then, in March, 1930, Stalin called a halt to frantic and extreme collectivization and made it clear that the artel, not the commune, was to be regarded as the proper form for an indeterminate time. The Proletarian Way came, like all collective farms, under more and more direct Soviet administrative control. It was required to adopt the same arrangements for incentive pay as artels, to pay out most of its net product instead of providing collective consumption, and to allow members to have their own household garden plots and limited livestock. It thus ceased to be a commune and recognized this fact by adopting the artel model statute in 1933.

Utopianism

The institution of the commune cannot be understood as a Russian peculiarity, as though a freak of the Slavic soul. In most lands of the civilized world there have been numerous experiments in communal living with more or less parallels and similarities to the Soviet communes. Some resulted from revolutionary flareups, but others were quite nonpolitical. Almost all, of course, have failed, breaking down, or retreating to milder forms of cooperation. A few, however, have shown considerable vitality and firm attachment to communistic living, in this respect outdoing most Soviet communes.

A glance at the better-known non-Russian communes should give a better perspective on the Soviet communes. The principal causes leading men to live in close association in the West all operated to some degree in post-Revolutionary Russia. There were similar irritants and problems in trying to reconcile ideals and realities. There was also ideological influence, since persons of revolutionary mood in Russia as elsewhere drew instruction and inspiration from radical ventures of the past. Furthermore, the analogy of the non-Russian communes is helpful because the writers on whom we must rely for information about Soviet communes are regrettably uninformative about social and psychological problems.

Three main urges, usually intermingled, have led men to form communal societies: the utopian dream of a happier life of brotherhood and justice without the poison of envy and unequal possession to divide spirits; the more materialistic desire to join closely for strength of unity and organization, especially in meeting extraordinary difficulties, as in pioneer life; and the religious urge toward a life of unselfish virtue pleasing to God. Other currents are less clearly definable: desire for economic security, emotional satisfaction of the close group, alienation from the mercenary and unfriendly world, or sheer gregariousness.

Plato was the inventor of utopia. In his *Republic* he drew up a blueprint for the perfect society, wherein not only property but the children of the élite were collectivized to avoid private ambitions. His vision was in large part inspired by the example of semicommunist Sparta, which had some communal eating and communal child-rearing for the aristocrats, but none of the equalitarianism so general in communisms. Of Plato's numerous imitators, virtually all, even worldly, successful men like Sir Thomas More, banished private property from their dream-worlds. Typical is the view of Campanella in *The City of the Sun* that inequality and poverty render men ignoble, that moral perfection can be sought only in common ownership. In general, the utopian holds that man is naturally good until degraded by property and other vices of civilization and that a new golden age will shine in the simplicity and purity of common ownership.

Of the many attempts to make real such dreams, perhaps the most celebrated were those of Robert Owen, who sacrificed a good portion of his hard-earned fortune to New Harmony (Indiana, 1825). That this community admitted all comers indiscriminately was enough to doom it, but labor indiscipline seems to have been the direct cause of downfall. Daily dances were well attended, but workers failed to show up at their jobs. Recriminations arose. Moral sanctions were the only admissible compulsion in the perfect society, but publishing the hours worked by each proved weak, and dissolution followed. (1) Somewhat more enduring was the Icarian experiment of Étienne Cabet (Texas, 1848), perhaps the only utopian colony ever founded by a utopian writer. This floundered on property instincts. There were quarrels over who got what, and the members, supposed to own nothing, accumulated such things as stores of wine made from community grapes. Through divisions and reorganizations, however, the Icarian society managed to exist for several decades and eventually become a joint-stock company.(2) The Llano Colony (California, 1914, later Louisiana) is of some interest in that the founder, Harriman, claimed to be a Marxist. Members worked together on the land and in small shops; housing, food and services were furnished according to need. Households lived separately and could, if they wished, take their food away from the common table. The community suffered from factionalism and declining membership until it dissolved in financial ruin in 1939.(3) Note may also be taken of a small colony established by a Russian anarchist in Southern France, somewhat similar in spirit to and contemporaneous with a Russian free-thinking commune, Krinitsa, founded on the Black Sea coast in 1880. In the anarchist colony, named the Society for the Creation of a Free Environment, work was to be done according to conscience; love was free; and children belonged to the society. Dedicated to utter freedom, after three years it broke up in bitter charges of dictatorship.(4)

As such examples indicate, the record of utopian communism is bleak. However, the attempts have called attention to their ideas. Owenism particularly contributed to the crystallization of socialist thinking in Western Europe, and through Marx and Engels (who, of course, rejected the utopian approach) indirectly influenced Russian Marxist communism. How much direct influence the utopians may have had upon Russian thinking is doubtful, but it was not negligible. The students and idealists who established the Krinitsa colony discussed at length the utopian socialists, especially Owen and St. Simon, and thought highly of them. A leading Russian economist, Tugan-Baranovskii, published a glowing account of communistic communities a few years before the Revolution; his *In Search of a New World* was much cited. At the time of the Revolution, Sergei Maslov, once Minister of Agriculture under Kerenskii, was at pains to draw lessons for socialized agriculture from utopian and other communities.(5)

Practical Communism

If some founded perfect communities in hopes that they might serve as models for the reconstruction of the evil world, others have looked to practical benefits: by uniting efforts, "One for all and all for one," men can more effectively fight or plow. The besieged city is necessarily collectivist, and hard times often drive even hardy individualists to the shelter of the group. Pioneering conditions are particularly favorable for communistic joining: partly, because old homes and habits are left behind, more, because of the necessity for joint effort. A good example is the Plymouth Colony in Massachusetts, in which, according to Governor Bradford, the land was at first farmed collectively, food and clothes were distributed equally, and cooking and laundering were done in common. Such arrangements may have helped the colony get started but soon met with the complaints to be expected: bachelors objected to working for other men's families; the strong and industrious felt they were carrying the less productive; the "aged and graver men" grumbled that they were demeaned; wives disliked serving men not their husbands. After three years, land was allotted to each to raise his own, and this "made all hands very industrious."(6)

It is significant that, while the modish "New Harmony," on which Owen lavished funds and attention, was a lamentable failure, the Owenite cooperative community organized by Irish tenant farmers, "Ralahine," had a splendid record. It is said that the members (who called themselves a "commune") showed great zeal in work, progressed admirably, and made advances in the use of machinery. A good economic purpose was here worth more than high-flown visions. The demise of the experiment came from no fault of the farmers, but a fortuitous capitalistic mishap: the owner of the land rented by the community held very bad cards one evening, and the new owner had no sympathy for radical economics.(7)

In a number of cases, governments have sponsored more or less collectivist farms to cope with hardship. Australia, in the Great

Depression, attempted communal farms for the unemployed, with the poor results that might have been expected.(8) The United States Department of Agriculture likewise set up a number of cooperative farms for relief of distressed tenant farmers. Pay was semi-equalitarian, generally on a straight work-time basis. As many as twenty-two were in existence before Congress liquidated them in 1943. In Italy, early in this century, landless agricultural laborers sought to help themselves by forming cooperatives to rent land. Some tilled individually; others, especially those dominated by socialists, had joint cultivation. There have been other experiments in joint farming in Spain, Scandinavia, and elsewhere.

Such associations for peasant mutual help, however less radical than Soviet communes, underline the economic functions of the latter. Russian peasants sometimes formed communes during the times of civil war because they were hungry and lacked equipment with which to farm. Similarly, drought in the Volga region in 1924-25 produced hundreds of communes, because in a commune the peasant could hope to survive when there were no horses for individual plowing.(9)

The Mexican ejidos aimed primarily at helping the small cultivator through cooperation. They showed some striking parallels to the Soviet communes, arising as a by-product of the Revolution of 1911 and the seizure of haciendas by peons, and deriving inspiration from ancient native communal traditions. It was claimed at one time that many ejidos were operating "with the greatest success upon purely communistic principles" of free sharing.(10)

Evidently, then, the Mexican Revolution gave birth to at least a few full communes. However, Mexico was not so radical as Russia, and the government gave little support to communism in the ejidos. In 1922, the leftists proposed a law which would have attacked private property in land and sponsored communal farming. But the conservatives carried the day, and the law enacted provided for individual cultivation under government protection, although ejidos were allowed to cultivate cooperatively if they chose. The number so doing increased to about 5,000 under the presidency of Lázaro Cárdenas (elected 1934), but even in collective ejidos consumption remained largely individual, and members, as in the Soviet artels, had their own pigs and poultry. Payment was usually by days worked, with equal shares of profits. The customary administrative structure was extraordinarily similar to that prescribed by the Soviet commune model statute: the assembly of members elected an executive committee of three (chairman, secretary, treasurer) and a supervisory committee, also of three.

The ejidos have not come up to the high expectations which they once aroused, but they have survived in substantial numbers. A visitor in 1953 thought that the standard of living, although varying widely among ejidos, averaged higher than that of the individual peons. But he noted an inclination to take advantage of better farming methods not so much to produce more for sale as to enjoy more relaxation.(11) A similar proclivity in Soviet communes helped to bring about their ultimate rejection.

Religious Communism

A third drive toward communal living involves a rejection of worldly values, a religious drive, or one expressed in religious terms. Of all communistic communities, the religious have been by far the most numerous and stable; this is not surprising as devotion to a faith can hardly be shown more emphatically than by renouncing conflicting interests—above all, family and property. Commonly, renunciation extends to sexual relations and leads to monastic orders. These would seem a far cry from Soviet communes, but semireligious impulses cannot be entirely excluded from worldly communisms and economic motives probably have had something to do with the background of the convents. Kautsky, for example, held that the original orders began in the early Middle Ages as unions of the poor seeking cooperative subsistence. However, noncelibate communisms are more instructive concerning Soviet communes.

Christian communism has a venerable history going back to the first Christian brotherhoods and even to the Essenes who preceded them. The passage in Acts 2: 44-46, much cited by Russian Sectarians, records: "And all that believed were together and had all things common; And sold their possessions and goods, and parted them to all men, as every man had need, And they, continuing daily with one accord in the temple, and breaking bread from house to house, did eat their meat with gladness and singleness of heart." This bespeaks a communism not of production but of consumption wherein the faithful gave freely to each other. Similarly, Acts 4: 34-35 states that all those who owned houses or land sold them and brought the proceeds and "laid them down at the apostles' feet: and distribution was made unto every man according as he had need." (Hence the communist motto, "To each according to his need.") The communism of charity did not long endure in the early church; but when, time and again, heresies arose in ancient and medieval times—Gnostics, Albigensians, Waldesians, Hussites, *et al.*—they uniformly denounced wealth and called for a return to some sort of communism, at least for the elect.(12)

These various heretical communisms, many of which are poorly known, may be passed over; but mention should be made of the first to achieve a powerful organization, that of the Taborites in Bohemia in the early fifteenth century. Proclaiming brotherly and sisterly equality, "No mine and thine, but all in common," they gained phenomenal military victories over much superior forces and so succeeded in holding off the feudal powers of Central Europe for a generation. (They have in fact been credited with organizing the first modern army.)(13) Of similar antipapal inspiration were the communistic Anabaptists who came to the fore in Germany a century later. In peasant uprisings they briefly controlled Münster and some other towns but never had sufficient peace to build their society. Engels considered them important enough as precursors of socialism to give them a sizable book, his *Peasant War in Germany*.

Many religious groups in Russia have shown communistic tendencies; those, having a direct bearing on the Soviet communes, will be considered in the next chapter. In the West, the United States was privileged during the nineteenth century to have the largest number of communistic colonies. Because of the liberality of its government and the availability of good land, this country was favored by both secular and religious communities; but the latter have had far more vitality. A survey in 1939 showed that half of the nonreligious communities came to grief in the first year, only 3 per cent lasted as long as 25 years, and none as long as 50 years. (14) Methusalahs among communities were the Shakers (1778-1940), the Rappists (1805-1905), and Amana (1842-1932, when it changed to a cooperative). The first two solved the question of family relations under communism by celibacy, although both sexes were admitted. They could be successful only so long as religious feeling brought in recruits.

If celibate denial is one obvious answer to the family-community conflict, an alternative is freedom of sexual relations. "Free love" was practiced successfully by the "Oneida Perfectionists" from 1848 to 1879; they felt that selfish possession of a person was as reprehensible as of material goods. It is significant that when, in 1879, the community felt constrained by public opinion to give up "common marriage," the residue of economic communism lasted only two years. The community then became a producers' cooperative.

As a successful "normal" community, Amana warrants more attention. Although the group was united by religion and left Germany partly for religious reasons, their principles did not dictate communism. Rather, they adopted it to maintain the integrity of the society when, in Iowa, men began drifting away to outside employment. Though religious feeling subsequently declined, it served at least to moderate the material desires of members; while the momentum of community living, once soundly established, was enough to maintain it. Members ate together, but had, as in the Soviet artel, individual houses with gardens. For minor purchases at the community store, they received cash allowances of $25 to $50 yearly, the amount depending partly upon work done. Amana was satisfactorily prosperous for a long time. The products of the handicraft shops enjoyed a reputation for excellent quality, but the society did not care to push sales or make a large profit. The rule was, in effect, "Take it easy." They worked at a leisurely pace and enjoyed a long midday rest and five good meals a day. Workers in the shops kept flowers in vases and had easy chairs at hand for ready rest. Eventually, this comfortable living in the midst of a commercial civilization broke down. Indolence became excessive, and the community had to hire outside labor to get jobs done (a sign of labor discipline problems seen in many Soviet communes). Some members were rueful of the transformation into a business-like cooperative but recognized that it could be avoided only by escaping to a more isolated spot.(15)

The Hutterites

The most interesting of religious communistic settlements are the Hutterite Brotherhoods. They have existed over four hundred years and prosper to this day, the oldest and stablest of all noncelibate communities. Arising in Bohemia early in the sixteenth century, the Hutterites were long persecuted and compelled to migrate hither and thither in Central Europe. Late in the eighteenth century they moved to Russia; in 1874, to avoid military service, they went to North Dakota. For the same reason, a majority moved to Canada during the First World War. As of 1954 they had about 120 villages with close to 10,000 inhabitants.

Hutterite communism is said to have begun in 1526 when a group of radical Protestants was fleeing from harassment. Four leaders spread out a mantle by the roadside and, like the Apostles, invited all to lay their worldly wealth thereon. Subsequently some groups deviated to limited communism; all such were soon wrecked by dissensions and disappeared. For a period in Hungary the main group gave up communal living, and again they did so for a few years during their Russian residence. In both cases they fell into a decline from which they recovered upon returning to pure communism. Pure and strict their communism remains, permitting no private households and no property, even of clothing. Children from age two and a half spend days in the nursery, although they sleep with their parents. Of necessity, the colonies buy and sell collectively, but they consider buying for resale or loaning at interest to be sinful.

The relation of their communism to their religion is unclear. Formally they are associated with the Mennonites, but the latter interpret the famous passages of Acts as suggesting whole-hearted charity, not communal living. The Hutterite religion is reported to be, in fact, rather dry and formal. Stress is on the "Hutterite way of life"; their religion is primarily a way of living, and the central beliefs concern life in the community.

The Hutterites have flourished. Partly because of frugality, they accumulate capital to buy the latest in farm machinery or outbid private farmers for land. Labor discipline seems to be no problem; they work earnestly and well, though without haste or compulsion, and very few complaints are heard that anyone fails to do his share. Crime of any kind is rare, and divorce unknown. Even mild quarreling is said to be infrequent, and suicide has never occurred. There are few symptoms of mental illness. Most Hutterites must be tolerably satisfied with the "way": though about a twentieth of the men leave the colonies at some time (aside from youths drafted for military service), nearly all of these return; and women almost never depart. As of 1957, only about a hundred had defected in the past thirty years.

Several factors seem to have combined to give the Hutterite Brotherhoods much more coherence than outwardly similar groups. One is the homogeneity of membership; members are born into the group and carefully educated in Hutterite tradition and ideals. Another is the insistence on isolation. Colonies go out into the desolate prairies and live, as far as humanly possible, to themselves. In Hutterite villages in Canada, some demoralization and disorganization have become evident; this is in inverse relation to the distance from the large city of Winnipeg. In colonies within twenty miles of the city, some begin to think of appropriating money for trips to town; women are infected with interest in stylish clothes; men shave their necks (all grow beards after marriage) or put on modern garb. On the other hand, villages far from the city lights escape corruption.

Also important is the close, family-like organization. Leadership is patriarchal; authority is informal. Decision-making is primarily a matter of talk, hashing things over until a consensus is reached. Thus the use of buttons instead of hooks may be broached by a few; when the rest swing around to accepting this modernism, the change is made. The internal accounting system is crude, but adequate for their simple life.

Informality and reliance on good will are possible only because colonies are kept small; a vital Hutterite institution is the splitting of villages. As soon as any colony approaches a hundred souls (and they grow rapidly, as the reproductive rate is near the biological maximum), it is divided into halves by lot. One half goes out, like a swarm from a crowded beehive, to found a new colony. Consequently, the average size is about eighty. Insistence on keeping colonies small and isolated is in contrast to the practice of Amana, which had villages of several hundred, surrounded, in densely settled Iowa, by drive-ins and noisy highways; this may be the great key to Hutterite success.(16) The average size of Soviet communes was similar, and small communes proved to be the most viably communistic.

Israeli Kibbutzim

The three main motifs of communistic communities entered into the kibbutz movement: they were held up as examples of an improved social order; they were formed by impoverished immigrants to meet pioneering hardships; they were inspired by Jewish religious nationalism. But formal religion was of secondary importance in their inspiration, and they were based upon socialistic ideology; hence they present close parallels with Soviet communes. They were not a few isolated villages, but a substantial movement roughly contemporaneous with Soviet communes, though preceding and outlasting them. From humble beginnings in the Palestine of 1907, they expanded to about 20,000 members in 79 settlements in 1940, and to over 60,000 members in over 200 settlements in 1954. At both dates they accounted for a third or more of Jewish-Israeli agricultural production.

The ideology of the kibbutz movement is variably compounded of Zionism, revolt against ghetto traditions, and utopian and Marxian socialism. Some kibbutzim are Orthodox Jewish, but most are anticlerical, and a few positively atheistic. Prime movers were young Jewish intellectuals of Eastern Europe who read Marx and Engels along with Proudhon and Robert Owen, and alloyed socialism with biblical precepts and Jewish tradition. Russian ideas played some part also. The founders of the first settlement,

Dagania, came from the town of Romni, east of Kiev, and at first, while merely a group of laborers, called themselves "The Commune of Romni." It was after a Russian writer, Soloviev, visited them for two days that they debated establishing a collective farm. Memories of Russian village commune and artel also influenced them.(17)

The real impetus to kibbutz communism, however, came from the realities of life in Palestine. Jews in Russia did not have village communes, and despite great poverty were strongly averse to artel associations in Tsarist times.(18) Some Jews formed kolkhozes after the Revolution—about 25,000 souls went into 207 Jewish collective farms in the Ukraine, 89 in Belorussia and 21 in the North Caucasus—but these were mostly artels. Unlike their co-nationals in Palestine, Jews in Russia formed few communes.(19)

At first, the Commune of Romni expected to retain private property, working cooperatively and dividing the profits. But there were no profits to divide, and they felt driven to a maximum of cooperation to fight at once against drought, waterlogging, disease, and Arabs. Hence they decided to eliminate ownership within their group. Their motto became the utopian, "From each according to his ability, to each according to his need," although their forms continued to develop in response to concrete situations.

Other kibbutzim similarly grew into a highly collectivized way of life. The land, owned first by the Jewish National Fund and then by the Israeli nation, was nominally rented for 99 years with an observance of the biblical declaration that, when the children of Israel received Canaan, the land remained the Lord's. In the kibbutz there are no wages; food, clothing, and housing are furnished without charge. In the early days often not much more than toothbrushes was privately owned. In the drive for absolute equality, some groups even tried complete communism in clothing: each took a garment from the top of the pile. This led to ludicrous misfits; the next step was to give each his proper size, and let him use a garment until it wore out. It was observed, of course, that some went through their clothes much more rapidly than others. The remedy was sometimes persuasion to care for clothes, sometimes rationing: so many shirts and pants per year for men, so many dresses and blouses for women.

For sundry personal needs there are small allowances, as in Amana. If a member travels out, he is granted additional sums according to necessity; demands are said to have been modest. The kibbutz also tries to provide small luxuries within the capacity of its budget: toys for children, musical instruments for the talented, books for students. Entrants turn over their property, but upon leaving ordinarily take with them only what is in their immediate personal possession. (Soviet communes began with this rule, but were compelled to retreat from it.) Similarly, if a member works outside the kibbutz, he should give his salary to it, except for his expenses.

Married couples have separate rooms, but children are largely cared for by the kibbutz, and very well, it would seem: the youngsters get the meat, dessert, and vacation trips, while the parents drudge and do without. In some kibbutzim the children live, or at least sleep, with their parents; in others, from an early age they live in "children's homes;" some parents are said to prefer this for practical convenience. In general there is a great attempt to maintain equality, simplicity, and a big-family spirit.(20)

Along with economic goes social equality. Ideally, managerial positions are supposed to rotate among the whole membership. (Such democratic rotation was also tried in some Soviet communes.) But in practice, responsible posts are likely to be confined to a small fraction. However, manual labor has higher prestige than administrative, and managers are not relieved of their regular duties. Hence, there is considerable reluctance to assume major responsibilities, and officers usually have to be drafted. But time and advancing economies erode pristine democracy: as more and more specialized knowledge is needed, the majority tend to leave matters to the expert few. Elections come to be automatic confirmations; one group becomes accustomed to giving orders, another to receiving them.(21)

Thus, neither economic gain nor ambition serves to stimulate kibbutz members to work well. Nor are shirkers subject to more than public disapproval, possibly a reprimand or a threat to discuss the fault in the assembly; only in the last rare extremity may they be expelled. Observers agree, however, that kibbutz members do exert themselves, and sometimes extremely hard; work may become a veritable compulsion. Absence leads to guilty feelings, despite heat and blisters. Even a foreign researcher felt burdened with shame when he took time off to write up his notes.(22) At times, overzealous workers may embarass the kibbutz economy by eagerness to get tools or supplies, as in the case of the pig-raiser who deprived the chickenhouse of feed. Supervision of work is slack, with an honor system of checking in and out; yet it is said that workers often overstay their hours. Shirking and malingering apparently are minimal. However, a recent (1959) observer finds devotion to the general welfare less compulsive on the part of those who resist being shifted to less desirable work; for example, a tractor driver would pretend to keep busy to avoid assignment to the dairy.(23)

Several reasons are cited for this earnest, at times almost fanatic devotion to labor. There has been an emotional revulsion against the one-time exclusion of Jews from all but commercial occupations, with consequent exaggerated esteem for manual labor. Hence, prestige is to be gained only through hard work—an advantage for the kibbutz missed by the Soviet commune. Another reason is the attachment of workers to specialties or branches, in the results of which they take pride; there is also competition with other kibbutzim. (One is reminded of the "socialist competition" the Soviet regime has been at great pains to promote in and between collective farms.) Group awareness is also important. Socially conscious members realize that the welfare of all depends upon the group; they fear that their bad example may hurt and hope that their good example may help their kibbutz. They appreciate the economic and social security it gives and wish to render their best efforts in return. As one said, "Somehow collective responsibility and the desire to be a productive force and a creative individual within my group have proved to be stronger motives than the prospect of remuneration for my personal pocket."(24)

That the kibbutzim in general have been rather successful economically is undeniable. Their long-continued growth in numbers has been impressive. All had to be subsidized at first, but most of them became fully self-sustaining after a few years. Their work in reclaiming land, in accommodating immigrants, and building up model farms, which were often combined with forts, has been vital to the new state of Israel. Living in the kibbutzim was at first a test of resolution, but they have gradually been able to soften the rigors and even to introduce comforts such as radios and heaters in every room. The kibbutzim have done well, also, in competition with the less highly collectivized agricultural cooperatives, the moshav villages. The moshav is somewhat like the Soviet toz: settlers have their own land, houses, and cattle, but cultivate and use machinery collectively. The two forms have coexisted for many years. For a long time the more communal kibbutz gained over the more individualistic moshav, but in recent years new immigrants, less dedicated to community life, have been going preferentially to the moshavim. In brief, it seems that the kibbutz has been remarkably successful in achieving the advantages of cooperative working and living without falling prey to the troubles that usually beset such utopian ventures.

However, even enthusiasts recognize that there are problems in the kitbbutz. Although some claim that parent-child relations are relieved of worry, boredom, and conflict, the separation of parents and children has grieved many, especially women. Not all appreciate the new style of married life, supposed to be a leisure-time and so unblemished relation free from artificiality and economic stress. The rejection of conventional moralities (it has been usual, for instance, to forego formalities of marriage; the fond couple would merely signify the desire to share a room) has not come easily to all. Women often yearn for their own home. The single job to which they may be assigned—most often cooking, sewing, or cleaning—is boring and low in prestige. They lack the importance and security of the homemaker. Hence turnover has been high, up to 25 per cent yearly in some kibbutzim, and it is usually the women who want to leave or who remain only for the sake of their husbands. Similarly, in the Soviet communes it was the women who most disliked the household arrangements supposed to emancipate them.

There has also been a decline of the kibbutz spirit of earlier days. Human vanity emerges in dressing, although makeup is slow to find acceptance. Greater prosperity has brought inroads of private property, as some members get valuable gifts from outside, e.g. refrigerators or record players. Formerly, it was the convention to spend evenings in the collective leisure of the common room; now members are inclined to drift in small groups to their own quarters, and may even take meals out of the dining room. The hiring of labor, a sign of some failure of the voluntary system, has become accepted in many kibbutzim. Weakening of community spirit shows up in low attendance at assemblies; while once nearly 100 per cent, it may now be only half. Thus comes a gradual demoralization and undermining of the glowing ideals of tougher days.

In the face of this creeping decadence, there are some favorable aspects. Discontent is often directed less at the basic institutions of group ownership than at the continuing lack of amenities. Poor rooms, bad showers, lack of walls and furniture are less tolerable now that the crisis is past; but such shortcomings the kibbutz can reasonably hope to ameliorate.

More fundamental is the fact that backsliding seems to be largely on the part of the older generation, which, after long years of sacrifice and self-denial, tends to revert to the values to which it was educated. Those born in the kibbutz show less tendency to accumulate property and usually lead the opposition to concessions to private ownership. Likewise, if older women doubt the desirability of collective child care, the younger seem to accept it wholeheartedly.(25) Women find it harder to adapt to kibbutz life than men, just as women were the most passionate opponents of collectivization in the Soviet Union. But among the Hutterites, women adhere to the communal way even more firmly than men. This suggests that the psychological difficulties of women in the close collective may derive from feminine conservatism in family relations which may not trouble the next generation.

Of a kibbutz founded in 1920 and studied in 1956 it was reported that no one raised entirely within it had ever abandoned it.(26) Not only are the kibbutz youth sheltered from contrary indoctrination, but they enjoy excellent treatment and may even be spoiled. They sometimes revolt when at age eighteen they are sent to the adult dining room and the poorer fare of their elders. It may be difficult for them to think of facing the insecurities and competitive hurly-burly of the big world after a coddled childhood, just as defection for a Hutterite means a dreadful leap into loneliness.

While the kibbutz can lay hopes on its coming generation, its future is shadowed by external factors. The stream of suitable immigrants, Zionist-inspired, educated but poor, purposeful, has dried up. Now neither the backward Jew from Yemen, to whom the kibbutz is incomprehensible, nor the European Jew whose fortunes have declined and who looks for a comfortable continuation in Israel of the old life is likely to wish to enter a kibbutz or to be welcomed there.(27)

At the same time, the place of the kibbutz in Israeli society has declined. Its usefulness as a recipient of immigrants and pioneers for Israeli settlement has largely evaporated. Financial backers who were never charmed with its social radicalism have tended to withdraw support. The government, at least in the estimation of kibbutz leaders, is no longer so friendly as it was when it badly needed their cooperation in securing the borders. In short, the kibbutz, having come up a hard road, no longer clearly sees the way ahead. But even if its great days lie behind it, one must marvel indeed that the full commune of the kibbutz, with no ideological backing from outside and little material support, rose so much more gloriously than Soviet communes.

Generalities

Even a hasty survey of communistic and near-communistic experiments offers some obvious lessons. One is that they have a strong bent to farming. With rare exceptions, modern communistic communities have been agricultural. Even town folk, wishing to set up a utopian colony, hie themselves to the country. There are practical reasons. Anyone can raise things, or, before the day of scientific mechanized agriculture, could presume himself capable of farming. More important, farmers are still the most self-sufficient people left in the world, and any group desirous of keeping uncontaminated by buying and selling no more than necessary must be farmers first of all. Only on the land is the communal life a practical possibility in the midst of a noncommunistic environment.

There is also an idealistic motive: growing animals and plants and working with nature is pure and ennobling compared with the degradation, exploitation, and artificiality of the city; it is healthful, productive physical labor and satisfies rebellious souls. As a Soviet newspaper wrote of an early commune, "The farmer's work is best loved, as through it one earns direct from nature the necessities of human existence, avoiding in the clearest and most definite way the exploitation of man by man."(28) The Soviet communes, like similar institutions elsewhere, were nearly all agricultural, although the Bolshevik Revolution was based upon the urban proletariat and the city workers were more accessible to communist ideology. There were, to be sure, in 1918 and again in 1930, some city communes of students or workers, but they seem to have been few and ephemeral.

If communes are naturally agricultural, they are not formed by a decision of small farmers to pool their own land and resources. They rent land or buy it for cooperative farming, or appropriate it in a virgin region, or confiscate it, or receive it from the government; idealism and hopes are very seldom strong enough to induce turning over one's own. On the other hand, when a group has received assets or acquired them jointly, the assets become a bond for the group. This was the case especially with the Amana, which remained firmly together when religious feeling was no longer strong simply because of the joint ownership of an economy.

Communism also thrives on poverty. The less with which one enters, the easier to reconcile himself to propertylessness. The less there is to divide, the simpler the division. If there is only enough for subsistence, no one objects to equality; when luxuries are to be had, the logic of equalitarianism is no longer so convincing. Pioneering hardships thus favor communistic arrangements, as does any great crisis. When times get better, communism may be felt burdensome, as in the Plymouth Colony. The Hutterite religion checks desires for material things, while the high reproductive rate keeps the standard of living modest. It was extraordinarily favorable for the kibbutzim that poor but cultured and inspired people went to a hostile land. Whether and how they can adjust communal living arrangements to high standards of comfort, if these are achieved, remains to be seen. The Marxian dream, on the contrary, is of a communism in which the problem of distribution is solved by abundance (and character education). No such communism has yet existed, of course.

It cannot be stated flatly whether economic incentives are vital in communal societies. Failure to reward work with goods has seemingly contributed to the downfall of utopian communities. Although it is appealing to say that all are equal and hence equally entitled to enjoyments, this would seem to hinge on an unrealistic assumption that all are equally responsible, capable, and productive. However, when the community is sound, equality of division is certainly not fatal and commends itself for simplicity and intuitive justice. The fully communistic Hutterites have kept their "way" intact while hundreds of less determinedly equalitarian religious societies have come and gone. The millenial stability of monastic orders may well be attributed to rigid denial of property. There is no obvious pressure in the kibbutzim against distribution by need, and in them unpaid labor runs fairly complex economies which are larger and more diversified than those of the Hutterite villages. Generally, laziness and lack of labor discipline do not seem to have been major problems; pressure of public expectation has usually been ample to keep men working as long as ideals were shared. The pre-Revolutionary Russian colony of Krinitsa seems to have been a veritable beehive of hard work before disillusionment set in. Members toiled diligently, it is reported, from 4 A.M. to 9 or 10 P.M. in the summer season; their enthusiasm led some to faint from exhaustion before yielding to weariness. For them, labor was the meaning of life, the first need; "Labor was not a burden but the dignity of man."(29)

But when idealism flags, payment can facilitate rational organization of the economy by accounting and stimulate close attention, development of skills, and productivity in general. Payment is not merely a means of acquiring goods; it is also a solid measure of status and prestige. An army would have to rely heavily on patriotism and love of medals if it gave no pay raises with merited promotions. Certainly, in a large, complicated and technologically advanced commune, need will be felt for monetary measures of achievements.

The failures of communistic societies have in most cases not been strictly economic, but psychological. That is, the communities have suffered more from factionalism and dissension than from inability to produce. Careless admission of unsuitable characters has added greatly to their woes. Motley membership has especially hurt utopian societies, generously inclined to the sanguine belief that every human is good at heart or can be educated to goodness. Soviet communes also suffered from the indiscriminate opening to all true-blue proletarians and had much trouble steering a course between abused hospitality and narrow exclusiveness. The Hutterite policy of recruiting only by birth serves them well, but it is no solution for the reformer.

The communal society should be cemented by idealism, a drive which may or may not be religious in expression, but which is certainly not strictly economic. It cannot base itself merely upon a desire for material betterment, but requires an ethical agreement. Where there are so many opportunities for abuse, there must be a mission to justify the submergence of self-assertiveness or a sense of duty to generate the required good will. Except in an emergency when men cling together to survive, such a drive is needed to make workable a society largely dependent upon conscience and public opinion. With varying effectiveness, socialist and religious communes in their moral revolt against an evil and unjust world have the purpose that all tears, or at least the bitter tears from injustice, should be wiped away.

The great vice of the iniquitous world repudiated by the commune is private property, the very stuff of pride, inequality, greed, and covetousness. But another fundamental institution comes under attack—the family. Many religious communities entirely reject family relations as incompatible with holiness. The family necessarily conflicts with communal life, as it leads a man to think first of his own. The marriage bond must inevitably be weakened by removal of the economic basis of the household, though the "leisure time" marriage may be happy. Moreover, aside from any ideology, the close integration of the individual in the larger group serves to loosen the bonds of the smaller. Some communities have taken the course of complete licence, as the Oneidaists and the anarchists. In the kibbutz there is some informality and scorn for sacraments, coupled with a certain Puritanism prohibiting public display of affection. In the Soviet commune one may guess that there was a good deal of unconventionality, if not sin, according to peasant conceptions. At the same time, communistic societies remove children more or less from the influence of their parents. It may be guessed that the Hutterites and kibbutzim keep children in nurseries more to ensure the development of good members of the community than to secure economic benefit. The Soviet communes gave economic reasons, such as saving of labor, or freeing of women for production. But it must be surmised that there, too, it was felt that good communards must be raised by the commune and that the commune itself should be the family of all its members.

In brief, the successful, truly communal society should be simple, not too large for intimacy, united in its main beliefs and especially in its rejection of individual exclusiveness, not divided into smaller groups, but a coherent whole with which each member can identify himself. It was not easy for the Soviet commune to satisfy these requirements and the demands of the Soviet state.

3 Background of Soviet Communes

Marxism

It may seem almost superfluous to seek the causes and ideological mainsprings of the Soviet communes apart from the motives of the Revolution in general. Radical institutions might readily spring up from the debris of any social cataclysm. In the French Revolution, Babeuf proposed sharing all property and distributing by need the fruits of labor. The Mexican Revolution fathered an ejido movement which could well have become much like the Soviet commune movement. In the British Cromwellian Revolution, the Diggers proclaimed equality and sharing of property. The Taiping revolt of mid-nineteenth century China advocated and to some small extent instituted communistic farming. Any massive assault on established rights is likely to inspire more extreme elements to attempt full communism, whether or not the national background, political thinking, or popular tradition were especially inclined that way.

In Russia, however, the stage was well set for communes. It is obvious that the Revolution was led by a Party that called itself Communist and followed the anti-capitalistic outlook of Marx. There were also old peasant cooperative institutions, the village commune and artel, infused with equalitarian feeling, weaker than that which was the mark of the Soviet commune, but akin to it. There were non-Bolshevik political programs inspired by such equalitarian institutions and sentiments. And not to be neglected were the anti-property, even revolutionary, attitudes of Russian religious dissenters. Although the Leninists led the Revolution, not everything done in it was dictated by Bolshevik political-economic theory, Lenin's exegesis of Marx.

In fact, anyone reading Marx to find a prescription for equalitarian communes will seek in vain. As the main concern of Marx and his alter ego, Engels, was industry and the city workers, they wrote little on agriculture. As they looked to the imminent overthrow of the old order, they wrote even less about the new order to be forged. If the peasant were simply an agricultural laborer, he could be bracketed with the city worker, who likewise toiled with means of production owned by others. However, whereas commonly the peasant was a small holder, he was a problem for Marxists, for he failed to fit into a neat category. The salvation of the peasant was, in any case, not to come from his own class; lacking the cement of economic cooperation, the peasants were, in Marx's figure, like a sack of potatoes. Made miserable by the division of land (which excluded modern agriculture), as well as by exploitation, the peasant would find salvation only in the fall of capitalism, which, Engels said, should bring to an end, "The separation of the city and country, [which has] doomed the inhabitants of the rural districts to a thousand years of stupidity."(1)

Although they placed few hopes on the peasants, Marx and Engels (who wrote at greater length on the subject) strongly favored cooperative agriculture, through which it should be possible to overcome both capitalistic relations in the countryside and the division of the land into small patches. Large estates should simply be turned over to associations of farm workers or expropriated and rented to "farming cooperatives under state control, and with the state remaining owner of the land."(2) Engels also praised a French socialist proposal for state renting of land to groups of landless families for collective farming.

The small holder required a different approach. Engels said that he would not be expropriated but would be lured to socialist agriculture by assistance and example. The examples might be co-operatively tilled estates, but exact conditions could not be fore-seen. In any event, Engels emphasized, state interests must be paramount, and land must be publicly owned.(3) The program was clear in broad outline: confiscation of estates; conversion of these into cooperatives under state ownership; efforts to persuade small farmers to merge for large-scale production.

Marx and Engels would thus have applauded the collective pro-duction of the Soviet commune and could only have said amen to the economic arguments in its favor, such as better use of tools and horses, large fields instead of the incredibly divided peasant strips, and better facilities for stockraising. But the commune mottoes of "Brotherhood and equality," and "To each according to his needs," would merit only Marxian condescension, if not scorn. The *Com-munist Manifesto* (1848) described utopian socialism as having "necessarily a reactionary character. It inculcated universal asceti-cism and social levelling in its crudest form." The aim of commu-nism, Marx stated clearly, was to deprive capital of "the power to subjugate others," not to do away with personal property. Much later, in the *Critique of the Gotha Program,* Marx rejected equali-tarian distribution for Germany, a society vastly more advanced than rural Russia: "As regards the division of consumption goods . . . the right of the producers is in proportion to the work they have put in; its equality consists in their work being measured by an equal measure." Communistic distribution according to need can come only much later. "In a higher phase of communist soci-ety, after the enslaving subordination of individuals in the division of labor and so also the contrast between physical and intellectual work have disappeared; after work has become not only a means to life but even the first need of life; after the productive powers of the individual have grown with his all-round development, and all the fountains of social wealth flow freely—only then can the narrow bourgeois horizon be quite transcended, and only then can society inscribe upon its banners: From each according to his abili-ties, to each according to his needs!"(4)

The Soviet communards, hardly so patient, boldly raised the banner of equalitarianism in circumstances utterly different from those predicated by Marx, not in progress and abundance but in backwardness and destitution. Moreover, communism under such conditions was totally at variance with the entire Marxist approach to history, which viewed society as advancing as a whole through historically necessary stages of development of productive forces to final communism. That the revolution should come in backward Russia rather than in advanced Germany or England was rationalized by Lenin on the grounds that capitalism was highly concentrated but weak in Russia. But there was no such justification for attempting to leap into pure communism on a small scale under conditions so far from those required by Marx.

Yet Marxism pointed to the glowing goal of communism; and the establishment of communes, if contrary to its doctrines, was in accord with its emotions. As a young man of twenty-five, Engels was enthusiastic about the utopian-communistic settlements of America. Their religious creeds were no matter, he wrote: what was significant was their prosperity, the pleasantness of working in them, the absence of compulsion, and the ideal distribution by needs. "We see thus that community of goods is nothing impossible, but that on the contrary all of these attempts have come out well. We see also that people who live in community live better with less work, have more leisure for cultivation of the spirit, and are better and more moral than their neighbors who retained property."(5)

That Marx and Engels might have been satisfied to suspend judgment and wish the commune well is indicated also by their unprejudiced approach to the Russian village commune and their willingness to see some possibilities for the growth of socialism from this precapitalistic institution. Russian Populists hoped that village communal land ownership would develop straight into socialism without any capitalistic interval. Russian Marxists vigorously rejected this idea, but Marx was not so sure. In answer to an inquiry of the Russian revolutionary heroine, Vera Zasulich, he wrote that he believed the village commune might be a "point of support for the social regeneration of Russia," if freed from negative influences. He stated in the preface to the Russian edition of the *Communist Manfesto* (1882) that, "If the Russian revolution serves as the signal for a proletarian revolution in the West, then the Russian community of property in land can be the point of departure for communist development." Thus, while the teachings of Marx were contrary to the quick leap into communism in the Russia of 1918, a communard might well feel that Marx would have sympathized.

Following Marx and Engels, the Social Democratic parties generally kept fairly close to the agrarian program of their teachers or modified it in the direction of moderation. Typical was Kautsky, long considered the leading Social Democratic theoretician. Estates in Germany, he proposed, should be bought by the state and made into socialized cooperatives or state farms. But socialization should proceed of itself. The advantages of the use of machinery would make small fields obviously senseless, and the peasants, seeing the good pay and short hours on state farms, would voluntarily join cooperatives. Discussing questions which were to arise in Soviet agriculture, Kautsky emphasized that "modern communism is not that of primitive Christianity," the former demanding not communality of housekeeping but socialization of production. Individual households should be kept, with garden plots. In specific demands Kautsky was modest: Social Democrats should oppose child labor in the fields, call for free legal services for poor peasants, cheap anti-hail insurance, etc.(6)

Others left the position of Marx and Engels farther behind. Some, as David, even came to find virtues in small landowning. The Mensheviks, who emerged as the moderate wing of the Russian Social Democratic Party at the Congress of 1903, endeavored to adapt Marxism to Russian conditions by a program of what they called "municipalization." As adopted by the Stockholm Congress (1906) the Menshevik program asked that lands belonging to the Russian Crown, Church, and private estates (over limits to be determined locally) should be confiscated and handed over to elected local governments, which would then rent them to the highest bidder. Some supposed these lands were to be rented to cooperatives, but this does not seem to have been the idea of the authors of the program. In proposing municipalization, the Mensheviks counted on being able to dominate the municipal authorities—a hope which Lenin considered ridiculous.(7) The aim was that the state (or local bodies, considered likely to be more democratic than the central government) should appropriate land rent;

it well demonstrates how far the Mensheviks, and most followers of Marx with them, drifted from the idea of the full commune.

Lenin's Program and the Commune

As a revolutionary in a peasant country, Lenin needed peasant support for his proletarian uprising; hence he wrote far more about peasant problems than Marx and Engels. The details and nuances of his ideas, developed in response to political needs and in interminable polemics with Mensheviks, Socialist-Revolutionaries and other opponents, mostly have little relevance for the commune. Like Marx, Lenin gave much attention to the conditions and tactics of political struggle and relatively little to the particulars of the future structure.

Hewing close to the line of Marx, Lenin held that only a social revolution would bring real improvement of the peasant's lot and scoffed at palliatives, such as the artels of the Populists. He believed in an inevitable capitalistic development for Russia, which should be hastened by sweeping away remnants of the old patriarchal and semi-feudal order in the countryside. Out-Marxing Marx, Lenin saw the village commune not as a potential "point of departure for communist development," but as an impediment to necessary historical sequences. Lenin agreed with other Russian Marxists that economic evolution would transform the peasant from small owner to laborer—opponents charged that the Marxists desired this degradation and hoped to bring it about.(8) In 1903 Lenin expressed his hopes for socialism in agriculture in about the same terms which he continued to use until the Revolution: the Party, upon gaining power, should organize cooperative farms on estates with extensive use of machinery; the peasants would be impressed by the good life of the cooperators.(9) This sounds quite like Engels or Kautsky.

The official program of the Russian Social Democratic Party in 1903, when Bolsheviks and Mensheviks were still formally united, limited itself to promising economic benefits for peasants, such as the return to them of redemption payments and lands lost at the time of the Emancipation (1861). In 1905 the revolutionary ferment in Russia led the Party to call for greater militancy; the program then adopted demanded support of peasant demonstrations and "revolutionary peasant committees to carry through all revolutionary-democratic transformations."(10) This emphasis on peasant organization, much favored by Lenin, vaguely foreshadowed the Committees of the Poor of 1918-19, or *Kombedy,* which gave great impetus to the communes; but in 1905 the program focused on stirring up revolution, not future collectivization. As the revolutionary tide was receding, at the Stockholm Congress (1906), Lenin proposed a strong agrarian program: handing over of Crown, estate, and church lands to peasant committees, pending disposition by constituent assembly; nationalization of all land if a democratic republic should be established. (This was turned down and the moderate Menshevik program was adopted.) Afterwards, Lenin reviewed his agrarian ideas as follows: he supported a political struggle for peasant support; was against municipalization as too weak; and for nationalization to sweep away all old restrictions and bring about a full revolution.(11)

Questions which had long been hypothetical became urgently practical when Tsardom collapsed in 1917. Upon his return from exile, Lenin trumpeted his April Theses, so radical as to shock his own Party. These included, "Confiscation of all estate land. Nationalization of *all* land in the country, under control of local councils of agricultural laborers' and peasants' deputies. Conversion of each large estate . . . into a model farm under control of agricultural laborers' deputies and on public account." This call for confiscation of large landholdings and the formation of model farms under government control was adopted as the agrarian program of the Bolshevik Party (now completely divorced from the Mensheviks) at their April, 1917, Congress; and Lenin, speaking and writing voluminously in the following months, reiterated and somewhat elaborated these ideas. He found nonsocialist and backward the division of the land in either of the two traditional ways, by number of mouths or of working hands. Socialism, on the contrary, required the organization of farm laborers and poor peasants and the collective, scientific cultivation of the estates. "If we sit old-style on little patches, even though free citizens on free land, all the same we are threatened with inevitable destruction."(12)

Lenin thus made clear his support for large-scale but non-capitalistic agriculture; but he did not attempt to sketch, even roughly, its organization. Possibly he might have called the future collective farms "communes," though without the equalitarianism associated with communes. More than once before the Revolution he spoke of "communes" in the future society and even used this word as an equivalent to soviet, or council of workers' deputies; by it he seems to have meant only a local self-government based on the lower classes and dominated by revolutionaries, perhaps something like the old village commune, which was a democratic administrative body. But while speaking of communes, he most emphatically rejected any idea of immediate communism, i.e. distribution by need, adopting the criticisms and even the wording used by Marx in the *Critique of the Gotha Program* against premature abandonment of socialistic distribution by work. In the first phase of the new society, Lenin wrote, there must remain differences of wealth, though exploitation is ended. Work according to ability and distribution according to need can come only, "when people are so accustomed to observing the basic rules of community living and when their labor is so productive that they will voluntarily labor *according to their abilities*."(13) Or, as Lenin wrote in April, 1917, "From capitalism mankind can go directly only to socialism, i.e., to social ownership of means of production and division of products according to the work of each."(14)

As the revolutionary situation ripened in 1917, more emphasis was laid on satisfying the peasants and less on the collective agriculture of socialist doctrine. In September, the Bolshevik paper *Rabochii* ("Worker," as *Pravda* was temporarily called because of suppression by the Provisional Government) headlined daily: "Immediate abolition of private property in estate land without compensation and transfer to the control of peasant committees," without mention of model farms. Presumably, the peasants would be free to do as they pleased and divide up the land. When Lenin and his Party came to power, October 25 (November 7), they proceeded forthwith to pass a land law shaped more by the need for peasant and Socialist-Revolutionary support than by theories about the socialization of agriculture. In effect, it was an invitation to the peasants to help themselves to the land, where they had not already done so. There was a hopeful provision that gardens, nurseries, and greenhouses should be kept intact and held by the government or village commune; but, for the rest, land was to be held equally; manner of utilization should be as locally determined, by farmstead, village commune, or, in the last place, by artels. A year later, Lenin spoke of the land law "which we passed by our own votes, saying openly that it did not correspond to our views, knowing that the idea of equal land use is held by the great majority, not wishing to foist anything upon them, waiting for the peasantry to outwear it and go farther ahead." There remained the consolation that the way had been left open for agriculture to develop "on a socialist basis."(15)

That "socialist basis" had much more to do with machines than with the "brotherhood and equality" of the communes. In the same speech, Lenin praised as forerunners of socialism in agriculture, "Those soviets and farms which in a planned way advance toward the collective working of the land on a large scale, toward the utilization of knowledge, science and technology." For Lenin, "Communism is the Soviet power plus the electrification of the whole country," not the brotherhood of communes.

Lenin failed to see the fully communistic society in the foreseeable future and so by inference opposed the communes. Nonetheless, he gave communes a great indirect boost. In April, 1917, he proposed that the Bolshevik section of the Russian Social Democratic Workers' Party be renamed the Russian Communist Party (Bolsheviks), and this change was made in March, 1918. Unlike the word "commune," the word "communist" is of modern coinage. It seems to have been invented in the 1840's by followers of Babeuf, who was beheaded for his equalitarian views in the French Revolution. From the beginning it implied negation of private property, in contrast to less extreme reforms advocated by socialism. Marx and Engels, however, often used "communism" loosely to mean militant socialism. For example, the *Communist Manifesto* asked concretely for many reforms which have become accepted in the most conservative countries, such as the graduated income tax and universal education. In the latter nineteenth century the various Marxist political parties of Europe had taken the less disquieting name of "Social Democratic"; Lenin reverted to the more revolutionary designation of early Marxism. His stated purposes were several: first, to proclaim the ultimate goal, a communistic society; second, to stress that the Soviet state was a government of a new type, patterned after the Paris Commune and a different genus from bourgeois governments; third, to cut off his movement from the old Social Democratic parties which he despised as revisionist and nationalist, traitors to the cause of the proletariat.(16) Of these reasons, the first was insignificant; Lenin dismissed it with a phrase. The most important was the last, the distinction he drew between the firmly revolutionary Communist Party and the faithless, compromising Social Democrats. The founding of the Comintern and the total, permanent schism of the international Marxist movement followed. The change of name may also have been a concession to Leftist Bolsheviks, much offended at this time by the signing of the Peace of Brest-Litovsk with Germany.

Naming the governing party "Communist" could not but increase confusion regarding communes. In 1918, official documents of the Party and the Soviet government sometimes called members of communes "communists," as though they were Party members. Similarly, all kolkhozes were occasionally called "communist collectives," and members of communes, artels, and tozes alike were given the honorific "communard." A peasant might well forget subtleties and suppose that the state ruled by the Communist Party wanted communes.

Village Commune

Marxism and the Leninist-Bolshevik program favored collective production and pay for work, not (except in some vague future) the total brotherly equality of the commune. It is also significant that communes were seldom formed in cities, but in the countryside, where Marxist-Bolshevik ideas were slow to penetrate. Peasant districts likewise seem to have been more prone to communes than those of mixed economy; at least in the Urals, it was reported in *Pravda* on December 29, 1929 that in mining-industrial sections there were few communes and many tozes, while the purely peasant regions had more communes and fewer tozes. This strongly suggests that the commune idea was based more on native Russian peasant institutions than upon Western socialist theories.

The peasants had strong tendencies toward equality and co-operation, as testified by many writers, in the nineteenth century, Russian and Western, conservative and radical. A disgusted Britisher even found that the communal system had "destroyed the peasants' capacity for individual thought and action."(17) Whether they were, in reality, more equalitarian in spirit than other backward and noncommercial peoples cannot be told. But they had, perhaps like many nations in like stages of development, sundry institutions which accented community, equality, and sharing. These were centered around two: the village commune, which was the village acting as a body; and the artel, or primitive cooperative group.

Russian peasants, like those of Europe generally, lived in small villages surrounded by fields and meadows. The village (strictly, the heads of household in assembly) constituted a primitive democratic body with elected elders, a peasant class organization, called in Russian *obshchina* or *mir,* and commonly translated "village commune." It had extensive administrative and disciplinary powers and was charged with such functions as maintaining roads, paying taxes, and controlling the travel of members. But its most striking attribute was a collective residual ownership of the land, in accordance with which it usually (at least in areas of Great Russian settlement) periodically redivided the fields among households. The basis for division was more or less equalitarian: by the number of persons under the latest census, by assessments for land taxes, by the number of workers, or, infrequently, by the number of eaters. Redistribution was not complete: building lots were not subject to it and could be inherited or sold, though not outside the village commune (but ownership of the lot depended on the building and reverted to the village if the building were abandoned or removed); garden plots near houses were as though privately owned and likewise exempt from redistribution. Pasture land was never divided, but used by the village as a whole, like the old English commons; a herdsman was hired collectively, and each household was permitted to pasture a certain number of animals.

Plowland, the most important factor, was redivided at intervals, usually of a dozen years. Great effort was made to give each household land corresponding in quantity, and equal in quality and distance from the village; each was to receive a due share of each of the three fields into which the plowland was usually divided—fallow, winter grain, and summer grain. This entailed cutting fields into an ever growing number of small strips; thus, each household might have dozens of widely separated narrow parcels. (In north and northwest Russia before the Revolution the average household had more than 20 separate strips; in the south and east, rather fewer.) Final assignment was made by lot. At the redivision, however, a possessor was supposed to be entitled to compensation for improvements he might have made, and could sometimes withhold specially fertilized land. Between full repartitions there might be adjustments to correct conspicuous inequalities. Hayfields were parcelled out like plowland, but more frequently, sometimes yearly; or the meadow was mowed in common, and the hay equally divided. Woods were also divided, or each household might be privileged to cut a fixed quantity of timber from the common woodlands. The principle of equal division was also extended to other resources; e.g., in areas where hunting was important, the village sometimes divided the grounds among its members. At times, the equalitarian impulse was strong enough to bring several villages together to share land, those with more per household yielding proportionately (but not always without protest) to their neighbors who had less.(18)

Russian peasants, like many primitive peoples, felt that land was not really subject to private ownership. When asked if they would not like to have land in permanent possession, they might reply, "That is impossible," or "Our children would curse us," or "That's not the Russian way." Peasants customarily called the land "God's," or "everybody's"; their idea of land ownership was the right to it of those who worked it. As the earth was mother of all, they said, how could it belong to anyone?(19)

Repartition was basically motivated by a sense of practical justice reinforced by taxation. Since Peter I introduced a head tax to pay for his program of modernization, it was considered only fair, if not indispensable, that the taxpayer should have land to work in order to be able to pay. At the same time, some families slowly swelled, while others shrank; some found themselves without enough land to live, while others had more than they could farm. It was presumably for this reason that the practice spread through the seventeenth century into the latter half of the nineteenth. In the Cossack borderlands of centuries past and in Siberia of recent times there was ample land for all to stake out as much as they could use; hence here repartition was not customary. But as population grew and free land had to be sought ever farther away, the peasants would undertake to redivide the fields.

Some incidents show that the logic of repartition was compelling. In the latter nineteenth century a group of German settlers in the Samara region was influenced to follow Russian practices regarding pastures and hayfields; other German colonists in the Saratov region after a few years petitioned to change from hereditary to repartitional tenure. Peasants migrating from Riazan, where need for fertilizer dictated long intervals between redistributions, to the black earth region, where fertilizer was not used, shifted to short, three-year intervals.(20) But after the Emancipation (1861) the growth of capitalism and commercialism caused repartition to fall into disuse in many places.

There was a good deal of communalism in the economy of the village, quite apart from the redistribution of land—a practice which was not universal and was uncommon in most non-Great Russian areas, as the Ukraine. Even under hereditary land tenure, the village commune more or less directed cultivation, as the intermingling of strips required all to follow a common crop cycle. After the harvest, all the strips were common pasture, and their enclosure was forbidden. Pastures, woods, and waters were always common domain. The village commune was also a beneficent institution, assuring its members against some of the ills of fortune: the homeless aged might be boarded around; widows were fed from common stores, or their strips cultivated for them; the burned-out hut was rebuilt collectively; taxes might be paid for the hard-pressed. A common granary was often put up for emergencies, filled by assessments in money or kind, or with the fruits of collective tilling of communal fields.(21)

Although subject to erosion before the Revolution, the village commune displayed remarkable vitality after it. Peasants not only expropriated estates for its benefit, but they brought back into its fold many of the small individual farms which had been established during the previous decade when Tsarist government policy had favored private over communal ownership and had facilitated withdrawal of individual farmsteads. The owners of such farmsteads were, if not dispossessed, often forced to rejoin the fold. Consolidated land holdings were resplit, and village communes which had been dissolved were restored. Redistributions became more frequent; for a few years after the Revolution they were even carried out yearly.(22) All this, of course, was independent of Bolshevik policy, which was unfriendly to the village commune. Toward the latter 1920's, the village commune was again weakened, redistributions lapsed, and many holdings were separated and consolidated. However, as late as 1927, 95 per cent of the cultivated acreage of the Soviet Union was still held by village communes, only about 4 per cent was in individual holdings, and somewhat over 1 per cent in state or collective farms.(23) The village commune perished only when swept away by full collectivization. The Soviet government did not try to turn village communes into collective farms, but transferred peasants from the former to the latter. A decree of July, 1930, provided that wherever 75 per cent or more of peasants were collectivized, the village commune should be dissolved, its remaining functions being handed over to the village soviet.

That the village commune made peasants more receptive to collectives cannot be doubted. A peasant accustomed to collectively owned land, equalitarianism, and joint action in the village commune would certainly find the full community of the Soviet commune vastly less monstrous than would a peasant accustomed to independence and love for the ancestral plot of ground. In the Smolensk district, in the mid-twenties, local Party policy led to extensive breakup of the village commune system and settlement of peasants on individual farmsteads. When the collectivization drive came in 1930, resistance was very much increased. The peasants asked why the Party had first urged them to leave the village commune and then summoned them to the collective farm;

evidently they found the one and the other somewhat alike.(24)

The village commune, however, was only a predisposing influence, not direct ancestor of the Soviet commune. Estates, convents, and state farms were frequently converted into Soviet communes, but village communes were seldom or never. Some communists, to be sure, thought that it was wasteful and negative to break up the old village, that it would be better to collectivize it as it stood. But the prevailing view—following Lenin's long-standing hostile attitude—was that the old village was too backward, that it had first to be taken apart in order to be reconstructed on the new basis.(25) Probably the village commune was simply too traditional to be amenable to Bolshevik refashioning.

Artels

The brotherhood of the village commune was adulterated by its formalism and its administrative relations with the Tsarist government, especially its tax-gathering functions. More suggestive of the Soviet commune was the artel. This term became, of course, the designation of one form of collective farm, ultimately the only one; but the Russian meaning was very broad. "Artel" came from a Turkic word, *orta* (from which derives the English "horde"), meaning community. (An earlier Russian term for the same thing, *vataga*, also had a Turkic source.) "Artel" was applied to a great variety of collective endeavors and associations; to do something "as an artel" might mean nothing more than doing it together. The word was applied to groups as diverse as the organizer-celebrators of a religious festival, eating and drinking together, or a purely financial partnership, wherein a dozen men might put up two hundred rubles apiece to buy a fishing boat, or the team of men pulling a barge up the Volga. But the popular artels tended to follow a pattern: they were small and simple, with rough equality among all members, informal relations (thus contrasting with modern cooperatives) and with little specialization. Ideally, the artel should be a little brotherly-familial community, sharing in work, eating, housing, and amusements. An elected leader stood somewhat like a father over the group, captaining them and representing them in dealings with outsiders. If invested capital was important, a share of artel income (as in fishing artels) went to those who supplied capital. Otherwise the product was almost always divided equally, and a member incapacitated without fault would receive his share, at least for a period.(26)

Artels were infinite in variety. There were artels of hunters, salt-breakers, lumberjacks, porters, harvesters, carpenters, stevedores, rag-collectors, bear-trainers, actors, etc. From the Caspian to the White Sea there were fisher artels; some hired out to owners of boats, others worked on their own. Port and transportation workers quite generally organized artels; they would have a meeting hall for before and after work, common eating and living quarters, and a chief who assigned jobs and maintained discipline. Originally established for the mutual help of country folk coming to cities to work, they became corporate monopolies, exacting high entry dues and even hiring workers for profit. Falconers who caught and trained birds for nobles' sport formed artels; they had a common purse but paid members a fixed sum per bird. Bands of thieves and musicians travelled, lived, played, or robbed as artels. Pilgrims to shrines clubbed savings, elected a leader, and made an artel. It is stated that, "Artels existed in all occupations and at all times of which there is record."(27)

Such prevalent primitive cooperation was far, of course, from the cooperative ideas cherished by Western socialists and reformers, from Robert Owen onward. The Western-style cooperatives, as credit unions or butter-producers' cooperatives, were introduced into Russia in the nineteenth century and proved decidedly successful; but they were hardly relevant for the development of communistic ideals. At the same time, the artels (unlike the village commune) owed nothing to official favor. The Tsarist government's attitude ranged from indifferent to hostile; at times it regarded artels as subversive.(28)

The artels can be traced to the needs of primitive life; they grew especially from the difficulties of working and living in the thinly-populated, bleak and inhospitable forests and steppes of Russia. Pressing long ago into territories held by Finnish hunters or subject to nomad raids, men had perforce to cooperate closely; the lone individual was too weak. Equal division, also, was the simplest and most pacific way when there was little enough for anyone and all did about the same kind of work. As in pioneer camps from Israel to Massachusetts, a sort of commune was the ready answer.

In another aspect, the artel was a carry-over from the large traditional family, in which lived not only wife and children, but brothers and cousins and their wives and relatives, all working and eating in common with no individual ownership (except for what the bride brought with her and could count conditionally her own). The great old Russian family, which remained largely intact until the Emancipation, was rather like an artel itself; it was more of a labor association than kin group, as it excluded daughters that married out and called the head not "father" but "boss"—*khoziain*. It was when Russians left the family that they were most disposed to organize themselves into artel-families. "All the hundreds of thousands of peasants who move from the villages in search of work either start by forming artels or join some artel when they reach their destination," said Stepniak.(29) For working in the city, they would engage a leader who made the collective contract, received all the earnings, and divided them among the men. Such artels of factory workers were often, like communes, given to collective consumption. The elder was charged with buying food and hiring a cook (suggestively called *Matka,* or "Little Mother"). Similarly, Russian students in the nineteenth century regularly joined to rent quarters and procure their daily needs, forming, as it were, "consumption communes." In a few cases, worker artels took over and managed factories when these were threatened with closure.(30)

The artel played a smaller role in agriculture than among peasants who had left home. This would be natural if the artel filled the place of the family. But the principle of cooperation "is applied as frequently and naturally to agricultural as to nonagricultural work." "Of late years," wrote Stepniak at the end of the nineteenth century, "cooperation in agriculture has become even more varied and extensive than ever before, partly because of the impoverishment of the people." There exists, he asserted, "no people on the face of the earth . . . who, as a body, are so well trained for collective labor as our moujiks (peasants) are. Whenever a group or crowd of them have some common economic interest to look after, or some common work to perform, they invariably form themselves into an artel."(31) Haxthausen, the German agronomist who toward the mid-nineteenth century made Russian intellectuals first aware of the Russian village commune, was struck by the "collective spirit" in Russian agriculture, the "Russian striving to communal work, the strength of the collective order shows itself in everything."(32) The British observer cited earlier found most estate cultivation to be carried on by share-cropping artels; peasants' reliance on the collective was so strong that they worked badly alone.(33)

The beginnings of artel and village commune were entwined in general primitive communism. Reportedly, collective working of the land was current in the Ukraine before serfdom, four hundred or more years ago, and was still customary in the northern forests of Russia in the middle of the nineteenth century. Various Cossack groups, or *Seches*, long lived communistically, having strict equality, an elected ataman, collective production, and property. This was practiced in large groups of thousands, as well as in small parties that went away to hunt and fish. Important Cossack bodies lived on artel principles until the end of the eighteenth century; they maintained private ownership of money but divided equally the booty of raids, and raised crops and livestock artel-style. Ural Cossacks are said to have kept up a communal organization (called *obshchina*) embracing as many as 50,000 persons into the middle of the nineteenth century. The cossack "obshchina" was neither artel nor village commune but a rather more primitive association. The communal existence was kept up by the danger of nomad attacks in the frontier areas; when pacification was complete, the Cossacks settled down and established separate households.(34) Perhaps from such memories, many Cossack villages (*Pravda* reported on February 23, 1921) went over to collective farming after the Bolshevik victory in the civil war.

Among native peoples of Siberia various degrees of early communism prevailed. Particularly is this recorded of the Buriats of Eastern Siberia. In their villages, all worked and sometimes ate together; villages joined for great hunts in which all game caught was shared equally. In Soviet times, it may be noted, communes were more frequent in the Buriat area than any other.

Rare village-artels were to be found in European Russia in

modern times. For example, a village in the Poltava region worked collectively its own and rented lands, while in the Kazan region a few Tatar villages farmed cooperatively, divided equally the harvest, and even moved into a single large building. In the latter part of the nineteenth century, a group of peasants migrating from Smolensk to Samara held all land in common (except building lots), worked together under elected leaders, and divided the product according to days worked.(35) Alexander I and Nicholas I both saw fit to set up military colonies in which all production was collectivized and all received equal rations; the justification for equalitarianism was the familiar one of avoiding envies.(36)

Less extensive cooperation was far commoner. As Witte, later Prime Minister and promoter of Russian industrialization, said early in the 1890's, "In artels or cooperative groups the peasants plow the land, sow the grain and harvest and thresh . . . mow hay, cut down forests and brushwood . . . In artels they buy horses and machines, hire blacksmiths, and so forth. Finally, the [village] commune works as a collective group in supplementary nonagricultural enterprises: in hunting, salt-distilling, stone-breaking, lime-extracting, fishing, and so on."(37) For centuries, peasants worked cooperatively on monastery, church, or estate lands, and did some of their own tasks in common, most frequently plowing. Tsarist officials often required common cultivation of part of the land prior to the Emancipation.(38) After it, artels sometimes arose because peasants were left landless; their forming an artel to rent or buy land was encouraged by the Peasant Bank's preference for a collective guarantee of loans.(39) Before the Revolution, about half of the non-allotment land owned by peasants was owned collectively, by village communes or, more often, artels. It is claimed that in the first decade of this century, as peasants came to see the disadvantages of individual farming of tiny strips, there was a growing, though still small movement toward artel farming, mostly on rented land.(40)

Other peasant cooperation, mostly quite informal, ranged from keeping a cooperative bull or team of oxen to doing field work by rotation, or bringing in the village hay together, or tilling land for village stores. Frequently, it seems, a few poorer families would join their means, sometimes eating together, sometimes dividing equally the harvest. An artel form which was common after the Revolution was the *supriaga*, whereby peasants, for the most part landless or horseless, joined to acquire and use a team. Each would have the team for a time corresponding to his contribution, feeding the animals while they worked for him. Though probably declining, this custom was still widespread in the 1920's in the Ukraine, Siberia, and the Middle Volga regions, in some places including a large majority of households.(41) Collective plowing was probably widespread; it had sufficiently impressive results that a number of local authorities debated making it compulsory before the Revolution.(42)

A few pre-Revolutionary farming artels presaged the future. In 1899 there was a large artel-farm founded in the Chernigov region; uniting more than 500 souls, it carried through tempestuous years to become finally a Soviet kolkhoz.(43) In that same district, the turbulent tide of 1906 brought a foretaste of the confiscation and collectivization to come: peasants expelled the mistress of an estate, took it over, and ran it as an artel with organized production and equal distribution. This experiment lasted, of course, only until the Tsarist government recovered sufficiently to smash it.(44)

It appears likely that collectivist practices were declining in the decades prior to the Revolution. Among the negative factors was the lack of machines to make large-scale cultivation an obvious advantage. There was also a growing inequality among the peasants which hindered cooperation, before as well as after the Stolypin Reforms of 1906. Perhaps the artel was a remnant of primitivism, due in the course of modernization to disappear or be replaced by trade unions and cooperatives in the Western manner; the artels themselves were tending to turn capitalistic, with less joint working and feeding and more monetary arrangements.(45) But the strength of artel-village commune principles was one of the facts of Russian life before the Revolution and had a great, though intangible effect on much that came out of it.

Peasant Ideologies in Politics—Populists

Native cooperative-brotherly-equalitarian ideals not only were part of peasant mentality, but contributed greatly to the outlook and programs of Russian political parties. Appealing folkways, often idealized, shone in contrast with the unhappy social realities of Tsardom. For the frustrated intellectuals, they were manna: if only the virtues of the peasants, who were an overwhelming majority of the country, could be made the basis of the social order, corruption and injustice would be swept away. Among the radicals, Nihilists, Populists (*Narodniks*), Socialist-Revolutionaries, anarchists, and others of varying shades drew ideological sustenance from peasant customs. Even the Marxists, who crowned the city worker, had to consider the peasant.

While Haxthausen and others of conservative sentiments saw in peasant cooperativism a bulwark of the old order, many Russian intellectuals were not slow to find it an easy road to socialism, a shortcut to a utopia of collective property, equality, and freedom. At first, however, views were not extreme. Chernyshevskii, in the 1850's, regarded the village commune chiefly as advantageous in the introduction of collective mechanical cultivation, but he expected this change to evolve over decades.(46) Following him, Herzen wanted means of production, not consumption goods, to be collectively owned. In 1862 a revolutionary "Young Russia" proclamation called for a society of "free communes," in which there should be private property except in land, but no inheritance; children and the aged would be maintained at public cost.(47)

There came a turn to greater radicalism with the "Going to the People" (1873), when thousands of idealists sought to carry their message directly to the villages. They worked with the peasants and preached subversion, passing out booklets on the absolute equality of all men and their equal right to life and fortune, telling of the new social order based on freedom and collective property, centered around the village commune with collective cultivation and consumption. The simple message was, "Down with bureaucracy and government, live to yourselves in the villages, work together as an artel, eat together, and you will be happy."(48) They believed fervently in the village commune, in which they acknowledged no faults that would not be purged by the coming revolution.

This remarkable mission lasted only a few years and proved no threat to authority; it was more of a sensation than a success. Probably for this reason, Tkachev, the succeeding prophet of

Populism, as the general radical pro-peasant movement was called, looked to conspiratorial rather than missionary methods, hoping for a revolution to be made not by a great surging popular uprising but by a small group of dedicated leaders. But the goal remained the same: the village commune, based on temporary possession, must be transformed into a full commune wherein all should work together and together enjoy the fruits of their work. This would bring about complete equality, making possible total freedom, the abolition of government, and the brotherhood of all mankind.(49)

The various schools and tendencies in and around Populism differed in emphasis and particularly in their ideas of how the future was to be achieved; but they agreed to a remarkable extent on the aim, a society of equalitarian communes, wherein all lived as brothers. The commune should be the vehicle of the modernization of agriculture. There were also hopes for small-scale socialist industrialization based on communes. Some added sexual passion to lust for gain as cause of the world's ills, and so would complete communization by abolishing marriage as well as private property.(50)

Beginning about 1870, a few communes were established to realize such ideals. An organization called Chaikovskii Friends, which was formed to help students obtain books and which came for a few years to lead radical Russian youth, was able to found several, in which a few persons lived as single households. In 1873-74 a commune which functioned in Kiev freely received radicals of all stripes and became a sort of revolutionary headquarters; it was reportedly dominated by Balkuninist anarchists.(51) Students considered it the height of socialism to live in communes in the 1870's. A commune was founded by those who were later to start the Krinitsa colony; in it, each contributed all his possessions and supposedly was to live wholly for the artel. The communards discussed endlessly, but soon felt isolated, lost faith, took to amusements instead of study, and began seeking individual pleasures. Drinking, laziness, and amorous conflicts crept in and broke up the venture. Failure, however, did not end the students' idealization of the communal way of life.(52) About this time in distant California there was a Russian commune called Cedar

Vale. It was very small and short-lived, but its constitution was remarkable in providing that, "The Commune should be considered as one family: all its members must toil together, turning over their property to the Commune; all the members live together and form a unitary home."(53)

In the 1880's "intellectual" communes declined in numbers, but in the 1890's more were formed, apparently in reaction to the government's forcible suppression of revolutionary activity. In 1899 a Populist writer saw fit to advise his fellows, "who cannot live otherwise," to join in brotherly communities as a means of agitation by example.(54) At least one "intelligentsia artel," presumably a commune, was said to be still extant in the Moscow region at the time of the Revolution in 1917.(55)

Of such communes, the star was Krinitsa, already mentioned. Founded in 1880 on unoccupied land of the Caucasian Black Sea coast, it lasted through tribulations, wars, and revolutions, and eventually became a Soviet state farm. As an intellectual influence, it must have been of some importance; during its flowering, 1886-1906, some 1500 persons spent more or less time in it. Its ideology was, "The more common, undivided interests people have, the more firmly they are united, the closer they come ethically; the more their interests are particularized, the more friction and misunderstanding." On this basis, the communards sought to come together in a search for inner perfection, in a cast of thought that tended to become a bit mystic. For about a generation the society flourished in its brotherhood, but decline set in after 1900 because of dissensions and the formation of cliques. There was antagonism between the older members, who stressed spiritual improvement, and the younger, who inclined to concentrate on economic improvement, within which they expected the personality to take care of itself. A strong point of the Krinitsa ethos was a powerful and lasting urge to physical labor on the part of intellectuals, much as in the kibbutzim. Its chief weakness was the lack of any clear meaning or sense of purpose, accentuated by a generous policy of admitting all who would be brothers.(56)

The chief importance of Populism lay in the ideas which it bequeathed to following movements. However, the memory of Populist agitation must have remained even after many decades.

In 1930 a Soviet writer attributed the urge of some peasants to form communes rather than artels in part to "seeds drifting, it may be, even from flaming times of *égalité, fraternité,* in any case from booklets and agitation of the Populists."(57) Perhaps the peasants remembered the Populists as the only educated persons who thought them of much importance.

Populism was never a coherent political group or doctrine, but a loose bundle of revolutionary tendencies resting on idealization of peasant ways. It began to lose spirit after the failure of the campaign of 1873-74 to raise the peasantry by word of mouth. Thereafter, it tended to turn to terrorism, which achieved its great pyrrhic victory in the assassination of Alexander II in 1881. There followed an era of successful police repression and all-around reaction. Prior to the Revolution, Populism had been replaced by three currents of revolutionary politics. One was Marxism, expounded by the Russian Social Democratic Party, itself split into Bolsheviks and Mensheviks. Another was the agrarianism of Socialist-Revolutionaries and related groups, which might be considered toned-down Populism. The third was anarchism, which most nearly followed the Populist spirit.

Marxism and Peasant Socialism

Marx and Engels were willing to see some socialist possibilities in the village commune under favorable conditions, but they were decidedly skeptical. Criticizing the Populist Tkachev in 1875, Engels wrote that the village commune was no Russian wonder but a primitive institution known to all Indo-Germanic peoples at one stage of development; moreover, it was "long past its flourishing period and to all appearances is moving toward its dissolution."(58) In 1892 he even suggested that it might become a fetter on progressive economic development.(59) Kautsky likewise, noting that there was a good deal of peasant joint ownership in Germany, rejected this "primitive communism" as a basis for "advanced socialism." It might represent, he thought, rather a step backward.(60)

This was the view of Plekhanov, dean of Russian Marxists. As late as the 1880's he shared the Populist outlook: in countries of strongly developed individualism, capitalism must precede socialism; but in Russia, individualism was so weak and collectivist customs so widespread that socialism could come directly. Hence, he supported equal division of the lands ("Black Repartition") and hoped for a free confederation of communes. But as this goal receded, despite the best efforts of many intellectuals, he decided that it was fundamentally wrong: repartition was ineffective, commonly more nominal than real in view of inequality of equipment and hiring of labor; artels were often capitalistic in spirit; the village commune and democratic-equalitarian institutions were decaying in the face of economic development and were no longer, if they ever had been, capable of providing a basis for the regeneration of Russia.(61) The economist, Tugan-Baranovskii, was equally ready to move away from the old idolization of peasant ways. Artels he would welcome only as unions of the poor, and of the village commune he chiefly regretted that it was a compulsory class organization.

Lenin grew up after illusions of an easy stride to socialism via the village commune had largely faded; he held stronger views. In his *Development of Capitalism in Russia,* one of his earliest works, he used masses of statistics to prove that Russia was definitely moving into capitalism in agriculture as well as industry, and attacked most vigorously the idea that artel or village commune could lead to socialism or even collective agriculture. He had no patience with Populist attempts to improve the peasant's situation by fostering artels. He found the village commune, with its antiquated landholding arrangements, only a barrier to progress. "It is necessary," Lenin wrote, "to 'clean up' the land of all the medieval rubbish." For this purpose he advocated the nationalization of all land, thus supposedly making way for the inevitable growth of a capitalistic economy in the village.(62) Lenin consistently maintained this attitude of scorn for peasant equalitarianism and primitive, small-scale communism or socialism; his later coolness to the communes was entirely in harmony with it.

At the time of the Revolution, the Bolsheviks would probably have been quite willing to abolish the village commune. Of course, they were in no position to do so, and the village commune saw a marked revival. But the Soviet government continued to regard it with disfavor. Thus, an official spokesman at the Ninth Congress of Soviets in December, 1921, decried the backwardness of village communes, the narrow strips, compulsory rotation, and technical immobility, but said it must be left to the peasants to decide their form of landholding. However, the Soviet government would limit repartitions to periods of nine years or more in order to give some security of tenure.(63)

Socialist-Revolutionaries

While some disappointed Populists turned to the schematic Marxist outlook, others drew back from extreme utopianism. In 1881, the "People's Will" movement asked only that all land be divided so that each peasant could work his share. Not long afterward, the paling Populism of Mikhailovskii was criticizing communes and artels as too rationalistic, not ends per se but only aids in the "struggle for individuality." Interest in unrealizable goals declined and attention shifted to more practicable plans, such as the fostering of consumer cooperatives, which would not bring a society of pure justice and harmony, but would give the peasant a bit more for his ruble.(64)

It was in this spirit that the Socialist-Revolutionaries developed their agrarian program. They emphasized the view that only work gives title to land and advocated "socialization" of the land as their main point. This meant abolition of private land ownership and control of land by village communes, which would divide it equally without permitting hired labor. Where village communes did not exist, they should be set up. It was a sufficiently radical program for Tsarist Russia, but not rankly utopian. In general, the Socialist-Revolutionaries were not eager for nationalization of industry; abolition of ownership in land would sufficiently undermine the foundations of capitalism. Nor did they have much to say about socialized, i.e. collective, agriculture. On the one hand, they thought that collective ownership of all land would open the gates to cooperative farming. On the other, they favored purely voluntary collectivization and expected individual cultivation to persist for decades.(65) It was typical that Chernov, leader of the Socialist-Revolutionaries, in 1917 wrote that, "Only collective work on socialized land can really bring a better life," but left this thought undeveloped and proceeded to expatiate on nearer problems.(66) In May, 1917, a Socialist-Revolutionary Congress proposed that the land committees then existing should promote collectivization, but nothing came of this.

Generally, the Socialist-Revolutionary program was vague, probably designed to appeal to as many as possible. However, in line with tradition, they proposed a few communes of a "higher" type with collective production to serve as models for the future. Hence, it may be guessed that if Socialist-Revolutionaries had made the Revolution, they would have done at least as much as the Bolsheviks to encourage communes.

But the Socialist-Revolutionaries, like many parties, found in the crisis that they were not of a single mind. In 1917, the moderates and rightists among them, led by Kerenskii, supported a nonrevolutionary Provisional Government; their left wing split away in opposition and became as radical as the Bolsheviks. In their brief and hectic existence as an independent group, the Left Socialist-Revolutionaries had little opportunity to expound anything as academic as a detailed agrarian program. In the months before the Bolshevik Revolution, they turned away from the old reliance on the village commune and, like the Bolsheviks, strongly favored the transfer of land to peasant committees.(67) After the Revolution, the Left Socialist-Revolutionaries devoted most of their attention to the question of war and peace and to their mounting conflict with the Bolsheviks, whom they had joined in a coalition for a few months. But, as thorough radicals, they strongly favored communes. Their leader, Maria Spiridonova, asked Lenin to appropriate money for fostering them,(68) and shortly afterwards, at the Fifth Congress of Soviets (at which there were 269 Left Socialist-Revolutionary delegates to 678 Bolsheviks) in July, 1918, sharply attacked the Bolshevik policy of making confiscated estates into state farms instead of communes. As Spiridonova wrote at this time, "It is necessary to deepen, broaden, and develop the revolutionary reform of the socialization of agriculture, and its marvelous glowing culmination will be the village commune on a new, holy basis, the commune of free, equal peasant-comrades."(69)

In 1919, when Left Socialist-Revolutionaries could no longer express their views freely inside Russia, they still advocated communes, in deep hostility to Bolshevik theory. The land, they said, could belong only to those who sweated on it, only to the peasants, never to the government. But the division of the land was only a step toward agricultural communism, for the peasants must join together to advance their own welfare. In the communes there should be not only schools and nurseries, but communal eating and living quarters. The commune should be governed by a council of all the senior members, but its only rule should be the spirit of equality; production and distribution should be simply as in the peasant family.(70)

The Socialist-Revolutionaries were the party of the peasants, and in the elections of November, 1917, they garnered the bulk of peasant votes. In standing for family communes instead of state farms, they stood for a peasant against a Marxist ideology.

Anarchists

It was easy to hate all government in a peasant country where for the peasants government meant dictatorial police officials ready to use the knout, bribable officeholders, insatiable tax-collectors, and life-long army service for unlucky sons. The truest heirs of Populism were the anarchists. It would perhaps be accurate to call the Populists themselves anarchists, although they usually did not use that designation. A large majority of them stood with Bakunin against Marx when these two feuded in the First International; and Bakunin held Populist views, except, perhaps, that he took unusual glee in violence. Bakunin was more moderate than most Populists in that he did not propose to abolish private ownership of consumption goods. Like Populists generally, Bakunin exalted the village commune as the prototype of socialism; his anarchist utopia was none other than the Populist vision of a federation of free communes.

Whereas at the time of the Revolution the Bolsheviks were somewhat aversely prepared to admit full communes and the Socialist-Revolutionaries gave them only incidental endorsement, until Left Socialist-Revolutionaries came out for communes after the Revolution, the anarchists boldly and loudly, before the Revolution and after, proclaimed the commune as their goal. And it was unequivocally a commune of fully collective production and consumption, brotherhood and equality, and distribution by need. (Anarchists, like Populists, often preferred the word for village commune, *obshchina,* to the Western-socialist *kommuna.*) "What is the basis of communism?" asked a manifesto, probably of 1917. "A simple and exact principle: to each according to his needs. This means that all members of society have equal right to the satisfaction of all their real needs," in contrast to the unjust collectivist principle, upheld by the Bolsheviks, of distribution according to labor. The only possible post-capitalistic social order is "collective ownership of all means of production and consumption goods."(71) According to Prince Kropotkin, the leading latter-day exponent of Russian anarchism, the ideal of all must be the "Anarchistic commune with collective working of the land and collective production in general, basing itself on the principle: from each according to his abilities, to each according to his needs."(72)

The first part of the anarchist program included such destructive measures as revolutionary general strikes, blowing up of armed camps and the smashing of prison gates, summary execution of police officers and other agents of coercion, and the destruction of all legal documents and proofs of ownership. Then, with the old order pulverized, each city should proclaim the Commune master of the new, establish relations with surrounding communes and expand the union, joining all into a great national or world-wide Federation of Communes, within which money should be abolished and goods exchanged freely. Without need of coercion, mere release from governmental pressures would permit the village to purify itself and become a perfect commune, so short the step from peasant equalitarian-cooperative traditions to distribution by need.(73)

The anarchists were thus the party of pure communism, but the extent of their influence cannot be assessed. They were conspicuous, with black banners waving over rowdy mobs, in the frothy days of 1917, but they despised anything so governmental as the elections of November, 1917, for the Constituent Assembly. Fragmentation reduced whatever effectiveness they might have had. Like the Populists, they represented an incoherent tendency rather than a united party; their very principles, in fact, kept them from organizing effectively. A conglomeration of "harmless idealists, active terrorists, groups of anarcho-syndicalists, partisans, theorists, and some criminal elements," they rejected discipline on principle as incompatible with political integrity. Locally, however, their influence was felt. The sailors of Petrograd were much swayed by them in 1917; they are said to have looked down upon the Bolsheviks as "sea-lawyers and spineless moderates."(74) The anarchist seamen of Kronstadt also published a ferocious little paper called *Kommuna,* which used "bourgeois" as a curse-word; and they led the sailor guard which sent the Constituent Assembly packing in January, 1918.(75) Anti-White, anti-Red movements like that of the anarchist guerrilla, Makhno, in the Ukraine, caused the Bolsheviks no little trouble, as did anarchist disturbances in Moscow in 1918. During the first years of Soviet rule, the anarchists, along with Left Socialist-Revolutionaries, Mensheviks and a few splinter groups, were among the parties half-tolerated. They had some representation in local Soviets through 1919 but were nearly wiped out in re-elections in 1920. Until March, 1921, some anarchist clubs kept open and anarchist papers appeared.(76) Anarchist influence inside the Communist Party was less tangible but may have been important. An official spokesman at the Eighth Party Congress in March, 1919 castigated partisans of anarchistic communism within the Party, who thought themselves the only true communists.(77)

Nothing would have been more natural for an anarchist than to have set about organizing communes as soon as the Revolution opened the gates. Some did. An anarchist writer claimed that many peasants came to him for instructions on forming communes; he himself lived in an anarchist commune in the Kharkov region, which he complained was closely watched by secret police and subject to vexatious discriminations by Soviet authorities.(78) In Soviet writings there is extraordinarily little mention of anarchist communes, as compared, for example, to those of Sectarians. This probably indicates that they were never very numerous; in any case, they may have avoided challenging Bolshevik authorities by an outward show of their politics. A Soviet writer complained of "anarchist sentiment" in some early communes, manifested in demands for communes "free and independent" of Soviet authorities; this sentiment was strongest in the western part of the country.(79) Usually, when Soviet writers censured communes' self-sufficiency, they did so without reference to politics; one can only guess to what extent political (or religious) inclinations were the cause.

Whatever overt anarchist communes may have existed, they seem shortly to have disappeared. Boris Pilniak, in *Naked Year,* described the forcible liquidation of an anarchist commune by Soviet agents; he seems to have chosen an anarchist commune as embodiment of the first ideals of the Revolution. Another anarchist commune, which was not molested by the Soviets, gradually turned into a mystic-religious society.(80) Probably most anarchists in communes, satisfied to be able to practice brotherly distribution, simply gave up political activity. This would be quite easy when, with the NEP, the Soviet state ceased to demand much of communes and let them go their own way. A time of crisis came only when far-reaching governmental controls were laid on all collectives and monetary methods and incentives, anathema to anarchists, were prescribed. Then, with their beloved communes being de-communized, any remaining anarchist consciences must have been sorely pained. But the pro-commune sentiment of this period was officially attributed to unnamed misguided leftists within the Party, not to Left Socialist-Revolutionaries or anarchists of the past.

As the only political group to make the commune the center of its program, the anarchists were the only ones to expound its rationale in detail. The argument is moral and ethical, religious in its intensity and in much of its tone. It has two main themes; rejection of all coercion and government as an instrument of force; and complete equality of the rights of all persons. Private ownership is sustained only by coercion or threats and is the worst expression of inequality. Hence, only collective ownership, to protect the rights of all, is permissible; the commune-family eats from a common pot and keeps no accounts. Such arrangements, of course, minimize administration, which is intrinsic to government; a socialist system requires detailed tally of work and pay or consumption, and separate property of individuals and community funds. Under Russian conditions the anarchist imagination naturally fixed upon the village commune, with its democratic equalitarianism, as the potential unit of the desired society. With regard to city workers, anarchists could fasten onto the trade unions and become syndicalists. Turning to the countryside, to the great bulk of the Russian population, anarchists had to be communists in the strict sense of the word.

Emphasizing equality, the anarchists denied the right of the worker to the fruit of his work (which Marxist theory said he should get, with deductions as necessary for social purposes) and would grant him only an equal share of the goods of society, to which he and all other humans were entitled as humans. Why should one not receive in proportion to his contribution? Anarchist pamphlets of 1917-18 answered as follows: the labor of many different skills is intermingled in every product, and it is wholly arbitrary to say that one worker has contributed more than his fellows when the efforts of all are indispensable; it is impossible rationally to compare different kinds of work, as shoemaking or teaching, in monetary terms. Even special skills of obvious value, such as engineering, do not merit special reward, for it is society as a whole that has made possible the necessary higher training—or, at least, the society of the future which will give suitable education to everyone without cost. If the effort of learning were, in itself, to merit reward, then a dullard would logically deserve more than a bright man, because the dullard had to strive more to pound his specialty into his brain; but this is an absurdity. Nor is monetary reward needed to encourage skills; some persons enjoy working at various special tasks, and society need only provide them with the necessary schooling. Training which raises productivity, as engineering study, should be simply counted as equivalent to the productive labor which society requires of all. If workers are to be drawn into certain lines or encouraged in dangerous or unpleasant occupations, this can be achieved merely by shortening work hours in these lines. In any event, workers will be able to do a variety of different jobs and will change about among themselves; factory and farm workers will trade places for variety's sake. Economic incentives for work are needed only in an unhealthy, debased society; in a healthy social environment, men work voluntarily, as shown by the enthusiasm of peasant mutual-help brigades. Moreover, different pay for different work is economic coercion; to be truly free, men must be free to choose their occupation without such pressure. Nor does greater productivity deserve compensation, because it is due either to inequality of tools (the usual case) or to greater mental or physical powers; the latter are blessings in themselves, not title to extra goods in addition. Just as children and the aged should receive their fair portion of the world's goods independently of what they may or may not produce, this principle should apply to all, weak or strong. The feelings of the masses, too, sanction the principles of equality.

Only if one produced entirely by his own efforts, the anarchist argument went, might he possibly claim the full fruit of his efforts. But this never happens in the modern world; even the poorest peasant uses tools invented and made by others. The only right rule is, "Everything belongs to everyone, and everyone needs goods and has worked for them according to his strength."(81) It is deeply ethical: all persons are of equal value and are entitled to receive by virtue of their humanity and inner good will, just as they have a right to life. (There is little thought that men can lack benevolence and the urge to produce. If they do so, according to Kropotkin, they will be excluded from society. This might not be coercion, but critics pointed out that under modern conditions it would amount to a death sentence.) A few skilled workers may be loth to renounce their special position and higher earnings; but they, too, will become convinced of the necessary justice of communism or will be too few to block it. Some anarchists hedged equalitarianism enough to permit extra rewards for unusually difficult work, but the complete anarchist would have none of this, not even conceding privileges to the worker who studies engineering instead of playing cards in his spare time, because rewarding some means coercing others. It is also unnecessary, because in the communist society people will naturally want to be productive. It is not clear how all are to obtain their needs, but exchange of goods between city and country would be on a help-yourself basis: peasants drive in with their surplus and cart away the offerings of the city workers.(82)

Furthermore, the anarchists warned of the regimented society certain to arise from "collectivism" and denounced the socialist order of work and pay according to work under a governmental bureaucracy in terms strikingly like much later criticism of the Soviet system. According to anarchists, the worker under collectivism will merely have changed bosses and so be little better off than in capitalist slavery. Indeed, the socialist bosses, fortified by a fiction of representing popular will and unrestrained by the competition which prevails among capitalists, will be even steelier than the capitalistic slave-drivers. Collectivism will become an overgrown state capitalism. After the aristocracy of feudal sword and bourgeois money-bags, it will be a new aristocracy of knowledge, and, "How horrible that will be, it is difficult to imagine."(83)

Sectarians and Communism

Instead of demanding equality of all humans, the right of all to goods, freedom from coercion, and the perfection of communal society, an anarchist could well have spoken of the preciousness of every soul, the sin of covetousness and possession, the evil powers of this world, and the coming reign of righteousness. Such terms were current centuries before anarchism and similar political doctrines were invented; they must have been always easier to understand and have reached and impressed a far larger number than listened to subversive political agitators in Old Russia.

From earliest Christian times into the modern age, numerous rebellions against established religion have been infused with economic and social radicalism, often extending to communism. Insurgence against the Church was an attack on an institution of enormous wealth, and any strong, consistent protest against the established order naturally found itself in opposition to the Church as a cornerstone of existing society. Moreover, discontent among those whose scanty education was mostly religious had to take on a religious cloak; religion was the philosophy and political theory of the uneducated. At times, heretical movements even turned their backs on conventional religion while retaining religious forms of expression. From attacks on the wealth and morals of the Church, heretics would move to assail dogma and even central ideas of Christianity. For example, some communities of the Anabaptists, once numerous in Germany, denied the divinity of Christ. For their leader, Thomas Münzer, the "Kingdom of God" was an anarchist's dream, with neither class differences, private property, nor oppression of government.(84) A few of the many communistic religious movements have already been mentioned; the still-thriving Hutterite Brotherhoods were born of the same Central European ferment which produced the Anabaptists.

In the West, since the Reformation, social agitation gradually lost its religious garb and became a political struggle. In Russia, the absence of representative institutions and political freedoms, together with the lack of education among the peasant masses, forced protests into a religious form at a much later date. The poor could hardly think of change, even in the nineteenth century, except in terms of religious teachings and biblical lessons. The precariousness of life and general misery brought murmurings and numberless outbursts against Orthodoxy, as well as against the government, taxes, and general oppression. Disappointment with the harsh conditions of the Emancipation of 1861 led to a great upsurge of Sectarianism. Persecution of dissidents was not systematic or severe enough to exterminate them but drove them farther into rebellion. It also gave practical reasons for economic radicalism: Sectarians were virtually compelled to unite closely when driven from their homes and transported to outlying areas; when leaders were exiled or penalized, it seemed only fair to unite to share the burdens.(85) Only in 1905, when the abortive revolution established some freedoms and an unrepresentative elected Duma, did restricted political outlets become available; then the growth of Sectarianism halted.(86)

The majority of dissenters from Orthodoxy were Old Believers, adherents of the ancient liturgy who considered themselves maintainers of the True Church against the innovations of the patriarch Nikon; they were formally detached in 1666. The Sectarians, a miscellaneous minority who frankly rejected Orthodoxy, were composed of numerous divergent, often short-lived groups, some of Western and some of Eastern inspiration. The Old Believers were the more moderate. Of them, however, a nineteenth century Populist wrote, "Communalism has always been the cornerstone of the native foundations of Russian society. It is natural, therefore, that the so-called Old Believers, as representatives and defenders of native thought and feeling of the Russian people, are at the same time representatives of strengthened communalism."(87) These schismatics, he claimed, absorbed the best living juices of Russia, and the result was their singular capacity for communism.

Especially in the seventeenth century, Old Believers had many communes (called "monasteries" but in reality mundane villages), mostly in the North of Russia, where cultivation was collective, and reportedly well done in the spirit of union and friendship. The brethren held themselves equal; property was either public (land and buildings) or private (clothes and furniture). Annually elected directors handled community affairs, and special officers supervised the education of the young. These communes persisted, so far as they could keep themselves isolated, at least until the 1880's but tended to lapse from full communism: they would work together and divide the product equally, but kept separate households with private consumption. More economic than strictly religious organizations, they respected freedom of faith and even invited Lutheran foreigners to join them.(88)

The Old Believers, lacking central organization, soon split into conservative and radical wings; some of the latter, for example, repudiated priesthood and were known as the "Priestless." In 1862 a leader of the Priestless went so far as to deny customs, ceremonies, even scriptural authority, saying that conventional religion "only served the government as an instrument to maintain order and exploit the ignorant."(89) The extremer Old Believer groups were hotbeds of free thought. The founder of one sect taught that, "The world has never been created at all, but has existed from all time," that the mind and body of man are perpetuated in children, or else perish utterly.(90) Such agnosticism was not general, of course, but its existence underlined the social nature of the movement. Less rationalistic Old Believers dreamed of the "White Waters," where there were no crimes, no taxes, and no government; they found the Number of the Apocalyptic Beast, 666, in the word for owner or employer (*khoziain*); and they wanted to run workshops along the socialistic lines of the village commune.(91)

Sectarianism, which was virtually confined to the peasantry, was even more involved in struggle against the economic order, which it abhorred as competitive and oppressive of the poor. Sectarians rejected all manner of distinctions and authority ("When the world turns righteous, the government will disappear of itself"); and they preferred collective to private property, sometimes going to complete communism. The majority denounced commerce and money, believing that a Godly world order meant primarily an absence of possessions; they, like the Bolsheviks, regarded the difference between rich and poor and the desire for private property as loathsome.(92)

Like Old Believers, Sectarians included the more moderate and the more radical. Among the former were Baptists and other Evangelicals; these made the Bible the cornerstone of their faith and were not much disposed to communism. The extremists comprised various diverse faiths, such as Khlysty ("Flagellants"), Dukhobors ("Spirit Wrestlers"), Molokane ("Milk Drinkers"), Novostundisty, Jehovists, Tolstoyans, and others. These would take what they wished of the Bible, but often regarded it merely as another book. Some understood God pantheistically, as a hazy, all-embracing love or "eternal good," or simply as an impersonal supervisor of the world. They commonly had tendencies toward communism.

In part, the separation was between richer and poorer. For example, the Baptist-Stundist movement, which was of Western origin, rather soon divided. The more prosperous retained a religious orientation, while the poorer stressed socio-economic concerns, demanding realization of ideals attributed to Christ. "Everything will be in common," they proclaimed, "all shops with silks and other goods will be open to all to take without payment. Jesus Christ suffered for all humanity, consequently his love for all is equal, therefore the goods of this world should be divided equally among all. Christ is only our elder brother; his children must be equal. People should live in brotherhoods; labor should be in common, the exchange of goods by barter; money should not exist, nor should exchanges and merchants. Everything should be produced in mutual agreement and brotherly fashion . . . Our creed will be this, 'Freedom, equality and brotherhood.' "(93) Their logic went, "Work is obligatory for everyone, it is the principal condition for happiness. But, as it is impossible to work without land, animals and plants, no one has a right to appropriate these things. They must be the possession of communes, of fraternal groups." So believed the Novostundisty. It is not surprising that at their meetings they read not only the Bible but Russian and foreign revolutionary and socialist writings. Practicing their preachings, they had some artels in which all worked, lived, and ate together.(94)

Famous among the radicals were the Dukhobors, a sect of obscure genesis. Their beliefs were not clearly stated, but seem to have been somewhat naturalistic. They denied postmortal life and sought immortality in the memory man leaves of himself; the scriptural promises of future life they interpreted as referring to the destinies of Mankind, not to individual resurrection. However, some thought souls might pass from the dead to young children. For them, Christ was the Son of God in the same sense that we are all sons of God. Their cardinal tenet was mutual love, which required that the goods of each be those of all.(95)

In 1804, Alexander I assigned them a tract of land in the Melitopol district; there they collectively worked the fields and divided the harvest equally. According to an observer of the time, they prospered greatly. In fact, prosperity brought adversity, for peasants were all too eager to join the flourishing community. The government took alarm and shipped them off, in 1830-39, to a highlands in the Caucasus. Conditions of soil and climate were very harsh there, but the diligent Dukhobors again built up a thriving settlement. In 1898-99 some 7,400 moved to Canada, where in part they farmed collectively, in part individually. Even in villages with individual farming they had common plowing, common purchase of supplies, stock, and machinery. Those who lived in collective villages—the ideal way of life—kept individual households and small garden plots, while equally dividing the harvest. However, they have not been immune from the troubles that commonly beset such groups. Frequently, the collectively owned horses would go unfed, and it is said that self-seeking has demoralized many villages.(96)

Akin to the Dukhobors were the Molokane. Their communities were not ordinarily communistic but had a common treasury into which each family had to give a tenth part of its income. However, a sect of Molokane stressed communism; they called themselves, in fact, "communists" (not *kommunisty,* but *obshchii,* from which *obshchina,* or village commune, derives). In their communes, each entrant surrendered his property, except for personal effects; sometimes even clothes and shoes were collectively owned. Women and children might keep articles they wove, and gifts, but part of these had to be given to charity. All earnings were kept in a common treasury; members owned nothing, it is reported, but wife and children. Each commune was divided into fraternal sectors, governed by elected headmen; all agricultural and domestic work as well was done in common. In each group a woman had charge of bread and distribution of food, a man of clothes and footgear. The Tsarist government decreed this sect "extra-pernicious" and arrested its leaders. Apparently, as in the case of the Dukhobors, prosperity of the Molokane-Communists led to the conversion of neighboring peasants and consequently to severer repression by the government. However, several villages still managed to exist in the 1880's.(97)

Another communistic group was the Stranniki ("Wanderers"). They travelled and preached, rather like a mendicant order, but mixed the sexes. They taught that "The phrase mine-thine is accursed and profane, for God created everything among you in common," but little is known of their ways. There were also Shaloputs, in whose villages the degree of collectivization varied widely. Some had only a chest for common needs; some had joint cultivation with equal distribution; some had full collective consumption with private ownership only of clothing. Their communal villages were small, like large families of about 40 persons.(98)

Suggestive of the pre-Revolutionary atmosphere was the frequency with which messianic movements arose against the social-economic order; in the ferment of the 19th century, radical preachers sprang up like mushrooms. One Zenia Kuzmin rose to

brief celebrity denouncing marriage, the official church, and animal food; she exhorted a new life based on community of goods
and social equality. In 1860, a certain Pushkin preached general
fraternity, abolition of property, and appropriation of the earth by
those who work it; despite his imprisonment, his teachings spread.
A former soldier revealed that the Kingdom of Heaven had already
come, so men should hasten to live like brothers, distribute their
goods among the poor, and shun worldly authorities. A crowd of
women left their families in Moscow to wander, preaching that
the Kingdom had arrived, that there was no need for Church and
images, but that people must live justly, renounce wealth, and join
in communes, sharing all things fraternally——food, clothing,
husbands, and wives. Such, we are told, were only a few of the
many examples rising from popular discontent.(99)

The Sectarians were a minority of Russians, and the extreme
radicals a fringe of these. But their number, though unknown, cannot have been insignificant. Tsarist officials gave very low estimates;
but Fülöp-Miller, who saw Bolshevism as essentially a religious
movement, thought dissenters (Old Believers and Sectarians) to
have been about fifty million; and sympathetic Russian writers
mentioned figures only a little less imposing. Probably a more sober
estimate was that of a Russian observer in 1928 who estimated Old
Believers at nine million and Sectarians at six at the time of the
Revolution, with the important comment that these numbers had
been growing since then.(100)

Whether it be true or not, as suggested above, that the dissenters
were the vital juices of the Russian nation, their attitudes indubi-
tably had a strong antiproperty, antigovernment bias. Certainly,
if anyone in Tsarist Russia mentioned communes, one could hardly
fail to think of Sectarians. This is apparent in the efforts of the
semireligious Krinitsa commune to spawn daughter communities.
One organized among agricultural workers of the vicinity found
itself floundering on the persistent attachment of members, especially women, to private property. Sectarians were brought in to
infuse the group with collectivist spirit. (The belated medicine
failed to save the undertaking.) The other daughter-commune was
purely Sectarian. It did well for a time, the only disagreements
being on issues of faith. After seven years, it broke up because of

difficulties with the water supply, but the regretful members planned to reunite.(101)

There was interaction between radical religious and political movements. Despite the gap between unlettered peasants and city students and revolutionary intellectuals, ideas flowed in both directions. Herzen and Bakunin both saw dissenters as potential leaders of uprisings. Subsequent radicals came to admire the dissenters not only for their political potential, but for their Christian principles; some even decided that the regeneration of society must be approached not intellectually but emotionally. Socialist-Populist circles contrasted the brotherly-democratic life of the Sectarians with the oppressive atmosphere of Tsardom, and read the New Testament and works of Russian Sectarians along with Proudhon and other French socialists. From the Sectarians more than any others they took the belief that spiritual truth could, in fact, be realized on earth. A Populist book, which was confiscated and whose author was imprisoned, cited socialists as heirs of the true old Christian tradition, and the New Testament was made the major sourcebook of the sensational political trials of the 1860's and 1870's.

Some radical leaders came to scorn Sectarians as passivists and non-resisters, but reciprocal influence continued. The political program of the "Land and Freedom" group, which rose from declining Populism, was said to have been taken straight from the Adventists, a communistic sect.(102) Many seminary students of this period managed to fill their heads with Sectarian idealism and emerged to become radical leaders.

Sectarianism had no such direct influence on Lenin and hard-headed Bolsheviks, but Lenin had a clear appreciation of its political possibilities. In 1899, he wrote of the peasant political protest appearing in religious guise and cited the strength of Sectarianism as proof of the revolutionary temper of the peasants.(103) The Party Statutes adopted in 1903 contained directions for greater efforts to draw Sectarians, as democratically inclined elements, into the Party. In 1904 publication was begun in Geneva of a journal called *Rassvet* (Dawn), written for and partly by Sectarians.

This seems to have been only political calculation. The tendency of Bolshevism is much more rationalistic than the semireligious motivation of the Russian anarchists. It seems more than a little mystic to maintain, as do some philosophically-minded interpreters, that, "Lenin's teaching is fundamentally the old Russian gospel and that its adherents are Sectarians"; or that Bolshevism is "very closely related in nature to those numerous brotherhoods which for centuries in Russia had carried on a similar hostile religious-rationalistic campaign against the prevailing faith."(104) But if Lenin's gospel had its inspiration elsewhere, no doubt emotions akin to Sectarianism inspired many of his followers.

Sectarian Communes under the Soviets

With the Revolution, Sectarianism by no means ceased to be, but increased. If communal living was still desired, there were no longer external obstacles but encouragement from political authorities. It might be supposed that at least a few thousand Sectarian communes would then sprout up. Some, not a great many, did arise. In 1928 an antireligious writer cited a claim that communes were mostly of Sectarian inspiration and countered with the statement, "We know many more non-Sectarian than Sectarian communes."(105) This weak declaration (omitted in a subsequent edition of the book) would hardly have been made had the Sectarian boast been entirely empty. It is recorded that in 1921 there was held in the North Caucasus an All-Union Congress of Sectarian Agricultural Communes and Artels; this represented 65 communes (called *obshchiny*) and 40 artels, most of which were perhaps de facto communes.(106) In all probability, many Sectarian communes were not affiliated because of their religious separatism, and the very hard times and the disinclination of the Soviet government to foster Sectarian union must have greatly reduced representation. Many religious communes also were very small and could not easily send delegates. Hence it is reasonable to suppose that the total number of religious communes must have been several times 65, at least a few hundred, when the total number of registered communes was about 3,000. In 1924 there were ambitious but unavailing moves to organize leagues of Baptist,

Mennonite, and other religious communes. The greater number of Sectarian communes were in the pre-Revolutionary strongholds of Sectarianism, especially the Caucasus and North Caucasus. They included Adventists, Baptists, Dukobors, Molokane, Sabbatists, and others.

More eccentric faiths also formed communes, as the Tolstoyans, who hoped to reform the world by good example, including continence and vegetarianism. Their communes and artels, unlike most Sectarian communes, tended to be unstable; one, however, was reported to have had 500 members.(107) There is an account of a Theosophist commune, opposed to property and money, and of a Theocratic society, which lived, worked, and consumed meatless soup in union. There was a Parsee commune, influenced by Islam, also vegetarian. There was the anarchist commune mentioned earlier, which turned religious in disillusionment at the failure of politics. It formally became an artel, but permitted no property at all and showed surpassing devotion to purity of principle. When some unprincipled members executed a few bedbugs, others cried out against such slaughter. There was also a row when some morally weaker souls robbed the bees of the honey laboriously gathered; those dedicated to equal justice fought against this exploitation of the toilers.(108)

Sometimes the religious was mingled with the nonreligious in communes. In 1918, seven families established a commune called Flame of the Revolution on a nunnery grounds in the Mid-Volga region. It was obliterated by Kolchak's White forces but was re-established when he was repulsed. The nuns remaining in the convent also formed a commune and then amalgamated with the Soviet commune. For some years two nuns and three Communists were on the board of the Flame of the Revolution. This peaceful coexistence lasted until what may be called the Stalinist Second Revolution after 1928, with frantic industrialization and collectivization, brought much heightened political tensions; then, after some internal struggles, the nuns and their partisans were expelled.(109)

Relations between the Soviet government and Sectarian communes were not bad during the first years. In December, 1920, a Sectarian leader spoke to the Eighth Congress of Soviets, greeting them and extolling the communistic spirit of his coreligionists. *Pravda* earlier had loaned its columns occasionally to Sectarian writers; for example, an article on July 20, 1919, stated that Soviet communes might strengthen their spirit by learning from Sectarians and urged that Dukhobors be lured back from Canada to advance communism. *Pravda* did not fully concur, pointing to Sectarian pacifism, but judged that their virtues would help reconstruction. Soviet writers of the first decade frequently cited the success of religious communes as proof of the possibilities of cooperative agriculture and fraternal living, just as pre-Revolutionary socialists had described communistic successes in America, and Engels once praised the utopian communities.

Efforts were made to enlist the Sectarians for Soviet causes, just as the Bolshevik party had attempted to recruit them before the Revolution. Soon after the seizure of power, the Commissariat of Agriculture called upon dissenters to occupy former estates, and there was formed a "Commission for Populating State Farms, Free Lands and Former Estates with Sectarians and Old Believers." (110) Supposedly communes would result. In 1919, an intimate of Lenin, Bonch-Bruevich, was asked to look into a religious commune, Sober Life. He did so and returned a favorable report to the Commissariat: they totally denied private property and agreed with Bolshevism in everything except their antimilitarism; he recommended cooperation.(111) A 1924 resolution of the Party praised the Sectarians for having suffered under the Tsar and urged that particular attention be given to them because of their numbers. In fulfillment of this policy, it is said, considerable aid was given to Sectarian as well as other communes.(112) Delegates at the Congress of Sectarian Communes and Artels complained of discrimination, but in 1926 a visitor to an Evangelical commune found it thriving in full communism (common table, clothing furnished by sewing room) on a former state farm, with much governmental assistance and tax reductions, just as granted nonreligious communes.(113)

Cordiality of Soviets toward Sectarians did not outlast the relaxation of the NEP. The question of military service caused friction, as it had under the Tsars. But the clash of philosophy was deeper. For earnestly religious Sectarians, the Soviet government and its collectives were godless and to be shunned. For the Soviets, the Sectarian communes represented an alien outlook. They were often dominated by religious conservatives, more interested in creed and ceremonies than in agricultural technology and production; most seriously, they sheltered the young from Soviet cultural and political influence. The conflict became acute as the tempo of collectivization rose after 1928. Then countless communes and artels must have been the stages of little dramas, as the Party wrestled against the resolution of the Sectarians to sustain their way. Sometimes the Soviet weapon was simply administrative decree; a small Evangelical commune in the Ukraine was dissolved when it tried to keep its children out of Soviet schools.(114) Sometimes non-Sectarians voted them out of the commune, as when Baptists tried to take over a North Caucasus commune.(115) Leaders were often arrested on various charges. Thus by arrests and pressure on the remaining members, the famed Krinitsa commune was made into a state farm. Frequently, Party stalwarts were sent to agitate and propagandize. Consequently, most of the religious communes were brought to an end in 1929 or 1930; probably the last were those of the Dukhobors, which survived stubbornly among the last communes, until 1933.(116)

An attack on a religious commune in 1930 was depicted by Kataev.(117) He found a group of "Joannites," celibates but of both sexes and all ages, running a livestock farm in the Kuban. For political reasons, they called themselves a "Union" rather than a commune, but in fact they owned all but clothing in common and ate together. A forceful Party man was sent to join them; he became president, presumably by the unwilling consent of the members. But he met silent hostility and made no progress toward converting them to Bolshevism. During the collectivization fever, a delegation from a neighboring village demanded that the Joannites join the giant collective farm being formed. The Communist president cautiously refused, even when the demands were pushed vigorously, on the grounds that he was subject to higher authority. He then went to that authority, the district Party committee, and with them worked out a strategy for de-religionizing the "Union": they turned over to the Joannites part of the cattle collectivized in the village and, on this basis, required them to admit a number of poor peasants and laborers who would vote with the Party. With the support of these and some Komsomols (Young Communists), they arranged the exclusion of the family which had been the mainstay of religious leadership and carried on antireligious propaganda among the others. When the time was ripe, they would consolidate victory by fusing the "Union" with nonreligious collective farms.

The religious communes were among the most efficient and stablest of all, and as such must have stiffened the whole movement. But the influence of Sectarianism was broader. In the NEP period a Sectarian leader claimed that most of the members of communes and artels in general were Sectarians, prepared for collectivism by their religion.(118) Even though this is perhaps much exaggerated, it would be wholly natural that a Sectarian background inclined many peasants to enter an artel or commune. The North Caucasus, the Urals, and Siberia, areas where communes were relatively strong, all had large numbers of Sectarians before the Revolution. Many communes were probably more or less Sectarian in content without any religious label, especially if the peasants were of a sect which scorned ritual and took a skeptical view of dogma in general. Nondogmatic Sectarians would likely join not only communes, but the Communist Party. Bonch-Bruevich, a prominent Bolshevik who specialized in Sectarian matters, testified that a large number of Sectarians did become Communists,(119) but data is lacking. For a Sectarian, long accustomed to opposing Tsardom, Orthodoxy, commercialism, and property in general, it would be no great jolt to join the Party at a time when familiarity with Marx was not requisite. Sectarians themselves, calling for Evangelical communism, sometimes stressed the identity of their own and Bolshevik goals. When naive peasants heard talk of an earthly paradise in the commune, they must have found the difference between Bolshevism and another sect a bit hazy.

Bolshevist expression, at least, was much influenced by the religious mood. While many advocates of communes put their case in economic terms, others stressed the ethical. Urging his native village to convert itself into a commune, a speaker said that the old order was bad, "because we did not have equality and brotherhood." For the future, "Our village should become one family, and we will all treat each other like brothers. We should live like the children of one father, and we will make the village soviet our father."(120) Sereda, Commissar of Agriculture, addressing a Congress of Communes and Artels in December, 1919, sounded like a preacher: "When you are imbued with the new religion of communism, then you will shine over those around you, you will thereby draw your neighbors into the new life . . . You yourselves know well that religious feelings are extraordinarily strong among the peasants. . . . they are all seeking now a new religion, not in the shape of a church, priests, etc., but in the shape of a new way of life. They regard communism as a kind of new religion. Indeed, one must make broad use of these searchings and the fact that here, in the communes, is being created a new communist religion, a religion of the new man."(121)

As the Sectarian communes were the more stable, their relative proportion must have grown after the aura of Revolution had faded. With passing years, many communes tended to compromise and give up strict equality; those that remained fully collective, with brotherly solidarity and distribution by need, were for the large part either small societies with familial cohesiveness, or religious or semireligious communes. Within the communes, also, there occurred a filtration of membership. In the very high turnover, it can only be supposed that those would stay whose religious convictions made the acceptance of brotherly sharing and the renunciation of individual gain easier, while those who joined to get through hard times, or from the flush of revolutionary enthusiasm, or simply because they thought it was the expected thing, would drop out. Hence the religious element in Soviet communes probably grew in relative weight until subjected to the great assault of 1929-30. It is possible that this was a reason for the ultimate rejection of the communes, and that the Sectarianism which at first greatly advanced the commune movement was a reason for its ultimate liquidation.

Conclusion

Marxism did not favor full communism in a backward society. The basic commune sentiment was hostility to property in general; Marxism branded not all ownership (at least for a transition period), but capitalistic use of property. Nor did "commune" in the language of Western socialists necessarily imply that all should sup from a common bowl. The Paris Commune, so much admired by Lenin, did not even move to socialize banks. Nor were the Soviet communes a creation of the proletariat, which Marx had anointed as standard bearers of the new society. There were almost no purely proletarian communes, and those with many workers were the least stable.(122) The program of Marxism nourished utopian dreams and its emotions rejoiced in brotherly communes, but they were contrary to its theories. As a Marxist, Lenin could take a pragmatic attitude toward them, but he could not advocate them as the immediate goal.

Peasant folkways of cooperation, village commune, and artel made fertile ground for the planting of communes. Their emphasis was more upon just division of the land, or distribution and sharing the fruits of labor or the lightening work by cooperation than on collective living, yet the cooperative-equalitarian spirit pointed toward the collective household, an extended or substitute peasant family. Soviet communes were, in fact, much less collectivist in practice than in theory; the harvest was more often shared out than consumed at a common board.

The extremist political movements rode on tides of feeling which they did not evoke. Neither Populists, anarchists, nor Left Socialist-Revolutionaries had any towering leaders to direct the current. They could have stood for communes only because little people, to and for whom they spoke, had such ideas. Likewise the Sectarian social outlook was the expression of deep discontent. When they voiced the commune's hatred of money and property relations, and the reverence for equality, Sectarians seem to have been asserting native values which peasants opposed to official Orthodoxy, encroaching commercialism, and haughty aristocracy.

It was to be expected that troubled times should see a resurgence of primitive values. The World War had brought huge losses; the "Little Father" Tsar and the whole regime had disappeared in discredit. The uncertain, agitated months of the Provisional Government; the Bolshevik Revolution; and the long, bitter civil conflict which followed; the years of cold, hunger, and isolation from the world, all meant the most profound unsettling of society. Burdened with so much trouble, in some ways thrown back to earlier centuries, men might well revive and exaggerate old values, seeking shelter and security in the old-new great family commune.

The communes of the Revolution may be so interpreted. But a less drastic dislocation of Russian society had been going on for many decades. Even in the seventeenth century the attack on old customs and rituals had produced the reaction, impassioned to self-immolation, of the Old Believers. Westernization, rampant especially in the latter half of the nineteenth century, meant the breakdown of old Russian institutions, the painful transformation of a primitive peasant culture into a commercial-industrial civilization. The new ways, the increasing dominance of monetary relations, and the strange ideas seeping into the village were threatening to the customary ways of thinking and living; they were deeply alien and fostered by a bureaucratic and half-foreign officialdom. This evoked a passionate reassertion of native virtues against Western vices. Those who acknowledged the technical superiority of the West, especially Germany, were often all the more determined to uphold the Russian moral superiority. Such was the reaction of religious groups, of conservative Slavophils, and radical Populists, of a mystic Dostoievsky, and a broad and enlightened Tolstoy. Even those who, like Tkachev, fervently loved Western science, equally and as fervently detested Western decadence. The anarchists' love of brothers was more than balanced by their hatred of the bourgeois. Brotherhood-equality seemed as much a refuge as a goal.

The winds of change were especially disturbing to the peasantry after the Emancipation of the serfs in 1861. The new money dues and taxes often fell more heavily on the peasants than the old labor dues which they replaced. The old "barin" had been a paternalistic, if sometimes abusive master; now he no longer felt responsible for his former subjects when they needed help in emergencies. Instead, he made them pay for wood and pasture; and, in case of need, the peasant had recourse to the usurer. The old nobility, for whom agriculture was a way of life, was gradually replaced by entrepreneurs for whom it was a business in which the utmost was to be squeezed from the peasant laborer. The large, old families, which had been kept together under serfdom, tended to crumble, bringing insecurity and inefficiency in farming. Spinning and other home industries, which supplemented incomes and gave occupation for winter months, were undercut by cheap factory production. Inequality grew, as some peasants sank into pauperism while a few, usually the most aggressive and grasping, were able to raise themselves to become small capitalists. Because of such dislocations and the increase of population, there was apparently some decline in the average standard of living in the decades after 1861, as shown by a decrease of the number of livestock in most provinces and mounting arrears of land payments and taxes, despite brutal methods of collection. The last decade before the Revolution was marked by an official attack on the village commune, and the Stolypin reforms, which fostered inequality and substituted commercial for the traditional relations of the village commune. (123)

It was no wonder then that the upheaval and overthrow of the old order should produce radical attempts to restore old forms and recover old virtues. It was in this direction that the mass of peasants moved to refortify the village commune, taking back the farmsteads carved out of it during the previous decade and making repartitions more frequent than they had ever been made before. It was not surprising that a minority should look to even greater communalism. Rather, a more massive communistic movement might well have been expected in such a revolution, powered by the lower classes and directed against property and privilege. Even the milder English, French, and Mexican Revolutions, for example, produced embryos of communism. Explanation is perhaps needed not for the fact that the Bolshevik Revolution fathered communes, but that they remained relatively few.

An obvious reason is that circumstances were adverse. Material shortages made it difficult to think of new arrangements. During the years of active commune-building, 1918-19, the bulk of the Russian domain was occupied at one time or another by White Russian forces without a whit of sympathy for communistic ideology. Canny peasants must have thought several times before committing their necks to a shaky cause by joining a commune. At the same time, the bearers of pro-commune sentiment, Left Socialist-Revolutionaries, and anarchists, who might in better times have led a great commune movement, had to devote their energies to a losing fight for survival against the Bolsheviks. By the time peace returned, they had been silenced.

But probably the chief check to the commune movement lay in the attitude of the Bolsheviks themselves, who were committed to a political theory which had no place for premature communes. It is to be remembered that almost all of the top leaders (Stalin excepted) spent many years in Western Europe before the Revolution, where peasant ideologies looked simply backward; and in those years utopianism was far weaker in Western Europe than it had been a half century earlier. Even if Bolsheviks did not positively dislike communes, they never gave them priority. There were a hundred more urgent tasks for the limited human and material resources of the Soviets: setting up the new regime, fighting the wars, procuring grain, keeping the economy from complete collapse, re-establishing some kind of order, and, not least, promoting the world revolution that was to rescue the Russian Revolution. Again and again, the last reserves were mobilized for far more vital things than communes.

At the same time, the Bolsheviks indirectly did much to choke the spontaneous commune movement by their policy of demanding a close affiliation between commune and government. Communes of old had been anti-government in spirit. Where they now came to be regarded in the countryside as instruments of a government acting chiefly for the supply of grain, they undoubtedly lost a major element of their primitive appeal.

After 1921 there began a slow return to something like normalcy; much of the revolutionary élan disappeared and the Soviets were forced to retreat to the mixed public-private economy of the NEP. The further history of the communes depended less and less upon elemental feelings and more and more upon the will of the Communist Party, which ultimately renounced them.

Long Live the Commune!

The more cautious Soviet leaders were prepared to admit that the commune was progressive but wanted to see its practical results; in any event, they held that state farms, which were wholly integrated into the governmental structure, were superior to somewhat separatist communes for the socialization of agriculture. Others practically identified Revolution with commune and longed to leap immediately into the millennial future.

At first, enthusiasm for the commune idea, or at least the label, seemed to be carrying the field. The Paris Commune was exalted as the glorious example for the Soviets; it received, for commemorations, celebrations and all manner of reflections on its brief heroism, an inordinate amount of space in the extremely thin newspapers of that penurious period, a single sheet which often failed to appear. To build upon the inspiration of her illustrious predecessor, Soviet Russia was sometimes called the "Russian Commune," and Petrograd was solemnly baptized as a commune, though the effect apparently only added a mite to the laurels of the incubator of the Revolution. Speakers at the party congress of July, 1918, proposed that the official title of the government be made "Commune," but this was turned down on grounds that "commune" referred to local government. When in the spring of 1919, consumer cooperatives were made obligatory distributors of the scanty rations, they were called "consumer communes." *Pravda* rejoiced at this great step: previously production had been organized but consumption left haphazard; with consumer communes the enjoyment of the goods of life would be assured for all.(1) Former bourgeois apartments were sometimes converted into "Workers' Communes," but this perhaps meant only cooperatively managed housing. One such "Workers' Commune" in Moscow comprised a block of 20 apartment buildings. Rent, just enough to cover maintenance, was evenly shared; management was by an elected committee. Communal services included a bakery and food-store, laundry and living room, but all these charged low fees. An orphanage became an "Orphans' Commune," and the Party urged the establishment of "Student Communes" to share housing, food, books, baths, even clothing, and shoes. A fishing commune was formed by fishers of Astrakhan, using boats and equipment they had previously rented; supposedly, this was the successor of a pre-Revolutionary artel.(2) A German journalist described the passionate equalitarianism of one of these consumption communes: the idealistic young members worked in sundry places but gave all their earnings to the communal purse in return for their sustenance, just as good children hand over their pay to their mother. They believed that everything possible should be in common; they long debated whether communist principles permitted individual love.(3)

Despite great fondness for the Paris Commune, the chief Party mouthpiece, *Pravda,* gave the agricultural communes a corner in its pages only occasionally even during the time of their greatest popularity, from May, 1918, to early 1919; but the eager tone of the articles, mostly about commune foundings, contrasted with the miserly allotment of space. The most substantial pro-commune statement was a series of eight articles in the summer of 1918 by Meshcheriakov, a vocal friend of the institution. Whereas in America communistic communities withered in the desert air of capitalism, he wrote, in non-capitalistic Russia they must thrive. Mere division of the land, the Socialist-Revolutionary program, is not socialism, which means collective agriculture and communes, the

models of the future. Hence communes are at the center of attention of the Commissariat of Agriculture, as the basic task of all
agrarian policy. Now they are mushrooming, and this is a con-
firmation of Marxist theory, as they are based on the agricultural
proletariat. "Only the commune can give all toilers a truly excellent human life." The principle that in the commune all belongs
to all needs no discussion, for, "These ideas are clear in themselves
and incontestable for every socialist."(4)

The number of communes grew steadily, and they did seem on
the march to triumph. In October, 1918, it was predicted that
they would thickly cover Russia by the following spring, and in
February, 1919, their expansion still seemed irresistible. Thereafter,
less enthusiasm for communes found its way to the pages of *Pravda*,
but as late as 1920 it was possible for a correspondent to call the
way of union and progress among the peasantry simply the commune, although artels were already much more numerous.(5) Even
in the following years, papers in the Ukraine gave much more
attention to the communes than to artels and tozes which far outnumbered them.(6)

The Commissariat of Agriculture supported the commune
strongly in 1918 and decreasingly thereafter. Its official organ,
Bednota ("The Poor") was the leading advocate of communes,
while other papers published under official auspices included "The
Agricultural Commune" and "The Farming Commune." In May,
1918, the Commissariat established a Commune Division, not a
Collective Agriculture Division. Early in July, telegrams went out
to land committees offering assistance and asking them to report
on their communes and to set up commune bureaus. From August,
Commune Divisions were functioning in local government bodies
over all of Russia controlled by the Soviets.(7) The Commune
Division of the Commissariat was to register communes, help them
so far as possible, and to control them, seeing that they followed
regulations and complied with agricultural plans. Help included
land assignment, instructions on organization, literature, and assistance in obtaining machinery and equipment. A regular stream
of peasant envoys, it is said, came trooping through the offices of
the Division.(8)

Ten million rubles were assigned for furthering the establishment of communes in July, 1918, and another fifty million in August—for communes, not artels or tozes.(9) At a time when the Soviet government was struggling to keep its head above water, this represented real generosity, if not extravagance. It was the more remarkable as a good deal of expenditure for communes was not directly productive. Thus, in the latter half of 1918, communes around Kursk received loans not only for stock and equipment but for eating halls, reading rooms, and clubhouses.(10)

In 1918, the Commissariat was not even registering artels but was frank in its preference for communes. In July 1918, the Commissariat published a model statute for the commune, fully sanctioning the ideals of proletarian brotherhood and communistic consumption, "All belongs to all." A following explanatory instruction gave the commune the lofty role of "leading to the full liberation of the toiling peasantry from the yoke of village kulaks and wealthy peasants, thus uprooting the age-old sentiments of property, the obstacle to the realization of the socialist order on earth."(11) In August, the Commissariat gave flat instructions, beyond the letter of the law, to give communes first preference in land assignment.(12) In October, it declared firmly that, "No support should be given to profit-seeking artels," but only to collectives "based on the principles of communism," that is, communistic distribution.(13) Communes were given official priority in machines, as "our advanced forts, fortresses of socialism, living models of it; they must have all preferments."(14)

However, exclusive love for the commune soon waned. At the end of 1918 the Commune Division became the Division of Collective Agriculture, and the artel was admitted along with the commune. Not until May, 1919, however, was a model statute published for the artel. The Commissariat's preference for the commune remained, though less overt, for in September, 1920, the artel statute was revised to make artels easy stepping stones to communes.(15)

Favor for the commune was strong not in the leadership of the Communist Party or the Soviet Government but in the Commissariat of Agriculture. This body seems to have radiated pro-commune influence for a number of years. On March 16, 1919, *Pravda* took note of this, rebuking the unnamed parties in the

Commissariat who seemed to fail to understand Soviet policy regarding the commune. The chief such party was probably Prof. A. N. Oganovskii, a one-time Populist, who was said to have been, as Vice-Commissar, the real head of the department. Despite *Pravda*'s shots, he remained in office until 1928.(16)

Top policy at all times preferred the government-run state farm to the commune, but the contrary opinion received a hearing. Some considered the commune, which was, after all, subject to great control, quite as serviceable to the state in producing and delivering grain as the state farm.(17) Others found the commune the proper nucleus of organization for the whole communal nation, since only in the commune was there brotherhood and equality. Hence, artels, cooperatives, and state farms should be organized only where communes were precluded by lack of conditions for brotherhood and equality. This almost anarchistic view appeared in *Izvestiia,* December 19, 1918.

The communards themselves did not hesitate to demand first consideration, calling themselves the only true builders of socialism in the village.(18) At a regional conference of communes and artels of the Orlov area, in November, 1918, the commune representatives opposed the artel-men and passed resolutions that all socialized farms (state farms apparently included) be made communes, that all agricultural specialists be sent to communes, that they be given state aid of a thousand rubles per household (a sum impressively larger than the niggardly subsidies then being passed out), and that they have priority in grain rations. They even resolved, "We need not only a dictatorship of the proletariat, but a dictatorship of the communards."(19)

A month later an All-Russian Congress of Land Offices, Committees of the Poor, and Communes saw a similar debate and another but less extreme victory for the communards—perhaps their last. Contrary to the wishes of Soviet authorities, they passed a resolution to amend the commune model statute to give communes unconditional priority in governmental assistance and voted down a resolution in favor of sovkhozes. Their principal conclusion was that, "The main task of agrarian policy is the thorough-going, unwavering organization of agricultural communes, Soviet communist farms and collective cultivation of the land, which in their development inevitably lead to the unified organization of the whole economy." The independent, pro-commune attitude was the more remarkable, as a majority of delegates were local Soviet officials.(20)

While anarchists wanted communes to be loosely federated, Soviet friends of communes spoke of giving them a great destiny through unification. Each commune, wrote Meshcheriakov, should not work "in its corner," but rather all should "form a close, unbreakable link between communes."(21) According to a pamphlet of 1918, communes must establish barter of goods between city and country, modernize farming, and eventually unite industry and agriculture in a single planned economy. This could be achieved when communes united to encompass the whole country.(22) The Soviet government under such a commune scheme would become a bit superfluous.

Some attempts were made to bring communes together. In August, 1918, the Commune Bureau was instructed to unite communes into a planned socialist economy, but at the time this could only mean requisitioning their grain. At a commune-artel congress in December, 1919, the Commissar of Agriculture said, "We will bring it about that communes and artels grow up and cover all Soviet Russia with a thick network. Then we will shift brigades of communards from one district to another for planting and harvesting. . . . When you imbue all with a psychology of unity, you can found and construct a united all-Russian commune. That is why you must direct your attention to local alliances and the All-Russian League." It is not recorded that shifting brigades of communards were ever formed to follow the seasons. But, as a step toward the new order in which "communes, state farms and individual peasants will be fused together and form a mighty commune," in the words of the Commissar,(23) there was established the All-Russian Union of Agricultural Producers' Collectives. This Union was based on local alliances previously formed, and its activities consisted not so much in the building of the All-Russian Commune as in keeping some contact with communes and artels, helping them to raise production and to procure equipment. Its most far-reaching practical aim was to manage the exchange of agricultural for industrial products. However, it never seemed to have achieved much and became only a minor appendage of the Commissariat of Agriculture. As such, it produced little more than bureaucracy and in February, 1921, was liquidated as duplicating other agencies of the Commissariat.(24) Thereupon, a new system less favorable to communes was tried: their members and those of artels, like the workers of state farms, were ascribed to the trade union of agricultural workers. This attempt to integrate collective farms into the trade union system was futile, for the unions could do nothing within the agricultural collectives. The arrangement soon lapsed, and kolkhozes were left largely to their own devices.(25)

While some thought that communes, welded into firm unity, would be the basis of the new society, others looked to a close co-ordination of commune and soviet, if not almost an identification. Thus, one writer found communes to be, because of their lack of private property, fully equivalent to the government.(26) An agitator in 1919 proposed that the village soviet register all peasant property and take charge of setting up the commune; later the village soviet should handle the exchange of commune-produced grain for city goods.(27) Meshcheriakov likewise stressed commune-soviet unity: the idea of communes organizing independently was wrong, for, "There are not and cannot be communes without soviets, outside the soviets, alongside the soviets (not to speak of against the soviets), independent of the soviets. The communes should become part of the soviets. Communes are true children of the soviets; the local network of communes is a network of soviet organizations with soviet tactics and program." Where the communes were inferior to the soviets, the former should raise themselves; "On the other hand, the commune should raise, improve, develop the soviets where the commune is higher, understands more, sees farther."(28) But the idea of commune tutelage over soviets was not taken up by Party organs.

The idea of close relations between commune and soviet was more workable than that of the mighty league of communes. The relation, however, was one of subordination. The Land Law of February 14, 1919, provided that communes (though not artels) must organize in obedience to plans of the local soviet and under the guidance of specialists in the service of the Soviet State. The

Commune (later, Collective Farm) Division of the Commissariat of Agriculture, also, of course, had full powers over communes; theoretically their independence was about nil. In days of mortal threat, August, 1918, as White armies were stabbing at the center of Soviet Russia, the Commissariat called upon all communes to furnish the utmost measure of food, evoking their "duty to come to the help of the workers' and peasants' government in this fearful hour, to give an example of civic valor and self-sacrifice. Therefore, the communes, as the vanguard of the socialist army, are unconditionally obliged to submit to all orders of the Soviet food administration," under pain of confiscation of all property.(29) That the communes should give all to the Soviets was endorsed also by the previously mentioned congress of communards and others in December, 1918. They demanded help, but only for the cause. Members of communes, they resolved, should spend for social needs only with the consent of local authority and consume of their produce no more than the regular rations allowed city workers.(30)

Some tried to bring about a virtual amalgamation of commune and soviet. The Congress of Soviets, turning estates over to communes, even provided that all commune income should go to a central treasury, closely controlled by the authorities.(31) It would not appear that this was ever effected. Nevertheless, some serious efforts were made locally to realize the fusion of commune and soviet. In March, 1918, the Samara regional Party congress passed resolutions for the development of a communal economy, the organization of poor peasants into communes, financial and other help for communes, and the "subordination of communes to the Soviet State and councils of national economy."(32) In this spirit, the local soviets of the Samara region tried to found model communes in every county, if not in every village. A few huge communes were actually set up, as the Eletskaia Proletarian Commune of 3,000 members and 3,300 hectares. Even bigger was the Novorepinsk Commune, with 8,474 members, including not only peasants but teachers, specialists, shoemakers, and tailors, and like occupations. Organized by the local Soviet Executive Committee in 1918, it met much enmity; the leaders were several times set upon. Composed of 508 artels and 26 councils, it had all manner of craft shops to produce virtually everything the population required. Specialists from outside were paid in bread. The commune was said to have cultivated 58,000 hectares, and it had great projects, such as a soap factory to utilize garbage, a woolen goods factory, and a scheme for large-scale barter of goods. Such a mammoth community could hardly have been effectively communistic. Distribution was apparently by workers, not by need. One report has it that food and other necessities were shared equally; however, another speaks of peasants receiving goods in exchange for grain. Collective eating was proposed but not established. Before the bold experiment could be well tested, it was smashed by counter-revolutionary Cossacks. (33)

Another huge commune, also of some 8,000 members, was formed in the vicinity of Tsaritsyn (Stalingrad, Volgograd) late in 1918 after White forces had been expelled. All cultivation was collective, and the grain was brought to communal storehouses. It seems to have been a compulsory mobilization, for it is recorded that all idlers were put to work. (34) If there were many such giant communes, there is no trace of them, and they must have all been short-lived. The idea of the commune-soviet seems to have been forgotten until, in the collectivization fever of 1930, it again flared briefly.

Cautious Soviet Policy

The body of opinion which ardently welcomed the commune appeared dominant for a few months, especially in the Commissariat of Agriculture. But Bolshevik doctrines never really subscribed to the communard's belief in "All belongs to all." For the real Bolshevik, communes might be useful for collectivization of production, not for bringing about collective consumption and communist distribution, brotherhood and equality. Indeed, there was an undercurrent of positive hostility, although this did not receive much expression until in the early 1930's Stalin vigorously censured equalitarianism and suggested the conversion of even model communes into artels. Usually the Party simply paid little attention to communes, doing little either to encourage or discourage them. Thus, in November, 1918, when pro-commune-ism was at its height, Zinoviev discoursed lengthily on the agricultural situation and the work of the Committees of the Poor (which were fostering communes) without once mentioning communes.(35) In March, 1919, a proposal to discuss communes at the Party Congress was rejected, and they received singularly little notice in Congress debates thereafter. By statements of long-term communistic aims, the Party may have stimulated commune enthusiasm, but the achievement of communism was always for an indefinite future. Thus, the authoritative Party Program, adopted in March, 1919, spoke for "equality of payment for all labor and full communism," but only the first steps in this direction were to be taken in the near future.

Before the Revolution, Lenin's ideas of socialist agriculture had room for the tractor but little for the ideal commune. He apparently never modified his views very much, and top Party policy followed in line. However, there was a certain evolution: in 1917, the Socialist-Revolutionary policy of division of the land was virtually adopted; in 1918-19 collectivization was rather ineffectually encouraged; in 1921-27, the NEP period, dreams of socializing agriculture in any form were postponed in favor of simple cooperatives.

Lenin's Decree on Land, passed immediately after the Revolution, did very little for collective agriculture and nothing specifically for communes. It provided merely that some cultures, as gardens, greenhouses, and nurseries, should be kept intact under government control and mentioned the possibility of artel farming. An instruction of December 4, 1917, asked land committees to give artels of poor peasants preference in land assignment(36) but did not mention communes, although some must have existed at this time. The more detailed law of February 19, 1918, stood for socialized agriculture, to supersede individual cultivation as "more economical and more productive," but it made slight practical provision for working this grand transformation. Communes were named and given the right to use land, along with peasant fellowships (tozes and artels), village communes, and individuals, but there were no special favors for collectives. However, a subsequent law of April 2, the joint work of Bolsheviks and Left Socialist-Revolutionaries then strong in the Commissariat of Agriculture, took the step of giving communes and other collectives priority in land assignment.(37)

These laws may have encouraged communes. A few were founded in the first months of 1918—at least 500, it is reported, by March 1—but little or nothing seems to have been done concretely in their favor until May, 1918. On May 11, the Commissariat received funds to help communes; a week later it set up the Commune Bureau and began the pro-commune activity already described, aided by appropriations of first ten and then fifty million rubles. The second half of 1918 was marked by the work of the Committees of the Poor and a growth of commune numbers. But in November the pro-commune tide was ready to begin to recede. Whereas previously sixty million rubles had been appropriated for communes only, on November 2 a fund of a billion (depreciated) rubles was set up for agricultural collectives of all varieties, with accent strictly on production: subsidies were to be given only for cultivation and to be repaid in produce.(38)

Although the Commissariat was hustling to build communes, Lenin during 1918 had little to say about them or socialized agriculture in general. He appeared, however, at the commune congress of December, 1918. But he did not flatter the communards: he spoke much of the Revolution, the wars, the lamentable state of agriculture, and a little of the advantages of collective cultivation, but not at all of the glorious role of communes and their brotherhood; on the contrary, he stressed that the transition to collective farming would be slow and must not be hastened.(39)

The shift away from the commune appeared at the end of 1918 and early 1919—not toward the individual peasants but toward the state farm as the preferred way to socialism. Enthusiasts for the commune thought it the straight, if not the only, road to socialist agriculture and doubted that anything carried on with hired labor and not directed by the workers themselves could be socialistic. Such was a widely expressed view through most of 1918, but *Izvestiia* carried a sharp rebuttal on December 6. This broadside against communes ridiculed the idea of making estates into little independent economies as an old Socialist-Revolutionary idea, calling it impractical as turning factories over to the independent administration of workers; "communes," it said (putting the word in quotation marks) played on the word "communist," but no more had the real content of communism than the Socialist-Revolutionary policy of "socialization" of the land had of socialism. Communes would turn into petty-bourgeois ownership societies, profiteering at the expense of the people; agriculture, like industry, must belong to the whole nation, not small, closed groups; communes (or artels) were progressive only when they united small peasant holdings; when formed on large estates, in lieu of state farms, they were essentially reactionary.

Bukharin, in *Pravda* a few days later, made a similar but less forceful statement. The state farm, he said, was the ideal form toward which the Soviets should work. However, peasant wishes must be considered, and thus the commune was to be accepted as a transitional form. At the December congress, the majority was pro-commune, but official policy favored the state farm, with the toz as an alternative.(40)

By early 1919, the decision in favor of the state farm was clear; the law of February 14 gave state farms, not communes, the privilege of preparing for communistic agriculture. In March, 1919, a peasant delegate at the Eighth Party Congress derided state farms as incredibly muddled and wasteful and urged more help for communes. The answering party speaker totally rejected these contentions. Some in the Party, he said, had been misled by petty-bourgeois equalitarianism, but this error had been corrected. They should rather begin with tozes and convert communes into state farms.(41)

The basic argument for the state farm over the commune was that the former belonged to the whole people incorporated in the state, whereas the latter was still private, albeit collective property. The commune was hence of necessity dominated by its group property interests, would want to get as much as possible for its grain, or would consume rather than sell. After 1918, despite occasional dissenting notes, the doctrine of the superiority of the state farm was consistently maintained, as it has been to this day. The commune, it was held, could not be more than an accessory to communist development; the state farm, closely bound to government and industry, represented socialism in agriculture.(42)

This preference for the state farm, which was entirely in accord with Lenin's pre-Revolutionary writings, was thus early established, and no reader of *Izvestiia* or *Pravda* could doubt that it, and not the more independent commune, was the darling of the Party. Even during the NEP period, when not only communes but artels and tozes as well seemed virtually forgotten, the sovkhoz or state farm was lauded from time to time. Later, in the period of collectivization, although artels and (for a time) communes were being formed, the lion's share of the glory still went to the state farms.

The state farm was and is a purely state-run enterprise, with hired labor, managers appointed from above, and no more autonomy than any state factory. While the commune was subject to more or less control, it was always in theory a voluntary farming cooperative, like artel and toz; its members received no wages but a share of the product. As an institution, the commune was comparable to artel and toz, not to state farm. There was once something of a commune vs. state farm debate, but the practical difficulties in the way of converting the mass of peasants into state farm employees meant that the real choice in collectivization was (despite Party fondness for state farms) between commune, artel, and toz as most suitable form. Ultimately, of course, the decision went against the commune.

Tokens of this decision began to appear after the first anti-commune articles in December, 1918. In the first months of 1919 several articles critical of communes appeared in *Pravda*—communes were too small, ineffectual, unstable, unpopular with peasants, not truly socialistic. The official program of the Communist Party, adopted in March, 1919, in a list of objectives in agriculture gave communes the honor of last place, after state farms, tozes, sowing of unused lands, and measures to increase production. Moreover, communes must not be formed by pressure. A resolution of the Party Congress at the same time made this point strongly enough to justify the belief that coercion had been practiced: "While encouraging cooperative associations of every kind, including agricultural communes of middle peasants, the representatives of the Soviet government must not resort to the slightest compulsion in the creation of such associations. Only those associations are valuable which are started by the peasants themselves on their own free initiative."

Lenin, addressing the same Party Congress, had harsh words for the commune. In it, he said, peasants often felt as though they were back toiling on an estate. Hastily built communes only served to antagonize them, and too many supporters of communes knew nothing about farming. He placed his bets on technology. A few days later, the Commissariat of Agriculture sent out a circular telegram, the authorship of which has been attributed to Lenin, strongly decrying compulsion in the formation of collective farms. Like Stalin's more famous message of eleven years later, this led in places to numerous withdrawals.(43)

Strangely enough, in the midst of these hostile opinions of the highest authorities there appeared the Land Law of February 14, 1919, more favorable to communes than any other Soviet statute. This gave clear preference to state farms and communes over artels and tozes, gave rules for the administration of communes, and defined them as voluntary unions "on a communist basis in production and distribution." It also stressed control of communes by official agencies.

How this law came to emphasize communes, in disharmony with leading Party opinion, one can only guess. It is said to have been based on the ideas of the Congress of December, 1918, dominated by pro-commune elements.(44) It must also be supposed to represent policy of the Commissariat. On March 16, 1919, *Pravda* wrote, "Among some local workers of the Commissariat of Agriculture, communes are still very popular as the highest and most perfect form of agriculture." But Soviet decrees, *Pravda* said with some exaggeration, were entirely opposed to this notion; "petty-bourgeois" communes were dominated by collective consumption; the wayward authorities should heed better the guidance of the center. It is likely that the waywardness was not in the field but in the center of the Commissariat.

Toward the end of 1919, Kalinin, one of the very few Bolshevik leaders of peasant origin, spoke out strongly for the commune as leading to socialism more quickly than the state farm while permitting local initiative. He warned, however, against commune apartness and advocated joining commune budgets to that of the government.(45) This, of course, would make the commune into a state farm with little room for local initiative. Lenin several times in the latter part of 1919 touched on the commune and collective farming; as always he favored collective production but not the consumption side of communes. He said that peasants must not be given the impression that communes live on subsidies; they must justify themselves by their results.(46) The main burden of his speech to an assembly of collective farmers in December, 1919, was that they must improve relations with the mass of peasants.

As the civil war drew to a close in 1920, there gradually developed a coolness not merely to the commune but to all collective farms. Voices were raised to point out realistically that individual peasants (those not in collective or state farms) accounted for ninety-seven per cent of production and deserved most attention. *Pravda* urged great caution in collectivization. Lenin, in a telegram to Ukrainian leaders, in October, 1920, even suggested that the commune should be put in last place as a form of collective farm, since "artificial false communes are most dangerous of all."(47) Soviet policy now was trying to win the cooperation of the peasants by helping them to restore production, with hopes that very gradually they might be drawn into socialism.

Retreat of the Middle Years

The New Economic Policy was a general turning away from the extremes of control and communization which had been introduced during the civil war for reasons of military necessity, mixed with ideology. Freeing trade and small industry, it invited private enterprise to restore production, which had fallen catastrophically. Monetary incentives again became respectable and even government enterprises were called upon to show a profit. The old slogans of brotherhood and equality were left behind, and dreams of quickly building a communist society faded in the face of the hard needs of getting a terribly sick economy back onto its feet.

In this atmosphere, the communes and all collective farms quickly declined from what little official esteem they enjoyed after

1919. This was clear at the Second All-Russian Congress of Agricultural Collectives, held in February, 1921. At previous such gatherings, Lenin, Kalinin, and the Commissar of Agriculture spoke. But the 1921 Congress was greeted only by the Vice-Commissar, and he only described the difficult times and hoped that the collective farms would do their best.(48) Lenin's negative attitude became still more outspoken as the first steps toward the New Economic Policy were made at the Party Congress of March, 1921. He said that the communes when mismanaged, actually played a negative part. In January, 1923, at the end of his active life, he delivered his last and strongest words on the subject. It was "harmful, even fatal for communism," he said, to try to put into effect prematurely, "purely and narrowly communistic ideals."(49)

During the first years of the NEP the government felt it must shed responsibility and put collective farms on their own. They became legally private organizations. The government would not help them, but neither would it make special demands upon them; those that could produce and survive were welcome to do so, while those that could not carry themselves should dissolve. Communards continued to clamor for the old semi-official status but were told to fend for themselves.(50) Allowed by a decree of November, 1921, to dispose freely of their harvests, collective farms were made liable for land rent. The Land Law of May, 1922, permitted collective farming but was individualistic in spirit.

In the NEP outlook, a commune should be judged not by its ideology but by its harvest. In September, 1921, a commune was in dispute between two groups of peasants, one wealthy, the other a landless proletarian. Local powers gave the property to the poor on class grounds. This was wrong, *Pravda* said: good communards might be bad producers; one should look at what the commune cost and what it delivered rather than at its class composition. Precisely from this point of view, many were prepared to assert that the commune had failed. It was even doubtful whether, in the market economy of the NEP, the existence of full communes was possible.(51)

In this period, the substitute for the commune or artel was the limited cooperative. The state farm, of course, was still cherished, but it had proved neither very successful nor easy to institute. On the other hand, cooperatives for credit, marketing, retail sales, or joint use of equipment were readily established and seemed to offer the best prospects for quick improvement of agriculture and gradual enticement of the peasant into socialism. In 1919 it had been possible to declare that the old style cooperatives were outworn and unsatisfactory compared with communes and state farms, but in 1920 this was reversed: communes were held to be too primitive and narrow; peasants could not be blamed for distrusting state farm, commune, and artel alike; and only by the growth of cooperatives under government guidance could agriculture be restored.(52) Doubts grew as to whether the collective farms would survive at all, though it was generally agreed they made valuable examples of socialism. Least viable of all seemed to be the communes.

Doubtful as to what to do with the collective farms, the Soviets tried to affiliate them with the marketing cooperatives; in December, 1921, it was decreed that all should be joined in one system. Like earlier attempts to integrate the communes, this one seems to have had no great effect. Apparently collective farms worked more or less with the cooperatives, buying from and selling to them, but largely went their own ways. During the NEP, the average commune received a fleeing visit from a representative of the cooperatives every year or so, and the artels and tozes received visits slightly less often.(53)

The type of collective farm now most favored was the least communal one, i.e., the toz. This category was vague and might mean little more than a group of peasants plowing together. But even the toz was advocated with great caution. A resolution of the Party Congress of May, 1924, after much about cooperatives, added a few words of support for joint plowing or joint reaping, "or even joint use of cattle in some field work or other," but warned against haste, for, "Real successes in the realm of cooperative production with present instruments of labor can be obtained only in the course of a number of years."(54)

If a communard followed official pronouncements over these years, he would have needed considerable independent will to remain faithful to the commune. Lenin, who wrote on cooperatives at length and in detail which contrast strikingly with his reticence on brotherly communes, gave the former a blessing he never conceded to the latter: "The system of civilized cooperation under socialized property in the means of production, with the class victory of the proletariat over the bourgeoisie—this is socialism."(55) This was written about the same time (January, 1923) as his statement that premature attempts at communism might be positively harmful. His preference for cooperative production rather than communist consumption cannot but remind one of his ideological rejection of the village commune a generation earlier in favor of a capitalistic development of agriculture.

Other leaders followed Lenin. In March, 1925, Bukharin had little cheer for a collective farm congress but advised them to work with the cooperatives, which represented the principal way to socialism in agriculture.(56) *Pravda,* commenting on that congress, March 4, 1925, even blamed collective farm leaders for hindering the advance of socialism in the countryside by misplaced emphasis on communization, which antagonized the middle peasants and caused neglect of the cooperatives. Molotov, then rising in the Party hierarchy, published a book in 1926 entitled, *The Policy of the Party in the Village,* in which he hardly mentioned collective farms except to call them illusory.

Local officials seem to have listened to such words and began treating collectives accordingly, with neglect if not downright hostility. Communes complained that they were denied supplies by cooperatives and soviets in some localities;(57) local bosses regarded commune property as theirs to use at will and would capriciously move communes from one place to another or deprive them of land entirely, while the communards had no recourse against arbitrary measures.(58) Collective farms had to pay rent for land, and it might be taken from them to be leased to private producers or turned over to state farms. Loans, if made, were sometimes usurious; in one case, a commune paid 18 per cent interest for a one-month loan and was refused permission to buy a tractor until the loan was repaid.(59) At times, the collective farms not only failed to get the modest tax reductions allowed them by law but were taxed more heavily than the peasants, perhaps because it was easier to collect from them.(60) If leadership appeared in a commune it was apt to be drafted out for work elsewhere on some Party or Soviet assignment.

However, even during the years when Soviet policy neglected or looked down on communes, there were slight nods of approval from time to time. Despite seemingly clear statements of Lenin, the Central Committee, and the Party organ, *Pravda*, there was a continuing tendency to regard communes as desirable. In 1921, Meshcheriakov, who in 1918 had pleaded vigorously for communes, still wrote that they were best, though the artels might be more acceptable to peasants. (61) Ukrainian authorities still gave collective farms first preference in seed, stock, and equipment; more surprisingly, in April, 1924, a Ukrainian district Party committee instructed Party members to work for the transformation of artels into communes. (62) In 1925, *Pravda* began publishing from time to time a "Collective Agriculture" corner, mostly given to short pieces in praise of communes. A typical such article on the "October" Commune spoke glowingly of its harmonious life as though in a single family and of eager work without pay or controls; the only defect found was a weakness for strong language. (63) In November, *Pravda* went so far as to declare that, since artel and toz presuppose some property, "The commune is the most suitable form of agricultural cooperative for the village proletariat." However, there must be provided incentives for work, as the poor peasants were not sufficiently selfless to exert themselves long without visible reward. (64)

Even when the fortunes of the commune seemed almost at their nadir, there were signs of a quickening of interest. Publications on all kolkhozes reached a low point in 1921 but rose steadily thereafter. In 1923, the Party Congress gave a hint of the future by stressing economic planning. The next Party Congress, in 1924, merely took note of some growth of collectives and expressed the caution already noted. However, in April, 1925, the Fourteenth Party Congress veered slightly toward collectivization: tozes, artels, and communes (in that order) should be given economic assistance, and cooperatives should foster their organization. *Pravda* occasionally printed flattering articles about communes, as models of progress and beacon lights in the dark countryside but continued to insist that they must adapt themselves to the market and expect no favors from the government. Editorializing on March 6, 1925, *Pravda* tried to draw a careful balance between over- and under-estimation: hopes of an earlier period must be given up, "lower" i.e., less communal forms of collective must not be neglected, and all should be valued as models for the peasantry. The Central Committee in October, 1925, took a similar position: support for toz and commune (artel being strangely omitted) with stress on the "simplest" forms of agricultural cooperation, joint use of machines, etc.(65)

Such expressions appeared at intervals through 1926, but the Party displayed no great interest in kolkhozes of any type. In the first half of the year, *Pravda,* devoted many times more space to the burning question of horse thievery than to all agricultural collectives. Certainly, little was expected of these; after all, they had progressed only slightly in the past five years. A *Pravda* article on May Day, 1926, imaginatively and boldly described the Soviet Union of 1940. It optimistically predicted that there would be ten million automobiles speeding along Soviet highways by then and that the wealthy peasants, or kulaks, would be feeling a shortage of cheap hired labor.

At this time, almost on the eve of the great Stalinist storm of collectivization, the party gave little attention to collective agriculture. So far as it concerned itself with kolkhozes, it favored the less communal forms. In 1925, a plan for collectivization contemplated that communes should increase only slightly in numbers, but that tozes should be multiplied.(66) The Central Committee in July, 1926 even omitted mention of communes among recommended collectives.(67) In April, 1927, Kalinin strongly attacked the collective consumption of the communes and urged that they limit themselves to production;(68) this, of course, was against their basic character. In December, Molotov told the Party Congress that communes were much less successful than artels and tozes and hence less deserving of assistance. Thus, as interest in collectivization slowly waxed toward the end of the NEP period, the commune was not marked as beneficiary.

5 The Commune Movement

The First Soviet Communes

On the very morrow of the fall of the Romanovs, February 28, 1917 (Old Style), the Petrograd Soviet, in the first issue of its *Izvestiia,* proclaimed among the aims of the new Russia: an eight-hour day, a constitutional assembly, and the confiscation and transfer to the people of monastery, estate, and Crown lands. The First All-Russian Congress of Soviets on June 23 (Old Style) approved the rules for local land committees, which should, among other things, take charge of estates. These committees had originally been sanctioned by the Provisional Government two months earlier, and were widely, though irregularly, at work by August. Some, it is reported, were conservative; but others organized peasants for their assault on the manors.(1) Peasant disorders were steadily on the rise through the spring, summer, and early fall of 1917, despite restraining efforts of the Provisional Government, which pleaded the need to await the constitutional assembly. Breaches of rights, ranging from refusal to pay rents or cutting the landlord's wood to occupation of his estate and burning his mansion, raged in October.

How many communes or similar collectives may have been established under such circumstances cannot be guessed. At least a few

Sectarian or anarchist communes must have been added to the sundry handful that came down from Tsarist days, although they were probably informal and certainly little noticed. Speakers at an All-Russian Agronomists Conference in Moscow, June, 1917, recognized that collective agriculture was likely to come in the wake of the prospective land reform.(2) But reports of communes founded are very meager. In the Irkutsk district a Tsarist exile organized a commune among fellow-exiles, mostly Petrograd workers, apparently in the first half of 1917.(3) A speaker at the December, 1919, Congress of Communes and Artels said that the first collectives in the Viatsk region had arisen in October, 1917.(4)

Although a few communes were probably organized earlier, the Bolshevik Revolution of November 7 cleared the way. Private ownership of land was abolished (although peasant possession, de facto ownership, was not disturbed), and shortly afterwards the local land committees were given instructions to favor artels in parceling out estates. In the Petrograd region, it is reported, 33 communes were organized in 1917,(5) but it is not clear how many of these followed the Revolution. By March 1, 1918, the Commissariat claimed there were more than 500 communes, on 233 of which it had information.

The first communes may have been helped by land committees or other local bodies, but they received hardly a glance from the central Soviet government. At the time when the Commissariat said there were over 500 communes, only 21 had presented statutes, only 3 (one for January and two for February) were officially registered, and only 26 had been rendered any assistance. There is very little information concerning these first, unregistered communes, except for one report indicating that they were of strongly peasant composition and mostly formed on peasant lands.(6)

Communes Fostered by the Soviets

The Land Law of February, 1918, gave only moral support to collective agriculture but was notable for making the first mention of commune in Soviet legislation. Despite the intentions expressed in this law, official interest continued low through March and April, when 5 and 7 communes were registered. Only in May did the Commissariat establish its Commune Division and begin pro-commune activities. In that month, twenty-five communes were registered, and the number leaped to an average of 220 in each of the next five months, dropping in the winter to less than half that figure.(7) In May, 1918, *Pravda* began taking notice of the formation of communes, printing occasional brief but laudatory accounts; these became more numerous after June. In a *Pravda* article of July 24, Meshcheriakov, the most persistent writer on communes of this period, tried to sum up the movement but found only diversity. There were communes of all sizes, of varying social constitution, some enjoying well-appointed estates, some settled on bare land, some purposeful and well-organized, some thoroughly befogged. In this heterogeneous mass he saw, however, the foundations for socialist agriculture.

To control the movement, the Commissariat in July published a model statute and in August issued more detailed instructions for registration, whereby the commune must present a copy of statutes in basic agreement with the model. Registration was made obligatory, in theory, by the provision that only registered communes were entitled to assistance and land.

The first official commune model statute was very collectivist and denied private property. This was in accord with the practice of the first communes, which generally required that the entrant hand over his possessions, including money.(8) Other provisions, for the most part corresponding to custom, were that no labor should be hired, and that those unable to work should be supported by the commune. It was also expected that the commune should turn surplus production over to Soviet organs, seek to improve agricultural technique, and cooperate with Soviet authorities in the class struggle. Administration was to be by a directorate chosen by the assembly of all members. A common kitchen should feed everyone.(9) The times were favorable for communistic distribution, with revolutionary disorder, growing shortages and rationing of food, and steady depreciation of the ruble. The communes were also small enough to be manageable without complicated administration. In mid-1918 they generally had 12 to 30 families and 45 to 90 hectares of land(10)—a size range within which they remained for most of their history. Some were midgets of 3 to 9 households. Peasants, according to a 1918 report, preferred communes of a few congenial people which could function like a large family.(11)

   Probably more effective than the work of the Commissariat was the action of the Committees of the Poor, or *Kombedy*. These were organized after June, 1918, and spread over all of Soviet-controlled Russia, especially during August and September. Their principal assignment was to carry the class war to the village and to requisition grain held by the more affluent peasants; they were also to overcome the influence of local soviets where these were still dominated by anti-Bolshevik elements. They were given the incidental task of organizing collectives of poor peasants. Specifically, the instructions were for collective plowing and harvesting, but the result seems to have been mostly the establishment of communes. The *Great Soviet Encyclopedia* credits the Committees of the Poor with several hundred—surely an understatement, for almost all the registered communes of 1918, well over a thousand, arose within the period of activity of those Committees, and active growth of commune numbers ceased in 1919 with the liquidation, or fusion of these Committees with local soviets.

   The Commune Division sent the Committees of the Poor literature about communes and instructions to assign them land, preferably more than the peasants had worked before on the ground that collectively they could use more.(12) Accordingly, a meeting of Committees of the Poor and local soviets in a Belorussian district resolved: "On all estates to organize working artel-communes of landless and landpoor citizens, to whom is to be given the right to plant all useful fallow land on communist principles. To proceed to the organization of communes tomorrow."(13) In their class warfare, the Committees of the Poor confiscated stock and tools from wealthier peasants; some were held for collectives in hopes of more effective utilization. When there were more applications for horses or equipment than could be satisfied, the remedy was often to tell applicants to organize a commune.(14)

   The Committees of the Poor were coercive against all designated as class enemies; the question arises to what extent they or other agencies applied coercion in the formation of communes. Strong pressure was certainly used at times. Lenin admitted there had been foolish attempts to drive peasants into communes,(15) and repeated party injunctions against compulsion (particularly the resolution of the Eighth Congress, March, 1919) were certainly not aimed at a non-existent evil. Leftists in the party thought a compulsory commune was better than none, and acceptance of the commune was sometimes made a test of loyalty: Will you join or are you against the Soviet State?(16) Forms of compulsion must have been various and have to be left mostly to the imagination. One writer said that local soviets decreed collectivization and then sent men around bearing a petition for the commune in one hand and a rifle in the other. Less dramatically, they would close cooperative shops and stop sales of kerosene, matches, and salt to peasants until they acceded.(17)

Such measures, however, must have been haphazard and local, probably important only for large official communes as described in Chapter IV. Forced collectivization would be impractical unless it were general; the authorities had no means of keeping peasants in communes once they were hustled there. The true commune, moreover, is unworkable unless the members are willing to make it work. That registered communes of this period did not exceed two thousand is sufficient evidence that dragooning was either sporadic or ineffective. The effect of official pressure would probably be the registration of a large number of more or less fictitious communes.

The evidence from official pronouncements suggests that the central authorities were not to blame for excesses committed; on the contrary they repeatedly emphasized the harm in pushing peasants into collectives against their will. Taken literally, the resolution of March, 1919 ("Only those associations are valuable which are started by the peasants themselves on their own free initiative") would restrain commune enthusiasts from even suggesting to peasants the desirability of starting a commune. Stalin, in a rather peremptory telegram of May, 1919 (his only known contribution at this time to a subject in which he was to act decisively a decade later), demanded to know whether compulsion in the formation of communes, artels, and tozes had not increased peasant disorders in a certain district.(18) It may be that the Party leadership considered it impolitic to associate the Soviet government closely with a movement which, if greeted with enthusiasm by some, probably aroused apprehension in many more, particularly the middle peasants, whom it was important to conciliate.

Why Join a Commune?

Those who went into communes must have done so largely of their own volition. Aside from vague psychological drives, stated reasons were various. Revolution inspired some. The first years of Soviet rule in Siberia were: "The time of enthusiasm for communes, when every Siberian partisan considered himself a communist, and socialism, if not already here, was a question of days; that was the time when minutes of general assemblies of communes were written in old church books. People united in glowing faith in the new life, but, receiving neither help nor advice from anywhere, on how to divide the collective bread and sweat, they consumed their stores and, cursing God and the government, went their separate ways."(19) Or, as a Saratov peasant put it, "Now that everything is in common and property isn't recognized anymore, we might as well join a commune."(20) In a communist revolution, why not join a commune?

But pure communist idealism was rare, and very few primarily sought to spread a political message. The chief Soviet argument for agricultural collectives, including communes, in 1918-19 was simply the advantage of more efficient cultivation on a larger scale, although it was hard to realize great economies in emergency conditions such as the civil war. They hoped to save labor by doing away with small strips; to use mechanical equipment, even tractors; to save on buildings and dwellings; to institute wider and more rational use of labor; to establish service establishments for the convenience of communards; to install facilities for processing agricultural produce, as creameries, mills, etc. Such economic improvements should bring cultural marvels. In the optimism of a commune statute: "The commune so far as possible will have its own agricultural, elementary, secondary, and higher educational institutions; the commune will establish living quarters, dining rooms, libraries, public lectures, readings, excursions and such educational institutions and outings, and also will publish newspapers and magazines."(21)

Economics and politics are mixed in the preface of an early (April, 1918) commune statute: "We, the village proletariat, without horses or tools, realizing that one truly cannot fight alone and that each working for himself can never be sure of even sufficient bread, and that only by uniting for cooperative and comradely toil in mutual agreement and unity is there a possibility of raising ourselves from our dire need; at the same time, having in view broad federal-republic support, we, in cooperation with the People's Commissars, in our general assembly determined: to unite in a single political-economic Commune on the basis of equality and brotherhood, standing on the platform of Soviet power and defending the cause of the revolutionary proletariat."(22) Some new communes might well pray for succor, as their lot was otherwise grim. For example, 45 peasants got hold of 35 hectares of land but had only a single cow. In another case, 117 communards had but one horse and no tools.(23) The financial help given by the Soviet government to all communes in the first years was trivial, but they could at least hope for preference in the allotment of confiscated property.

The main help and inducement the government could offer was confiscated estates; indeed, communes of workers and other landless persons could easily be established only on government lands of some kind. For example, the famous Communist Lighthouse commune began when workers, made jobless by the closure of a mill, asked for and were given a sheep ranch that formally had been turned into a collective farm by the owner and his family.(24) Typically, a local soviet executive committee would take charge of an estate to prevent its partition and to keep its assets together, and move to convert it into a commune "in the full sense of the word."(25) The commune was psychologically much easier to accept when it meant not sacrifice of one's own home and farm but joint use of land, buildings, and equipment furnished by the authorities. Where no estates remained, local authorities tried dutifully to establish communes but found it much more difficult. Consequently, it was to be expected that most of the early communes would be based on confiscated holdings and composed of persons who had not been farming for themselves. This became the official image of the commune—a group of workers, partisans, or landless peasants on former estate lands.

Who Started Communes?

Most of the registered, official communes of 1918-20 seem to have been constituted more or less according to the official image, as indicated by statistics given later. But the only information on the very first communes, before the Soviet government began to intervene actively indicates that they were quite different. A memorandum of the Commissariat indicates that a large majority of these first unofficial communes were formed by peasants on peasant land. On March 1, 1918, as stated above, 233 communes had furnished information about themselves. Of these, 177 were composed of local peasants, 27 partly or entirely of migrating peasants, 3 of intelligentsia, and 1 was credited to an estate owner. The number established on peasant land, 172, was almost the same as that of those composed of local peasants. An additional 11 were going to Siberia in the old tradition of eastward movement. There were 30 founded on estate lands, 3 on monastery and 1 on kulak lands.(26) Those communes which told the Commissariat about themselves were less than half the communes supposedly in existence, but it is unlikely that the unreported majority were nearer the official image. The complete absence of workers as founders of communes at this time is remarkable; equally so is the large majority on peasant land. That many communes were founded without assistance by peasants on their own land bespeaks the release of powerful impulses.

The character of the commune movement changed during the civil war as a result of several factors. First, the steady deterioration of the economic situation of the cities, with bread shortages and near paralysis of industry, drove many workers out looking for sustenance; some went into communes. Second, consolidation of the Soviet government and extension of Bolshevik power in the countryside, especially as a result of the work of the Committees of the Poor, gave the Soviets increasing control over the use of estates for state farms or communes. Third, the definite break between Bolsheviks and Left Socialist-Revolutionaries in June, 1918, sent the peasant pro-commune party into opposition and then impotence. Fourth, the determination to subordinate communes strictly to governmental authorities and to take all their produce above minimum rations would cool any peasant's original enthusiasm for them (in a commune the peasant could hardly withhold anything from the increasingly oppressive requisitions). Those most strongly attached to the Soviet government or lured by what it could offer might enter communes none the less, but they could no longer appeal to the ordinary peasants. Consequently, the proportion of communes in the "official image" must have risen steadily, while many or most of the elemental little peasant communes (reportedly quite small compared to large communes on former estates) disappeared. The Soviet government gradually extended its control. It was reported on March 1, 1918, that more than 500 communes were in existence, but only 3 had been registered. On July 1, 242 had been registered, out of 1600 reportedly in existence.(27) Thereafter registration was made obligatory in theory, and the unregistered proportion must have declined.

There seem, then, to have been two basic directions in the commune movement. The small peasant brotherhoods without official connections, possibly sparked by Left Socialist-Revolutionaries or anarchists, were dominant at the time when Bolshevik control over the countryside was weak. As control was established from mid-1918, more or less politically oriented communes were founded with some help from Soviet authorities and thus owed them allegiance. Purposes of the first were probably those of traditional peasant societies, with ethical and religious overtones. The latter were more political and economic, with thoughts of world revolution and mechanization of agriculture.

By Marxist theory it might have been expected that estate laborers would take over estates and form communes upon them, just as workers in the early Soviet period often took collective charge of the factory in which they had been employed. This does not seem to have happened; communes made up purely of estate laborers did not exist.(28) The proletarian communes which did arise were rather different. Before the Revolution, an anonymous anarchist had prophesied, "The peasantry will take into its collective possession all land and estate equipment. Part of the population living in the cities will hasten out onto the communized land, the more so, the more unemployment there is in the revolutionary period and the longer it takes to organize city production."(29) This happened; many a city worker, lacking a job and bread, hastened back to the country, where he probably had ties, and many entered artels or communes. Or they formed a commune in the city, then went together to a chosen site to start farming. These, sometimes called "potato collectives," were especially numerous around cities, and workers were an important element in communes founded during the civil war.

Veterans of the Red Army or guerrilla fighters also figured prominently. Communal military life and political dedication were excellent preparation for the commune. Lenin believed that acquaintance with military technology would stir peasants to a desire for the reconstruction of agriculture, and separating a peasant from his old milieu would make it harder for him to go back to old ways.(30) There was also overt indoctrination. A peasant who joined a commune years later testified that he had done so because an army lecturer had convinced him that individual farming was doomed.(31) When returning soldiers found the old village devastated, it was all the easier to think of collectivization. A delegate from the Rising Sun Commune told the Congress of December, 1918, "When I got back from the front, I saw right away we couldn't go on as we had been. The poor peasants were in a bad way, the huts were falling down, there was no grain, no cows, no horses, no tools . . . I got together peasants who had no land or very little, widows and orphans, and told them how I thought we must live. . . . Thirteen families signed up for the commune."(32) The share of ex-fighters, like that of ex-workers, was substantial in the commune movement.

There were diverse other groups. War widows sometimes formed communes to sustain each other. The Fortress of Communism was started in Siberia by seven widows or wives; later a few husbands joined on their release from service. These communards were virtually compelled to full communism; they had only one good pair of boots and one presentable suit, to be worn by whoever had to go to town.(33) Other hard-pressed persons, as refugees from German-occupied territories, entered communes or formed their own. Interestingly, there also were "intelligentsia" communes in small numbers. They were mostly composed of teachers, but agronomists and students also entered.

Another type of communard, numerically few but much celebrated, was the returning emigrant. "International" communes
could not appear until borders were reopened after the civil war
and they were founded only while revolutionary ardor was high;
hence they date from the early 1920's. In 1922-25 there were 18
such communes with about 2,500 souls.(34) A congress of "international" communes was held in Kharkov in 1924.(35) Some seem
to have been little Cominterns, with communists from many lands,
as one with 500 members of seven nationalities, led by Hungarians
who had lived in America. Russians coming back from the New
World usually formed the nucleus. Several such communes became,
because of their relatively high cultural level, outstanding models
and so are mentioned more than once in the following pages. These
included the Lenin Commune (one of many "Lenin" Communes)
founded by 150 Russians and Galicians, returning from the United
States and Canada in 1922. Their membership grew to 500 in 1930,
and their estate meanwhile rose from almost nothing to twenty
buildings, foundry, cheesery, sawmill, power plant, etc.(36) Another model was the Seattle Commune, otherwise known as the
"American" Commune. It was started by 77 Russians and Finns in
Seattle, Washington, many of them members of the American Communist Party. They were lucky enough to bring with them a good
deal of machinery, including a combine (then a rarity in Russia)
and 21 tractors. Like other "international" communes, they were
given abundant land by the Soviet government, 5,291 hectares in the
North Caucasus. However, they had troubles. There were snarls and
shortages, and at first they had to live in tents. Organizational difficulties arose, as in almost all communes; many members left, and
there were numberless changes of administration. Slowly they got
on their feet and became sufficiently prosperous to impress the
Webbs in 1935.(37)

Some communes were less in tune with Soviet ideology. There
were numerous Sectarian communes, at first welcomed or tolerated
but attacked after the NEP period. Monasteries often became artels
or communes in hopes of keeping their establishments intact; as
late as 1925, 5 per cent of communes in the Moscow district and 11
per cent of artels were of such origin. Estate owners also used, or
tried to use, the same device, incorporating themselves and rela-

tives and adherents as communes—although with few exceptions they had supposedly been dispossessed by Soviet laws. Lenin took a mild position in this regard and proposed allowing former estate owners, if favorably known to the peasants, to remain in estate-communes on the ground that they were useful agricultural specialists.(38) Some communes and artels were also formed by peasants without intentions of collectivization. As the decrees of 1919 and 1920 permitted collective farms to obtain land in a single block, peasants who desired to separate from the village commune could adopt this tactic. After the collective had obtained its land (no short or easy task), they would dissolve and partition it into individual holdings.

Troubles

If the first communes were poor as Job, the envisioned improvements were slow to appear. Probably typical is the story of a commune, which, founded in 1920 in hopes of a tractor, waited nine years before the authorities took any notice of its existence. First harvests were usually bad, sometimes only 20 per cent to 30 per cent of normal.(39) During the civil war, communes suffered not only the general burdens but also were called upon for an extra measure of devotion. With the NEP, workers again began receiving wages in money, instead of primarily in rations; peasants generally were no longer obliged to deliver all surpluses but to pay a grain tax. The commune idea was undermined, as the economy was virtually back on a monetary basis. As unemployment gradually declined, the idea of working without pay became less enchanting. For such reasons, the number of communes fell in half between 1921 and 1924. In the Ukraine about half of those which dissolved in 1922, the worse year for communes, were workers' "potato communes."(40) At the same time, official help for communes was terminated and attitudes became doubtful if not unfriendly. In some places, mortality was all but total. In a district of the Kuban, in the North Caucasus, of 70 communes in 1920, only 3 survived the following years.(41)

A basic difficulty was finding something to take the place of waning enthusiasm. A commune founded in 1922 pulled through initial hardships and got some good harvests but then found productivity steadily declining, instead of rising as expected. Growing enough to eat without great exertion, the members felt no incentive to do more and simply took it easy.(42) All communes of which there is detailed record underwent organizational sickness at some time. Thus, the Communist Lighthouse, later a model, suffered fly-by-night membership, and many who entered to keep warm and fed during the winter showed their heels at plowing time. After the famine of 1921, it was almost dissolved, having at one time only two families and a few individuals. Later, those who wanted to share out the assets converted it into an artel; when they had gone, taking their horses and belongings with them, the remainder reorganized into a commune.(43)

The price of stability was usually the loss of a large part of the membership. The Red Orphans Commune sank from 150 in 1920 to 68 in 1922 but even then suffered lack of incentives and only slowly straightened itself out.(44) The Free World Commune had up to 300 members in 1920 but did not begin to find organizational firmness until a few years later when only 36 were left.(45) A commune which received a large estate in 1924 was given a loan for working capital but imbibed it in a grand celebration that became a fracas with neighboring peasants. Membership was diverse and divided; the president was ejected by intrigues, fought his way back, and was finally thrown out as a class enemy after a veritable battle. At length membership was purged, quarrels over land with the peasants were settled, and things went better.(46)

Communes suffered from internal and external political conflicts. Although not located in a battle zone, the Dacha Commune of the Tambov district was entirely destroyed three times by anti-Soviet bands, 1919-21.(47) Such happenings were common in the civil war and the immediately following years. There were frequent troubles with Soviet authorities, also, when these were dissatisfied with the character of the commune. For example, a commune founded on government land at Sviatoslavsk had, after the usual hardships, only eight of the original several dozen men. These few holdouts now felt themselves owners of the domain and refused to consider any but wealthy applicants. When the local Party committee demanded that they admit some poor peasants, they acceded but kept them in the position of laborers. The latter protested; the "old communards" threatened to withdraw but demanded return of their share of commune property, which the commune was unable to pay. The Party then took charge and presumably corrected the class composition of the commune.(48)

Uncertainty of Commune Numbers

Figures give realism and exactness, and statistics of communes and their population tell much of the interacting effects of Party policy, the changing economic and political situation, and the maturing commune movement. Although its birth and its passing are enveloped in statistical darkness, a good many figures were published during the 1920's.

These must, however, be treated with the greatest caution. They can indicate general trends where samples are more or less comparable, or show approximate magnitudes as of the dates referred to. But they cannot be used as a basis for detailed analysis, and inferences based on small percentage changes may be quite misleading.

There are several reasons for such reserve. Disorder and disorganization of the early years made accurate counts in the countryside quite impossible. Different sources, as the Commissariats of Agriculture and Finance, the Kolkhoz Center, the Central Statistical Board, and the Worker's-Peasants' Inspectorate, gathered data and often gave contradictory results. Only with the collectivization drive after 1928 were statistics coordinated and only a single set published; but it cannot be assumed that uniformity meant accuracy. Much of the detailed data, especially that of collective farm economics, was based on samples, and there is no reason to suppose that sampling was scientific. Much information came from questionnaires filled out by officers of collectives. From the questionnaires returned—a large proportion were not—information might be reliable for some matters like the number of members but not for complex or doubtful questions.

Even regarding the simplest and most ascertainable objective fact about collective farms, their numbers, there were large doubts in opposite directions. As in the first part of 1918, the estimated number of communes continued to be greater than the number registered; for years, many declared that a large part of the commune population was not on the rolls. Legally, registration was made obligatory in July, 1918, but this was effective only if the commune wanted something from Soviet authorities. It may be supposed that many, especially religious communes, remained aloof. Bukharin noted that by December, 1918, there had been registered 1,384 communes but declared that there must be in fact over 2,000.(49) In February, 1921, when there had been ample time for registration, a delegate to a kolkhoz congress reported that 40 per cent of the collectives in the area around Moscow—perhaps the most accessible of all to Soviet influence—were unregistered, and another delegate from the North Caucasus claimed to speak for 300 unregistered in addition to 448 registered collectives.(50) A writer of 1925 claimed that the Commissariat of Finance had gathered taxes from 33,000 collective farms, whereas official statistics showed only about 15,000.(51) Indicative of the confusion was a reverse report for 1926: although only 15,000 collective farms had been taxed, the Agricultural League claimed that 22,000 existed.(52) Until the latter 1920's, numbers were also reduced by the simple fact that they did not cover all of the Soviet Union.

Those less fond of collectivization were inclined to stress the inflation of the rolls with collectives which had never really come into existence or had fallen apart without cancelling the registration or were not collectives in the spirit of Soviet laws. In 1925 it was found that only half of the supposed collective farms of the Moscow district were actually operating.(53) In 1928, workers of the Statistical Board found about 40 per cent of communes, artels, and tozes on the rolls to have been liquidated de facto.(54) There was also an indefinite but sizable proportion of "pseudo-kolkhozes." These were more or less fictitious collectives, formed as a means of saving landholdings of wealthier peasants or even landlords, or as a means of obtaining credits or other favors without really collectivizing. In some places in the mid-1920's they were allegedly half of all registered collective farms.(55) But this was probably much exaggerated; it was easy to brand as "pseudo" any kolkhoz that did not measure up to particular political standards.

No less uncertain was the classification of collectives. That is, it is impossible to know, when figures speak of communes or artels, how many really were communes or artels. So far as statistics go, a commune was a kolkhoz registered as a commune. But, until all were drawn under strict control in the 1930's, there was no real obligation to follow closely the prescribed rules. By definition, they were reasonably distinct: in communes all production and consumption were socialized; in artels, basic means of production were socialized but households remained separate and had garden plots and some livestock; in tozes, means of production were only partly socialized but basic cultivation was done jointly. But all types departed frequently from these rough rules, and variations were legion. Only in a minority of communes was all consumption collective; some formal communes were run like artels, some artels like communes; even tozes like communes with collective eating and living existed. In 1919 *Pravda* wrote of communes and artels as being generally indistinguishable.(56) Ukrainian writers in 1923 claimed that the dominant form was really the commune (though only 6 per cent by statistics) simply because most collectives distributed by eater or by need.(57) For a long time, even after the formal extinction of communes, there were strong tendencies to equalitarian distribution in artels and even tozes; this brought them closer to the commune spirit though it did not, of course, make them real communes. It is curious that when Gaister in 1928-29 investigated 13 kolkhozes, 7 of them formal communes, the only full-blooded true commune among them was formally an artel.(58)

Even if the statutes were correct, there is no surety that they were followed. Astoundingly, it was learned at a Crimean Congress of Artels and Communes in 1924 that not only members but even officers were most ignorant of their own statutes.(59) Kindeev found, in the mid-1920's, that about a tenth of communes and artels had no written rules, while over half paid their statutes little heed.(60) But communes seem to have run truer to type, as a rule, then artels and tozes. Studies in various regions from 1925 to 1929 showed about nine-tenths of communes were carried on more or less as communes, while a quarter or more of artels were actually tozes or fictitious.(61)

Even if there were a serious effort to list each type accurately, ceaseless change soon outmoded the data. There were always foundings, dissolutions, mergers, and transformations. An idea may be gained from shifts in a single district during the eight months following October 1, 1928. At the beginning there were 470 communes; 281 more were organized; 101 artels and tozes took on commune form; 89 merged to form 31; 2 changed to "lower" forms; 12 were dissolved. The net change was an increase from 470 to 781.(62)

For such reasons, much of the numerical data on kolkhozes must be considered only a semblance of reality, its accuracy much dependent upon luck. Despite this, the many figures generally give a fairly consistent picture of the differences between types and their development, and they are consequently worth attention.

Numbers of Communes

Communes registered monthly during 1918 were as follows:(63)

January	1	July	134
February	2	August	235
March	5	September	57
April	7	October	672
May	25	November	77
June	202	December	84

It cannot be told how much of the upsurge after May represents formation of new communes or registration of existing ones. During 1918 it was not considered necessary to register artels at all.

Total numbers for 1919-22 for the Russian Soviet Republic (RSFSR) show the growth of artels and tozes alongside communes. As given by the Commissariat of Agriculture, they are:(64)

	Sept. 1919	Sept. 1920	March 1921	Jan. 1922	Dec. 1922
Communes	1,961	1,892	2,114	2,459	1,672
Artels	3,606	7,722	11,136	9,238	8,130
Tozes	622	886	1,356	2,431	1,605

The communes, it appears, had a tendency to increase until well after the beginning of the NEP early in 1921. But already in 1919 they had yielded first place, and the increase of artels was much sharper. Before the end of 1920, large areas were affected by civil conflict, and not all parts of Russia were under Soviet rule until late 1922. Most of the growth of kolkhozes in these years was in the reoccupied lands.

Another set of figures, covering the whole Soviet Union, begins with 1920: (65)

	1920	1921	1922	1923	1924	1925	1926
Communes	1,759	3,015	1,943	1,874	1,571	1,829	1,742
Artels	8,067	9,777	8,459	6,809	7,381	8,802	9,081
Tozes	695	2,497	5,038	5,319	4,571	4,547	4,072

Communes and artels remained fairly steady after 1922, with a small rise for the latter and a small decline for the former. The low figure for communes in 1924 is said to represent a purging of the rolls of those long inactive. (66)

From 1927 onwards there no longer exists a multiplicity but only a single set of figures: (67)

	1927	1928	1929	1929	1930	1931	1932	1933
Communes	1,335	1,796	3,537	4,654	7,564	7,600	4,200	4,000
Artels	7,135	11,574	19,167	20,773	63,517	193,600	202,400	216,200
Tozes	6,362	19,888	34,341	42,019	14,869	9,900	4,500	4,300

These refer to June 1, except the second figure for 1929, which is for October 1. The totals, rising so sharply, 1929 and thereafter, tell eloquently the story of collectivization. Tozes, as the easiest form to establish, dominated at first but were turned into artels as political pressure mounted in 1930. Communes were numerically less important but reached their height just as tozes were being relegated to second place. Communes then declined as the artel pattern was made the rule.

After 1933, no statistical separation of types of collective was made. In any case, by then all were pretty nearly shaped to the common mold.

Some idea of the regional distribution of communes may be

gained from the following table, showing percentages of the total number of kolkhozes for the Soviet Union and the chief regions, 1923 to 1933:(68)

	1923	1924	1925	1927	1928	1929	1930	1931	1932	1933
USSR	12.2%	11.0%	9.7%	9.0%	5.4%	6.2%	8.8%	3.6%	2.0%	1.8%
Ukraine	4.6	5.9	6.7	4.6	2.7	2.9	4.3	3.7	3.1	2.9
Belorussia	18.0	16.0	14.3	11.1	6.6	7.7	11.7	3.8	2.0	1.9
Moscow Olb.		12.7	11.7	20.3	8.9	6.3	5.8	1.2	.9	1.0
Ural Oblast		41.6	38.6	25.6	14.7	14.5	16.1	7.7	3.7	
N. Caucasus		47.0	10.8	9.2	3.4	4.2	11.5	9.9	8.1	
Mid-Volga		4.0	5.5	6.9	3.0	3.7	4.6	6.2	2.6	2.2
Siberia	57.4	59.6	42.9	28.4	16.0	21.6	31.9	9.0	3.9	2.1
Far East		8.0	15.9		10.8	15.6	29.8	7.9	4.5	1.4
Transcaucasus					2.9	2.0	1.4	0.7		0.4
Uzbek Rep.					1.6	0.4	0.5		0.2	0.1

These figures confirm that communes relatively abounded from the Urals eastward. In the non-Slavic Transcaucasus and Central Asia they were very few. Their proportion fell everywhere in 1931 as Stalin turned away from the commune.

In general, according to this and other information, communes were most numerous in Great Russian areas, somewhat less so in the Ukraine. They were important in less densely settled areas, as Siberia, the Lower Volga, and the North Caucasus. They also clustered around Moscow and to a less extent Leningrad.(69) Their greatest dominance was in the Buriat Mongol region in Siberia, where in 1929 they had 52 per cent of all collective farmers and 82 per cent of collectivized land.(70) This may be attributed to the old tribal communism of those peoples, just as the absence of communes among Central Asiatics must have been due to their different background.

Membership

The average commune was about 50 souls until pressure for collectivization began in 1927. Average size, so far as can be judged, varied little from 1918 through 1926. Significantly, artels and tozes also most commonly had 20 to 30 workers and an equal number of dependents; also, it was reported in 1925, in all regions, the average was about the same. (71) This no doubt shows that peasants generally found such a group most satisfactory. There was considerable range; some communes were midgets, a few were giants of 200 or more, those of over 400 members were rare. But a survey of 1921, for example, showed 70 per cent to have between 25 and 100 souls. (72)

In 1926 and after, the membership of collective farms was counted in households, no longer by individuals. This was a reversion to the custom of the village commune, which was composed of households; it was contrary to the provisions of the statutes that joining a collective was an individual matter. The average household varied but may be taken as 4 to 5 persons—smaller than the usual family because unattached persons were also counted as households. The following table of average membership in households shows the effects of the collectivization campaign: (73)

	1926	1927	1928	1929	1930
Communes	12	18	19	28	71
Artels	11	18	12	16	73
Tozes	13	21	12	17	57

The communes seem to have outstripped artels and tozes in 1929, when Party policy was most favorable to the former. The big spurt came in 1930, when all three forms reached dimensions about six times greater than had been usual when membership was quite voluntary. This signified, of course, a basic change in the collective farm movement. The communes in particular were swollen far over the size which could make full communism workable.

Social Origins of Communards

The commune offered the greatest appeal to the rootless and homeless, to orphans, refugees, and workers unable to find a livelihood in the city. Giving no return on property, but expecting help from the government, the commune offered most to those who had least to lose. To the extent that it was politically oriented and associated with the Soviet regime, the commune was presumably most attractive to the groups more sympathetic with Bolshevism, more to the working classes than the peasantry. All of these reasons should have made the commune, more than the artel, a non-peasant group.

The somewhat contradictory data indicate that this was to some extent the case. However, despite expectations to the contrary, the communes were usually of dominantly peasant composition. The very first communes prior to March, 1918, as has been pointed out, seem to have been overwhelmingly peasant groups. And even after the Soviet government had moved to take charge of the communes, they had quite as much a peasant make-up as the artels. A study of lists of founders of 590 communes and 877 artels established in 1918-19 showed that peasants made up 55 per cent of those going into communes, but only 45 per cent of those going into artels. Only in 1920-21, when city life was near its lowest ebb, did the non-peasant tendencies of the commune appear strong enough to reverse these proportions.(74) In 1919 in the Moscow area there was a surprising tendency for workers to shun the communes; 40 per cent of agricultural artels but only 14 per cent of communes were classified as dominantly "worker."(75)

Later, the proportion of workers declined in all kolkhozes but less in communes than in artels and tozes. For example, in 1925 communes were reported to have 10 per cent workers, while artels had 6 per cent and tozes 3 per cent.(76) In 1927-28, when industry was back near the prewar level, communes were found to have only 5 per cent workers, while artels and tozes were down to 3 per cent and 1 per cent.(77) Communes apparently still held some attraction for nonpeasants, especially workers, who now shied away from artels. A survey of entrants into a group of communes and artels in 1927-28 showed that a tenth of those going into communes were workers but almost no workers entered artels. The communes also received a large number of orphans.(78)

There were more peasants of the poorest strata in communes than in other collectives, especially the tozes, which were best able to attract middle peasants. Various surveys showed about nine-tenths of commune entrants officially in the "poor" category, against about three-quarters of artel entrants and half of toz entrants. "Poor" meant nearly destitute; as many as three-quarters of commune entrants, for example, owned no horse.(79) There was thus clearly a difference of composition between communes and tozes, with artels standing between. But it was a difference of shade; many poor peasants went into tozes, and a few middle or prosperous peasants went into communes.

6 Organization

The Prescribed Statutes

Communes were far from uniform and had diverse arrangements for joint production and consumption. Nor were they immutable but ever altered in response to the changing surroundings and pressures directed upon them; it might be said that the commune of 1933 had ceased to be a commune in the sense in which the word was used in 1918-19. However, the commune movement had at least a formal unity in that all communes were expected to conform to a pattern prescribed by the Soviet government.

In order to register with local officials, the commune (or artel or toz) had to deposit a copy of its statute or charter, which defined it as a juridical entity and set forth its formal structure and rules in basic agreement with the officially decreed model. Supposedly, then, the model statutes should tell how communes were run. But in the first years many communes did not bother with statutes at all, and the statutes adopted might differ widely from the model or be more or less ignored. Hence, the model statutes indicate better what the Soviet government hoped communes to be than what they really were. Only after 1929 was it seriously attempted to control the collective farms through the model statute, and for years thereafter accusations indicated that the control was much less effective than desired.

But as long as collectives were voluntary, the model statute could not deviate very far from what peasants understood commune or artel to be. In view of the weakness of the Soviet regime in the countryside, this was especially true of the first commune model statute, issued on July 21, 1918, by the Commissariat of Agriculture. This model is also of particular interest as it represents something close to the commune ideal; subsequent changes were nearly all retreats from its aspirations. Its principal provisions were:

1. There is established in . . . an agricultural commune under the name of . . .
2. The commune is organized in order to a) increase to the maximum the production of food by raising the productivity of agriculture and increasing the cultivated area; b) make the fullest and best use of agricultural machinery, tools, and other equipment; c) build the economic bases for the transition to socialist agriculture; d) form model demonstration farms.
3. The following principles must be fully carried out in the life of the commune: a) everything belongs to everyone, and no one in the commune can call anything his, except objects of personal use; b) each member of the commune labors according to his ability and receives according to his needs, in keeping with the economic possibilities of the commune; c) work is done jointly; d) surplus production after covering all needs of the commune is delivered for social use through the local food administration of the Soviet government in exchange for goods needed by the commune; e) the commune cannot use hired labor.
4. Every able-bodied citizen over 18 years of age has a right to enter the commune. The entrant is confirmed by the assembly or council of the commune.
5. The members of the commune undertake to follow the general principles of communism and to obey the rules established in the commune concerning work, the use of goods, etc. Those who disobey the rules of the commune may be expelled by the general assembly . . .
7. Those who leave, voluntarily or expelled by the general assembly, cannot demand any of the property of the commune, except articles of immediate personal use. Note: the general assembly may arrange assistance if the motives of withdrawal are justified.

8. If direct exchange of goods is impossible, the commune may sell its products, but only as absolutely necessary to buy goods not obtainable by exchange . . .

11. The commune will organize shops (smithy, carpentry shop, etc.) so far as possible for the satisfaction of its needs.

12. The commune will train specialists in all branches of agriculture from among its members, for this purpose establishing courses, schools, etc. Note: at first, the commune may invite outside specialists as instructors . . .

14. All the business matters of the commune and its internal order are governed by the general assembly of members . . .

17. To save labor, food and fuel, the commune will organize collective eating facilities.

18. All administration is in the hands of the general assembly and council . . .

20. It is obligatory for all members to attend assembly meetings . . .

27. The council consists of . . . members chosen for (period) from the members of the commune.

28. The council chooses from its members a president, secretary and treasurer . . .

31. The rights and duties of the council are fixed by the assembly . . .

34. Personal effects of members are not subject to liquidation. In case of dissolution, all property of the commune is turned over to the local soviet.(1)

This statute is an obvious hybrid. In part, it expresses Soviet policy: the commune should serve to improve agriculture; all surpluses should be handed over to the government; the commune property should be turned over to the local soviet in case of liquidation. Yet communist ideals received their full due: all belongs to all; distribution is to be by need; hired labor is forbidden, except for instructors; the "general principles of communism" are to be followed; those who leave cannot demand return of property; goods are to be obtained, so far as possible, by barter; communal eating recommended; for self-sufficiency, the commune should have its own shops. References to shops, courses, and schools may indicate that authorities contemplated large communes.

The model soon required amplification; supplementary instructions were issued two weeks later. These underlined the character of the commune by requiring that entrants surrender all their possessions, money included. Whereas the model statute had declared everyone eligible to join, the instructions accented political bias by forbidding entry of classes associated with the old regime—capitalists, merchants, priests, police, etc. The list of recommended communal facilities was also enlarged to include residence-hall, school, medical services, library, etc.(2) Such hopes, at a time when industrial production was down to a small fraction of the prewar level and rapidly sinking and the greater part of Russia was occupied by anti-Soviet forces, were extremely visionary but indicate the spirit with which it was hoped to infuse the communes.

Six months later a new commune model statute was published, that of February 19, 1919. This attention to the commune is the more notable as no artel statute was produced until May of that year, and no official toz statute, apparently, until 1922, although an unofficial model appeared in 1919. Such neglect cannot be attributed to Soviet indifference to the "lower" forms, as they were consistently mentioned in legislation. It was probably felt that they were not so politically usable; artel and toz seem at first to have been regarded as associations which could make their own way, while the commune was a means of communist mobilization.

The Land Law of February 14, 1919, it will be recalled, went counter to the tendency of Soviet policy since late 1918 to de-emphasize the commune. Similarly, the model statute of February 19 showed a remarkable heightening of tone at the very time when the Party was making it clear that communes had fallen from esteem. It gave the communes a loftier "final goal," no longer mere preparation for socialism but the transformation of all Russian agriculture to communist bases, collective labor, and "just" distribution of the results of labor. For this, the commune must "carry on the struggle with capitalism by all means." The commune was not to be regarded as a separate unit but must work to unite industry and agriculture and join with other communes, peasants, and state farms for the collectivization of the whole economy under the guidance of the authorities. Educational and cultural facilities of the commune must be open to peasants as well as commune members. All nationalities must be welcomed, and only opponents of the Soviet way of life rejected. There should be established a common residence and eating place, and facilities for making and cleaning clothing.

Women should be made equal to men; to achieve this, sewing rooms, nurseries, communal kitchens, and laundries should free women from domestic drudgery.

The authors of this statute evidently hoped the communes would be very useful for Soviet political development. But there were some retreats from primitive communism. Entrants were to surrender only such property as was useful to the commune; hiring of labor was permitted for special tasks or in times of shortage, as at harvest; communards were promised freedom in personal life as long as they did not infringe the rights of others; persons departing might take household goods. But the commune was still to be a model of "brotherly equality."(3)

The artel model statute of May 19, 1919, was contrastingly non-political. It stated purely economic aims of improving farming practices and had no words about equality, or socialist agriculture, or union for general collectivization. It required entrants to contribute not their whole property but a fixed quota in money or equipment, and members might provisionally retain individual farms within limits to be fixed. Those leaving the artel were entitled to their share of the harvest, the return of their entry contribution, and allotment of land outside the artel. Religious and political freedom was promised, and there was no warning against anti-Soviet elements. The rules for distribution were vague but left the door open for equalitarianism: the harvest should be used first to fill the needs of members and their stock; the surplus, if any, should be divided according to labor or as the assembly might determine.(4) The mixture of individual and collective ownership required involved rules regarding the different kinds of capital. Blanket collectivization in the commune rendered such details needless; commune statutes were always briefer and simpler than those of artel and toz.

According to the model statute of May, 1919, the artel differed from the commune not only in lack of political slant but in allowing members to keep private property, even their own farms. Much of the difference was erased by the next artel model statute, that of September 29, 1920. This required the entrant to give up all equipment and stock and even to turn over to the artel any outside earnings. It also required that the artel, like the commune, should deliver to the government its entire product over the needs of its members. If the artel were liquidated, its property, like that of the commune, should go to the government. Consequently, some artels became virtual communes, and others converted to the laxer toz form.(5)

When the NEP brought a milder atmosphere, the commune was made more attractive to middle peasants. Model statutes of 1922 and 1923 provided that only agricultural equipment and household goods useful to the commune should be collectivized; these should be assessed and credited to the communard. When he left, he should have back his tools and the value of his other contributions. The heavy political emphasis of 1919, the goals of communism in agriculture and class struggle, were left behind. But the fundamental tenets remained: "Equal division among the members of all products of their labors," and "The collective satisfaction of their needs," for which common living quarters, laundry, kindergarten, eating facilities, etc., should be provided. It was optimistically specified that each family should have its separate room. The commune was to remain close to the government, NEP to the contrary, for its economic plan was subject to approval by the local soviet.(6)

The artel model statute of 1923 likewise loosened the requirements of collectivism. No longer did members have to give up all individual farming. The basic capital of the artel was to be formed from non-returnable entrance dues, but the degree of collectivization was left up to the artel. Each had full freedom to divide its harvest as it pleased, by labor, by mouths, or any other method. Formally, the toz statute of the same time was little different from that of the artel. But it specified that lands might be worked by individually, as well as collectively, owned means of production, and part of the harvest should be used to pay dividends on members' contributions. The toz assembly was free to distribute by mouths if it wished but might even let each member take in the harvest from his own fields.(7)

The evolving commune model statute provided in 1926 that those leaving the commune were entitled not only to return of property they had brought in but to an assignment of land. More important, it recommended that the commune pay workers in accordance with the quantity and quality of their work. But this was only a recommendation qualified by the concession that the commune might distribute by need or by mouths in accordance with its capabilities. It was also mitigated by the statement of purpose, that the commune should provide (presumably without charge) communal living, eating, laundry, and other such facilities.(8) Supplementary rules issued at the same time suggested unequal pay with an increase of one-third for the most skilled. To make money mean something, the commune should charge market prices for goods furnished to members.(9)

The 1928 statute took the commune another step from the old ideals of communism. Mention of collective eating and living, kindergartens, laundries, and the like was dropped entirely, except for vague "cultural facilities." Work was to be rewarded by payment for quantity and quality, and bonuses might be given in addition. Not more than 75 per cent of income should be spent for social purposes; presumably, at least 25 per cent must be paid out for work. However, probably in deference to unaltered practice of many communes, it was still allowed that the assembly might authorize distribution by need or by mouths.

Model statutes for artel and toz during these years were not significantly changed. Amount of collectivization and methods of distribution were still largely left up to the collective farm. But supplementary rules for the artel in 1926 recommended crediting work time according to age classes and establishing pay rates up to 50 per cent over the basic scale. There might also be premiums for quality. Interest should be paid on everything brought in by entrants over the minimum quota.(10) But these rules seem to have been only suggestions.

Late in 1929, the pressures for collectivization were rising toward the violent storm of January and February, 1930, when there was something near civil war in the countryside. New model statutes were hence required. On December 21, they were issued for commune, artel and toz; for commune and toz these were the last ever to appear. That for the commune moved still farther from communist ideals. Members were flatly given the right to payment for their labor "by quantity and quality"; although they were entitled to commune services, they should be charged for these. Moreover, payment was preferably to be made in money, not in kind, despite the old commune abhorrence for money. As collectivization was becoming a political struggle, kulaks were forbidden entry, just as in 1918 the classes associated with Tsardom had been excluded. As collectives were getting ever bigger, for communes of over 500 members provision was made for additional governing organs including an assembly of elected delegates.

While this brought the commune much closer to the artel, the artel statute approved at the same time brought the artel closer to the commune. It went back to the artel statute of 1920 by requiring collectivization of all land, equipment, and draft animals—no more individual farming. Those leaving the artel were to be given no artel land. Pay should be by quantity and quality of work, with bonuses as deserved. As in the commune, kulaks were excluded, and there were provisions for delegate assemblies for large artels.

This was inadequate for the political demands of the feverish collectivization drive. At its height, February 6, 1930, a new artel model statute was issued. This was almost as political as the commune statute of 1919. It opened with a flaming declaration of purpose: "To ensure real and complete victory over the kulak, over all exploiters and enemies of the toilers, real and complete victory over poverty and ignorance, over the backwardness of small individual farming. . . ." Not only kulaks, but any peasants who had sold or otherwise disposed of their equipment or stock were excluded. The land of the artel was sacred; it must never be decreased. No longer was there to be a fixed quota for entry, over which property brought in would be considered a returnable deposit. Rather, the entrant had to turn over a quarter to a half of his property to the "indivisible fund," the proportion, higher for the wealthier. All work animals, equipment, seeds, and farm buildings were to be collectivized. Regarding payment, the same statute took a step backward. Payment was to be by labor, but quality was not mentioned. Perhaps to give the Party a freer hand in directing the kolkhoz, the general assembly was degraded, its functions being reduced to the formal election of officers.

This artel statute reflected the brief upsurge of the commune spirit, and often the commune title, at the beginning of 1930. It clearly encouraged the excesses of rudely forced collectivization, which continued through January and February with loss of much livestock and turmoil among the peasantry. It did not definitely require that the peasant's cow and chicken be collectivized, but it gave no hint to the contrary and so implicitly sanctioned the efforts to form practical communes.

Change of policy was signalled by Stalin, who in a brief article published on March 2 rebuked those who had allegedly exceeded instructions by using force and carrying collectivization too far. A new model statute was required, of course. Published in the same papers that displayed Stalin's article, it provided that households should be left with their garden plots and tools, plus poultry, pigs, cows, etc., within limits to be fixed. It also went back to the payment of work by quantity and quality and urged piecework so far as possible.

This compromise must have proved more workable, as it has essentially endured to this date. The principal modifications made were to increase economic incentives. An instruction of April, 1930, required that 5 per cent of gross income be paid as interest on property brought in; various rules of 1930 and following years strengthened the system of piecework payment and made rewards increasingly unequal according to type and amount of work.(11) Finally, in 1935 there was proclaimed a new model statute, more detailed than that of 1930 but basically unchanged; this has remained the universal code. Under it, garden plots should be given to households which had none. As before, families were permitted to keep necessary tools and fixed amounts of livestock. A brigade organization was established. Piecework pay was made the rule and strengthened by such provisions as stated that not more than 2 per cent of gross income should be spent on social purposes, such as help for invalids, nurseries and the like. Such was the Stalinist kolkhoz statute which the last communes had to adopt.

The Actual Statutes

The successive model statutes issued to guide collectives show a good deal of Soviet policy but much less of actual organization. A group of farmers sharing customs and ideals might function best without formal rules, as suggested by the Left Socialist-Revolutionaries and as the village commune always functioned; and many kolkhozes were long grossly indifferent to statutes. In 1919 a peasant delegate at the Eighth Party Congress, apparently unaware of model statutes and instructions, stated that there was no set pattern for communes, that each just decided on its own form.(12) Communes sometimes went directly counter to the model, as in 1924 a Ukrainian commune adopted the rule that departers could take with them only immediate personal property, although model statutes for two years had provided just the contrary.(13) The journalist Tretiakov, who has given a rather detailed account of the Communist Lighthouse, a leading commune of the North Caucasus, tells of many discussions of matters of internal order, but he never mentions the model statute supposed to guide them.

The Soviet government recognized that the models were not to be followed strictly. When in July, 1918, registration was required, it was specified only that statutes be in "basic" agreement with the model. The artel statute of 1924 conceded in its introduction that it was only a model, to be modified as desired within the laws. As late as 1930, the Commissar of Agriculture said that collective farmers should work out "their own" statutes on the basis of the model.(14) Only in 1935 did the artel statute become totally rigid. Even the few details not fixed for all had to follow norms set by regional authorities. Thus, collective farmers in Kirghizia would be allowed to keep more horses than in the Ukraine, but only as officially determined.

Unfortunately, it is not possible to compare the rules of actual communes at different periods. A few appeared in peasant newspapers prior to the publication of the official model; one of these, of May, 1918, was so similar to the official model of July as to suggest common inspiration. (15) Later it was not considered necessary to publish crude peasant rules. An exception was the forthright regulations of a commune founded by army veterans in the Ukraine in April, 1924: (16)

1. Everyone entering the commune must understand clearly that he who works eats, so he should take pains to do the job assigned him, knowing that, if he works for all, all work for him.
2. No matter what job anyone has, he receives equal shares with everybody else.
3. Everyone must be careful to look after the interests and property of the commune.
4. No one must leave his daily task unfinished.
5. Everyone must listen to the directions of his senior comrade.
6. Follow the practical instructions of a comrade.
7. Be polite to everybody, remember you are a proletarian with the title of communard, and this is your social obligation.
8. Don't use strong drinks and don't go on a binge.
9. Don't start arguments in the commune, either about goods or politics.
10. Use your free time sensibly.
11. Keep yourself and your surroundings orderly.
12. Keep the dormitory, grounds and buildings clean.
13. Help all you can with the political, educational, and physical development of young communards growing up.
14. All property brought into the commune is for common use, except articles of prime necessity.
15. In case of voluntary or compulsory departure from the commune, you have the right to take away the property you brought, but your work stays with the commune.
16. Everyone entering the commune promises (in writing) unconditionally to fulfill the above rules. Violation will be punished by expulsion, if necessary.

Government of the Commune

Since most communes had only a few dozen members, no complex structure of authority was needed. Written statutes to the contrary, decision-making was probably mostly informal. Kalinin, for example, noted that the smaller communes were ruled by patriarchal authority and opinion over the dinner table. Only larger communes bothered with formalities of elections and the like. Artels and tozes tended even more to be informally run, as artels of old, by the accepted headman.(17)

The prescribed structure was simple. Supreme power lay in the general assembly of members, which elected a governing council or board. In order to check abuse of authority, there was to be a "revision committee" to review administration and finances. Only the last commune model statute provided for two-step elections in communes of over 500, a delegate assembly to choose the directors.

The powers of the general assembly were theoretically un-limited. It adopted the rules to regulate the commune. It elected officers, admitted or expelled members, ratified accounts, es-tablished work regulations, provided for the division of the com-mune income.(18) Model statutes required that it meet only twice or thrice yearly, but special assemblies might be called by the council or some fraction (as a fifth) of the membership. Voting was open by custom, as always in the old peasant institutions, and this was specifically decreed by the last model statute.

The assembly seems ordinarily to have asserted itself more than intended by the model statutes. If it met only twice a year it could do little, but more frequent assemblies were common. It appears that monthly or even weekly meetings were usual. In 1925 in the Kuban, communes averaged 19 assembly meetings; artels had 11 and tozes a mere 4. As women were usually shy in speaking out, some had special feminine assemblies.(19) Topics discussed were, in descending order of frequency, the commune economy, organization, violations of labor discipline, accounts, cultural-educational questions, finances, social-political matters, economic improvements, and construction.(20) Assembly discus-sion could be serious and lively. The American Commune regu-larly had stormy sessions, which for a time were so tempestuous that the chairman might be changed four or five times in a single night. Bickerings and quarrels often stirred up the meetings, and they were criticized for trying to discuss everything, no matter how trivial.(21) No doubt, the proposals of the directorate were usually sanctioned without difficulty, but restive assemblies might rebel and expel the officers at any time, causing serious discontinuity of policy. It was often provided, in order to maintain the independence of the assembly, that its president could not belong to the council.(22)

If the commune were large enough to have a delegate assembly, this took over the functions of the general assembly of members. Thus, in the huge Fortress of Communism Commune, each ten members chose one delegate.(23) This was reminiscent of peasant self-government in Tsarist Russia. Whereas village communes had assemblies of all heads of household, several villages together would elect a *volost* assembly, sending one delegate for each ten heads of household.

The ordinary business of the commune was carried on by the council or directorate. This varied in size, from three for small communes to five or more for some larger ones. Communes of more than 100 members were by the later model statutes to have at least fifteen councilmen; for the Fortress of Communism, there was a cabinet of thirty. The term of office was one year, but re-election was allowed and probably frequent. Positions of chief manager or president, secretary, treasurer, bookkeeper, and the like were usually bestowed by the general assembly, despite the model statutes, which instructed that the board or council should apportion duties and designate president, treasurer, and other major officials from among themselves. In the Fortress of Communism, the council chose a presidium of president, field director, property manager, financial director, and cultural supervisor. Board meetings might be open to any member to attend, as they were in the American Commune.(24) Sometimes, despite statutory provisions, all members were made equal in responsibility as in all else. That is, offices rotated daily or weekly, making every communard chief administrator in turn.(25) It is of interest that this practice of rotating responsibility with short terms was adopted by a Populist society in the mid-nineteenth century.(26)

The revision committee, which was to see to the correctness of the actions of the officers, watch expenditures, and report to the general assembly, was smaller, with only two or three members. This watchdog group was seldom mentioned and probably of tertiary importance. In the Kuban in 1925, half the artels and tozes, but only a tenth of the communes, lacked a revision committee.(27)

Management of the commune was no doubt more complicated than that of the artel or toz, because of the greater degree of integration. Futhermore, the strength of the Party fraction in most communes meant far more political direction. In form, however, the system of administration laid down in the model statutes was exactly the same for all types.

Entry of Members

A prime organizational question for any close group is the control of membership. For the commune, this was complicated by ideology. As a utopian community with faith in its social magic, it should welcome everyone; but experience soon taught that many were not assets to the group. As a militant proletarian-revolutionary organization, the commune should exclude all non-proletarians and admit freely all the poor and underprivileged; but it had sometimes to be allowed that peasants who had bettered themselves were superior agriculturists.

Aside from the injunction of the 1919 model statute to bar certain criminals and classes considered counterrevolutionary and that of the last statute, of December, 1929, to keep out kulaks selection of members was largely left up to the individual communes, although the party occasionally exerted pressure for the admission of poor peasants and Party members. High turnover of membership, especially in the first years, showed that many unsuitable persons found their way in, but the commune had only itself to blame. Candidates were customarily put on probation for three months to a year; only after this mutual acquaintance did the assembly vote on the applications. The Communist Lighthouse tested candidates by hiring them for a period. Probation might be dispensed if a communard vouched for the candidate or if he were well-known. Sometimes, if a peasant was reputed to have valuable skills, the commune sent emissaries to urge him to join. Often communes, especially if prosperous, were choosy about admissions. According to one investigation, communes turned away over ten times as many as the artels. The reason given was usually lack of industry. But shortage of living space was frequently cited, and those with many dependents were viewed coldly.(28)

Another question with which the commune wrestled was that of the entrant's property. If a peasant surrendered irrevocably his worldly goods, he was solidly bound to the collective and would have to identify himself with its fortunes. If his property was reclaimable, he might regard his association with the commune as temporary and unworthy of great efforts; if it turned sour, he could pack up and leave. As Tretiakov tells, communards of the Communist Lighthouse would keep their eyes on their "own" horse or cow and give it special care for four or five years; such tendencies were overcome only slowly as the commune's "own" or "indivisible" fund grew in importance.(29) Yet, if property were not returnable, few but the poorest peasants could be expected to be so rash as to leap into a commune, risking destitution if things went badly. So it was at first; by the statute of 1918, the candidate had to turn in everything but his clothes and was promised nothing when he left. The 1919 statute softened this severity, allowing the entrant to retain money and to take household goods with him. But generally in the early period the departer received only partial or delayed compensation at best.

In the NEP period, it was usual to take away clothes, household goods, and provisions. Any contribution over the entry fee was to be returned in cash equivalent (perhaps minus a charge, as 10 per cent). The valuation was made at the time of entry; this was likely to lead to a long haggle, with the new communard contending that his horse was strong and sleek, the commune chairman finding it lame and half-blind.(30) But the departer's lot was not happy. There was inadequate provision for assigning him land, and in order not to disturb commune finances, the monetary return was to be made only after settling the year's accounts or within a few years. The American Commune, in a departure from usual practice, paid interest on deposited property of members, but if they left promised to return its value only in installments over five years. In exceptional cases, leaders of communes were able to credit themselves with considerable sums and take out enough to go into farming on their own. Tretiakov spoke of the division of the commune into two classes in the early 1920's, those who considered it a permanent home and those who hoped it would help them safeguard their property for fairer weather.

Artels and tozes always and communes usually had a nonreturnable entrance fee, designed to enlarge the "indivisible" capital of the collective. It was usually not high, perhaps ten to thirty rubles, and there were exceptions for the very poor, army veterans, etc. However, it might be used as a barrier; the wealthy American Commune had a prohibitive entry quota of a thousand rubles.(31)

Collectivization of the Economy

According to the model statutes, Soviet policy, and the general notion of what a commune should be, those entering should give up all tools and stocks and thereafter farm only collectively. Commune practice was very close to theory in this respect; collectivization of production seems to have been at all times nearly total. For example, percentages of collectivization in the major categories were reported as follows in 1926:(32)

	Land	Tools	Work Animals	Other Animals	Buildings	Total Capital
Communes	100%	99.6%	98%	95%	98.5%	98%
Artels	55.5	75	15	13	31	30
Tozes	33	53	3	4	6.5	15

The contrast between communes and other forms is glaring. At the time, communes were practically the only collective farms to collectivize thoroughly in any category, especially in livestock. The artels and tozes were very lax by comparison, at this time, as permitted by the model statutes.

Few communes were as remiss as one near Smolensk, the members of which made good money in 1925 keeping individual cows and selling milk in the city.(33) But it was in regard to cows, pigs, and poultry that collectivization was least complete. This is understandable in view of the fact that most communards ate in their own households and not from communal kitchens. Even so, according to a study of 1926, communes collectivized 90 per cent of their pigs and 80 per cent of poultry; artels collectivized only 13 per cent of pigs and 18 per cent of poultry; tozes, almost none.(34) Likewise it is a reflection of the usual lack of communal eating arrangements that in 1927, 25 per cent of commune vegetable gardening and 48 per cent of fruit-growing were reportedly individual, although field crops were 100 per cent collectively cultivated.(35)

The effect of the drive for general collectivization was to bring the artels and tozes nearer the commune level of socialization. The following percentages are reported for June 1929, when collectivization was still relatively mild(36):

	Plowland	Draft Animals	Cows
Communes	99.5%	99.3%	98.6%
Artels	90	63	40
Tozes	74	24	3

Collectivization in the communes was only a shade more complete, but it had advanced considerably in the artels and tozes, despite the fact that a great many new ones had been formed. During the following months it doubtless continued to rise, and in the stormiest weeks of the campaign, January and February, 1930, nearly everything down to the last chicken seems to have been thrown into the common pot. In March, 1931, Stalin changed policy to permit individual ownership of limited "productive stock" and household garden plots in artels. In the spring of 1930 collectivization of cows in communes was still 90 per cent complete.(37) But permission for the peasant to keep a cow, pigs, and chickens was gradually extended to communes, and a series of decrees pushed communes toward the artel form in the next few years, with every household to have its garden plot and domestic livestock.

Collective Consumption

In the ideal commune, all lived like brothers in residence halls, all ate in dining halls food from the big kitchen, wore clothes from the sewing room, and enjoyed collective recreation, culture, and education. Toddling communards played and perhaps slept in the nursery; their brothers went to the commune kindergarten or school. Model communes sometimes may have come close to this ideal image, but the average was far behind. Probably because official policy was less concerned with collective dining than collective plowing, there is less information about the former. But it is clear that consumption was much less fully collectivized than production. Reasons are not far to seek. Joint housekeeping meant a much more radical break with customary peasant ways than joint cultivation. It also required heavy expenditures, usually without much promise of quick economic return. Party policy never favored collective consumption very much and came to view it as positively detrimental to productivity. Successive model statutes gave it less and less sanction.

It is remarkable, in view of the obvious costs, that communes were more successful in communizing housing than other services. As of 1925, it was reported that 80 per cent of communes had communal dwellings (against 22 per cent of artels and no tozes).(38) But this does not mean that a fifth of communards called their home their own. Even though detached, 98 per cent of living space in communes (against 31 per cent in artels and 16 per cent in tozes) was reported collective property in the RSFSR in 1926.(39)

Community feeding was much less the rule. It was reported for about half of communes in 1925, very few artels and no tozes.(40) In the Tomsk district in that year Kalinin found "most" communes to have dining halls for adults, while almost all did for children. Later, with the formation of many new collectives, the proportion with community eating apparently declined somewhat, but the scattered data are inconclusive. In 1930, about a third of communes, but only one to three per cent of artels and tozes reportedly had collective eating.(41) Very often there was a communal pot only in the busiest season, when labor was most in demand and many workers ate in the fields.

It is surprising that there should have been much less joint eating than joint housing in communes, as the mess hall might require less expenditure and would promise much greater savings of labor. A German attaché cited a commune which had suitable space for a dining room but for no evident reason failed to use it.(42) Resistance was probably psychological, especially the reluctance of women to give up their household functions. They did not like the communal kitchen. Of the Comintern Commune in Siberia it is told that men returning from the fields sometimes found no dinner because the women assigned to the kitchen refused to show up. The kitchen was also the chief breeding-grounds for quarrels, whence they spread through the commune.(43) On the other hand, the dining hall is frequently referred to as the heart of the commune, its center for discussion and contact among the members. Without such a focus, the commune would not seem to be a genuine commune.

Equally characteristic was the nursery or "children's home," which should partially or wholly relieve mothers of the chores of child care and give fledgling communards suitable upbringing. There is surprisingly little information about them, but it appears, from various regional samples of the 1920's, that a fifth to a third of communes had pre-school institutions of some sort; very few artels and almost no tozes were so graced.

Undoubtedly, the same conservatism that held back community eating checked the establishment of children's institutions, although the Party liked the nursery as much as it disliked the dining hall. Kalinin, a strong critic of collective consumption, approved warmly of "children's homes."(44) However, if housewives hesitated to give up their kitchens, even more did they resist—as Kalinin also remarked—surrendering their offspring to strange hands. Rumors that communes socialized babies and fears that children suffered lack of maternal care, while mothers were deprived of their darlings, were very common and must have contributed greatly to anti-commune feeling. A peasant woman rebuked another who had joined a commune, "Unnatural mother, letting your baby go to a nursery. I always have my baby before my eyes."(45) Despite the advantages Communists saw in the nursery, the more such institutions there were, the more peasants would find confirmed their fears that the commune meant the end of the family.

Nor was the nursery simple to organize. Although the model Communist Lighthouse supplied all the wants of the children and gave them special care and attention (to some annoyance of the bachelors), the nursery caused many headaches. At first, the communards thought to keep children in the nursery at night but were dissuaded by a visiting nurse who told them the little ones needed the comfort of nearness to their mothers. Later it was again decided to make the nursery full-time despite much maternal opposition. Sad not to hear the child's breathing near them at night, mothers would steal their precious ones from the nursery, which greeted the dawn with empty beds. But after a time, they became accustomed, or reconciled to the absences, and in the summer rush were glad to be relieved of children. The authorities gave a prize of 500 rubles which served to improve the nursery by providing metal cots. Then several of the neighboring kolkhozes began imitating the Communist Lighthouse by setting up nurseries of their own. However, the question of management was still vexatious. Mothers took turns, but they did not like it, although it was an easy assignment and rated equal to field work. There was a great squabble whether all mothers should share it equally, or give time proportional to the number of their children. This was settled only by getting a professional from Moscow.(46)

Communes might logically have many other service establishments, from maternity wards to barber shops, but there is little information regarding such facilities. For 1929 it is reported that 1 per cent of communes had medical stations and 2 per cent—a small number—had community laundries.(47) It may be assumed that material backwardness prevented such frills and usually limited the commune to basic services. Culturally, the commune shone with libraries, clubs, etc., much excelling artels and tozes; but these probably served political ends for the most part.

Absolute Equality

Total brotherhood means total sharing. In some communes, the spirit seems at first to have gone far beyond the first most communistic model statute, which permitted personal property in articles of individual use; and equalitarianism led to the ridiculous. The novelist Panferov, perhaps with literary hyperbole, related that all members of the Siberian Proletarian Will Commune wore identical garb; he was more surprised to be introduced to Masha Proletwill and Ivan Proletwill, all communards having taken that identical surname.(48) Contrary to the rules, in some communes all communards alike became president for a week. In the youth commune visited by Mehnert, it was agreed that boys and girls should do the same household tasks, but when the former proved clumsy at ironing, they were given only heavy clothes to smooth, while the girls did the laces and blouses.(49) In the Ukrainian Plow and Hammer Commune, it was decided to socialize the pillow-stuffings. All pillows were opened and equalized in size and fluffiness. In this thorough commune, everyone lined up on Saturday at the store, took off his used garments and put on newly issued ones.(50)

Clothes caused the most trouble. Since city workers entering the Communist Lighthouse had wearable clothes, whereas farm laborers often had only rags, some protested, "Why do I have no boots, and my wife has nothing on her back, while others have plenty?" No true commune could permit such a state of affairs, so they agreed to socialize clothing. This proceeded smoothly enough with the men, but women raised a storm at having to hand over extra dresses to less fortunate sisters. When sharing time came, some tried to wear all their dresses at once; others, led by the wife of the Party secretary, stuffed clothes up stovepipes. Afterwards, the former owners were furious to see other women parading in their erstwhile finery but had to swallow their gall.(51) (A kibbutz made a similar levelling gesture with contrasting results: American girls who had many dresses proposed sharing wardrobes with Israeli girls; the latter turned up their noses in disdain at the cast-offs.)

Extreme equalitarianism did not satisfy for long. A Ukrainian commune began by giving out clothing that was not only equal but uniform; at first the communards found the standard blue pants and skirts a pleasing badge, but soon wearied of it, and demanded a choice of style and color.(52) As in the kibbutzim, the first step away from completely communistic distribution was to allow each one to keep the set of clothes issued to him. But still there was discontent. Inevitably, some used up and discarded clothing and shoes much faster than others; some communards found others to be careless or believed that they deliberately ruined boots or pants in order to avoid having to work. The solution was to ration clothes or, to permit flexibility, to give members a money allowance to buy. Thus, to meet criticism, the Krupskaia Commune credited each member with 65 rubles yearly for clothing or whatever he wanted; later this was raised to 15 rubles monthly, of which seven rubles was charged for food.(53) Such a system seems to have been common in the latter 1920's, but, subsequently, the communes had to go over to straight pay for work.

It must have been difficult to decide just what should be furnished free. For example, gallants of a Siberian commune requested horses to search for wives. After considering that, unless he had already located a girl, the swain was likely to waste his trip, the commune decided and incorporated in its statutes: "To find a sweetheart, a communard must provide horses on his own account; but when going to visit a sweetheart he has found, he will be allowed three horses without cost."(54)

The Payment of Labor

In the brotherhood of the commune, which forbade that one should have more than another, it was hard to decide whether or how far economic incentives should be used to stimulate production. After the first period of accepted equalitarianism, Soviet discussion of communes usually centered on the question of incentives. Nearly all writers expressed belief that some economic incentives were desirable, but Party policy long remained imprecise, and little was done concretely to regulate labor management in the collective farms until the campaign for mass collectivization was well under way.

The rule of the first communes, unequivocally sanctioned by model statutes, was equal sharing or distribution by need, although perhaps not many were so liberal as the youth commune which kept a cash box open on the table for anyone to supply his needs.(55) Despite the commercialism of the NEP, the attack on commune idealism did not begin until January, 1925, when an All-Union Council of Kolkhozes admitted the possibility that communes should distribute according to quality and quantity of labor.

This was recommended by the model statute of 1926, with the weakening qualification that communes might distribute by need if they felt able to do so. Thereafter, if communes distributed by need or mouth it was their own doing and not because of any instructions. Subsequent model statutes, including the last, of December, 1929, emphasized payment for work, though distribution by need was still permitted. In 1929 the Party issued a strong call for material incentives in collective farms in general. In June, 1930, the accounting measure of the "labor-day" was introduced, and it was made theoretically universal in 1931.(56)

The kolkhoz "labor-day" was very far from equalitarian; credits were given not merely in accordance with quantity and type of work, but on a progressive scale. Thus, not only did a tractor driver earn several times more than a milkmaid, but his earnings rose steeply as he did more. For example, for plowing one hectare over 20 cm. deep he received only 0.65 "labor-days," but he earned 2.20 for his fourth, if he managed to plow four in one day.(57) Through 1931 and 1932 there was a strong campaign to generalize this system, but it could be said to have become universal only in 1933.(58) The "labor-day" accounting and distribution system, along with the requirement that communards be allowed their own garden and livestock, meant the virtual end of the communes.

Thus, until 1930, the communes were allowed to cut their cake as they saw fit, subject only to general exhortation from the authorities. There was much experiment and groping; even when a need for incentives was recognized, there was uncertainty how they should be arranged. There was resistance to attacks on equalitarianism, and sometimes reversion to an earlier equal practice because of fear of creating differences and privileges, an aristocracy within the fraternal commune. There were ignorance and inexperience, shortage of managers and bookkeepers, and the difficulty of paying wages when the commune income was in doubt until after the harvest.

Probably typical was the labored learning of the Communist Lighthouse, located near Piatigorsk in the North Caucasus and chronicled by Sergei Tretiakov, a minor author. It began in 1920 with full communism but soon found itself suffering from many eaters who only hibernated there. To control those who were not serious communards, the membership was divided into "actives" and "passives," the latter having no vote and no share of commune property. In the NEP, some of the "actives" decided that the time had come to take away their shares. When the more affluent had removed themselves, the communists recovered the upper hand and again tried to follow the rule, "To each according to his needs." Designated senior comrades made suggestions as to what ought to be done, but work went badly, and the plows barely scratched the earth. Reasoning and persuasion proved ineffective, especially as many counted on remaining in the commune no longer than necessary. Some needed boots after a few months; others made theirs last a year or more, and resented the difference. Non-smokers did not understand why they should furnish smokers with tobacco, and bachelors saw themselves supporting the large families. So there was established a compromise: everyone should receive an "existence-minimum," and for extras there should be pay for days worked. But board and room were free, the "existence-minimum" was only for clothing, and there was little else to buy. Workdays were added up on an honor system and often neglected, as they stood for little.

For lack of a sound currency, the "existence-minimum" was measured in wheat until 1924; then, with the currency stabilized, it was made a ruble allowance. An agronomist at this time introduced other reforms: charges were levied for food consumed in excess of the general ration, and strict control of days worked was instituted. This the good communards resented, saying, "We are our own bosses, let's just work and let it go at that!" The recalcitrant refused to enter their workdays, but resistance collapsed when others, especially women, received more at harvest.

There was still no reward for quality of work. An experienced blacksmith was paid just the same as a beginning helper, the industrious the same as slackers. The commune was still small, with some 25 workers and 70 mouths, but more stimulus was plainly needed. So they divided into sectors (livestock, field crops, gardens, etc.) headed by leaders on fixed pay, with a production plan for each, and attached communards permanently to sectors. Then the workers in a sector received a bonus of 20 per cent to 50 per cent of any net production over the plan. Thus each one was interested in raising production and seeing that his mates cooperated, it was no longer necessary to drag them out late in the morning, and they took better care of stock and equipment. There were premiums of as much as 200 rubles over the regular wage of 240 rubles.

This was still not satisfactory. If things went badly in any sector, workers lost interest entirely as they had no hope of bonus yet were sure of the "existence-minimum" in any event. Conflicts of interest arose, as when swineherds tried to monopolize fodder to the detriment of horses and cows. So the commune took a short step backward: there was to be no premium for any sector unless the whole commune showed a profit; this meant that each sector had a stake in the success of the others. The leadership also wanted to abolish the "existence-minimum." As long as it was retained, there could be little real difference of pay or reward for skill or effort. But resistance was very strong, as communards thought this would be the death of socialism.

Finally in 1929, after a year of argument and persuasion, they accepted its abolition and went over to piecework pay: fixed rewards in "conditional rubles" (to be evaluated after the harvest and settling of accounts, a forerunner of the "labor-day") per chicken raised, per liter milked, per hectare harrowed, etc. This stimulated production and also facilitated close accounting of costs and results. Still, the communards continued to hope that, with the increasing wealth of the commune and the growth of social services, they would one day be able to overcome the repugnant inequalities.(59)

Such were the concessions to self-interest hesitantly introduced and reluctantly accepted as lapses from principle. Changes came slowly; in 1925 a commune that decided to give some pay for work done, in addition to the usual share of the common pot, was pointed out as a novel example.(60) Introduction of a pay system brought serious dissension in many cases. In the Plow and Hammer Commune, many comrades refused to accept the innovation and left, while others who had pulled out decided to return.(61) And the inequality of wages was at first very mild. One commune, upon determining that labor should be rewarded, decreed that all alike, young and old, should have 0.10 rubles per hour.(62) A commune cited in 1927 as an example of progressive management gave everyone 5 rubles monthly plus provisions, and only 10 per cent of the net income was divided as incentive pay.(63) The Peasant International Commune established in 1925 a system of incentive pay by branches. The net income of each branch was apportioned as follows: 10 per cent for improvements, 15 per cent for non-workers; 40 per cent for collective eating; only 35 per cent for the workers. Even this was held an immoral compulsion to be abolished when the commune grew stronger.(64) A commune in the Buriat-Mongol region had, in the early 1920's, the usual troubles with full communism. Under the wage system adopted, women received 13.50 rubles monthly, and men, 16.50 rubles; one twenty-fourth of these amounts was deducted for any day missed, and work was made voluntary except at the rush season.(65) Division by days worked, also, was more equalitarian in practice than in theory, for most of the year there was a surplus of labor; common practice was to divide the available work more or less in accordance with the number of eaters in the household.(66)

The movement away from equalitarianism often halted entirely. In 1925, Kalinin wrote of a striking example of persistent commune spirit. The commune had decided to pay extra for extra time worked, but accounts at year's end showed that most had done more than the norm. Hence they resolved to do away with premiums as an insult to the good communard and despicable ruble-chasing. Instead, they bestowed honors. In 1922, Kalinin stated, there had been some scorn for the old motto, "To each according to his needs," but in 1925 it was firmly established. And with the rule, the commune became firmly prosperous, with many applicants and no more departures. Social pressure took the place of grosser compulsions. Each communard was obliged to work 300 days of eight hours, with quotas for what should be accomplished per day; punishment for poor performance was the name on the blackboard, loss of days credited, and expulsion for repeated offenses. Kalinin, no friend of communist distribution, found this admirable but not practical for the average peasant.(67) A commune in the Orlov district was reported going back to full communism in 1927; they decided that inequality, especially in clothes and shoes, caused bad feeling, and sought to remedy this by outfitting all alike.(68) *Pravda* on February 13, 1927, wrote of an "international" commune in the Ukraine: since 1920 they had kept full communism, and no one owned so much as a handkerchief; those leaving could take only the clothes on their backs (in flagrant disaccord with model statutes of many years standing); when the president worked in the local soviet, he had to turn his pay over to the commune. With such arrangements, the commune was reported to be quite a success and beloved of the peasants. The *Pravda* correspondent, at least, noted it all with much enthusiasm not in harmony with Party exhortations toward incentive pay.

The introduction of wages was often a response to a specific practical need. The Krupskaia Commune decided to give a regular monthly allowance to all members of 15 rubles, to solve the clothing problem. But when a state farm was established nearby, skilled workers began drifting away to earn good wages there, and the commune in defense was compelled to meet the state farm rates.(69) Another commune remained fully communal until 1927; then, in accord with the drive for collectivization, it admitted many peasants. These were weak in commune spirit, so a system of pay was needed: they were paid by the day, charged for food, and given a share of year-end profits according to days worked. Children and the aged were still cared for free.(70) The growing practice of hiring hands served as a stimulus to payment of wages; it was an obvious anomaly, in the Communist Lighthouse and others, that outsiders received pay while members did not.

Even in times of mass collectivization, despite strong official demands for incentives, communes were reluctant to admit substantial inequality. The American Commune in 1929 had equal pay of 0.15 rubles per hour for everyone, gave an equal yearly allowance of 50 rubles for clothes, shoes, etc., and took care of children. In 1930 they finally established pay classes with a spread of 0.15 to 0.30 rubles hourly. Another leading commune in 1930 paid the president only 1.50 rubles daily against 1.00 rubles for the beginning worker.(71) In that same year, the Stalin Commune, despite the strictures of that leader against equalitarianism, still distributed manufactured goods partly by need and counted on censure on the bulletin board and assembly to prevent malingering.(72) At the beginning of 1930, the model Lenin Commune, founded by workers who returned from America, paid 360 rubles yearly to all workers alike, while nonworkers received 280 rubles; skilled workers and directors received small bonuses. Everyone was fed and housed free. Even in 1933, although it had bowed to regulations and was dividing money income among members according to conventional "labor-days," the Lenin Commune furnished free light, housing, heat, and furniture, and it made a charge for food only sufficient to cover the cost of service, not provisions.(73)

Statistics of Distribution

There was such a variety of schemes as to defy classification; precise arrangements in any one commune might be different from those of any other. The Kolkhoz Union in 1928 found some twenty forms of distribution, ranging from pure communism to downright capitalism. But the limited numerical data available confirm the general picture of increasing incentive pay in communes and the trend away from equalitarianism. The drift was already indicated by a study of bases of distribution in collective farms of the Altai district in 1920-23(74):

Basis of Distribution	1920	1921	1922	1923
Collective or by need	40%	40%	20%	15%
Equal rations	60	60	30	20
Workdays, rations for nonworkers			40	40
Other (incl. dividends on contribution)			10	25

Prior to the NEP, all collective farms, at least of this region, were communistic or equalitarian. With the coming of the NEP, workdays became the leading basis, but it may be guessed that the change was more in artels and tozes than communes.

A sample group of Russian kolkhozes in 1925 was separated by types, with the following results(75):

Basis of Distribution	Communes	Artels	Tozes
Collective or need	32%	0%	0%
Equal rations	55	37	22
Workdays and rations	10	31	0
Workdays	3	24	4
Other (incl. contributions)	0	8	74

The proportion of communes distributing by need was of about the same magnitude as those with collective eating, but most communes merely divided equally the harvest for each household to use. Even where work was taken into account, its quality or difficulty was not usually considered.

But change crept on. In 1925, 48 per cent of collective farms in the North Caucasus according to the number of mouths, 11 per cent by the number of workers; in 1927, only 26 per cent by mouths, 44 per cent by workers; so effective seemingly had been the Party call for payment by work. In 1928, half of RSFSR communes reportedly took into account time worked, while a quarter still distributed by need.(76) Among the seven communes examined by Gaister in 1928-29 there was a wide range; in some, up to 90 per cent of net income was given out according to work performed; in almost all there were wage rates for different jobs; in one distribution was entirely by need or collective consumption. In 1930, figures for the Mid-Volga, Central Black Earth and North Caucasus showed 45 per cent of communes taking piecework into account and 30 per cent paying by straight time.(77) Subsequently, the Party undoubtedly made its will increasingly effective, but no statistics were published. Repeated pronouncements and edicts against equalitarian practices showed that it was no easy task to make the piecework "labor-day" supreme in the collective.

The Obligation to Work

When communes promised to give to all according to their need, they required that all should contribute their labor to the extent of their capacities. The rule was simply that all had to work; statutes typically laid this obligation on those between ages 12 and 60, except the sick, pregnant women, and recent mothers. Responsible heads were to assign specific duties. For breaches of discipline, there were social remedies: discussion in the general assembly, formal reprimand, and possible expulsion. The wayward communard might also be assigned to less pleasant tasks. Social pressure was exercised on a member of the Communist Lighthouse who was found sleeping under his tractor. The assembly condemned him to have no job for three days. Wherever he went, the communards asked, "How did you sleep?" until he was so humiliated that a chance to go back to work seemed heaven.(78) At first there was little specialization in jobs; each communard would have a daily task as assigned by a list posted the night before. Gradually there developed the practice of making monthly or weekly assignments, and as the economy developed it was found desirable to keep workers permanently at their specialties.(79)

Payment for work reduced the need to make work obligatory. However, at least through 1928 very few communes permitted members to work or not as they chose. Even the Buriat-Mongol communes which allowed members to idle at a sacrifice of one twenty-fourth of the months's pay had to call on everyone during the busy season. In all seven communes investigated by Gaister, work was compulsory; only in the one which paid most by work-time, women were free to work or not. Generally, in the communes the obligation to work was individual, while in tozes this was a household obligation, according to old custom. The greater complexity of the communes also required more specialization. According to a survey of 1928, in communes 83 per cent were assigned to special branches, against 41 per cent in artels and 26 per cent in tozes.

The Grounds of Equalitarianism

During the first years of the Soviets, the stark lack of almost everything made sharing a necessity. With far less deprivation all countries in wartime have some sort of rationing of scarce goods. Not only communes but artels and tozes were then equalitarian, and, so far as the requisitioning agencies of the Soviet government could bring it about, individual peasants were also limited to rations until 1921. When the NEP brought a market economy, change set in, but the earlier attitudes and practices were persistent. The belief seemed to remain, despite pronouncements, that official policy favored communist division. Even in the late 1920's when a commune sought to arrange distribution by work-time, local officials informed them that this was not allowed, that as a commune they must be communistic.

Not only the shortages but also the primitiveness of the Russian countryside checked any elaborate wage schemes. For example, when it was proposed to keep an account of hours worked in the Communist Lighthouse, no one had a watch. Finally some alarm clocks were procured from the local cooperative, and workers carried these in their pockets. The measurement of areas plowed depended upon who paced them off until a measuring tape was obtained.(80) Lack of standards and experience also impeded accounting. This could be solved only crudely, as in the Plow and Hammer Commune. When they decided to establish work norms, the president went out to see how many carts of manure he could load in one day, how many cows he could milk, etc. Then, as he was an unusually able worker, they made the norms somewhat less.(81)

More serious was the technical problem of bookkeeping. When everyone ate together, or the harvest was portioned by simply adding mouths or working hands, no fancy books were needed. It was the old peasant custom to carry accounts in the head, and this was done with great virtuosity, but memory could not tell how much each had done throughout the year. Yet bookkeepers were scarce, and bookkeeping was expensive; indeed, it might comprise the bulk of administrative costs. The professional bookkeeping of the Communist Lighthouse was extremely complicated; every transaction had to be entered in seven different accounts. It is no wonder that communes would be slow to undertake adequate bookkeeping and most of them got along with very little.

The practical difficulty of paying wages in the collective farm was inherently greater than in, say, a fishing artel, which would receive income at frequent intervals. Russian agriculture was based, not on livestock, which returns a fairly steady income, but on crops yielding a single harvest per year. Wages given out were advances on prospective results; to avoid overpaying, they had to be kept small. But for an effective incentive, the reward should correspond to real achievement and be prompt. Some communes tried giving stamps or bonds to be redeemed at a rate determined by the year's profits. But as of 1930, very few had adopted such a scheme or a labor-book in which the earnings of the communard were noted.(82) It is not surprising that selfless communards would shrug their shoulders and say, "Let's divide it evenly."

Under simpler schemes, everyone at least understood what his share was and should have been satisfied if he accepted the rationale of distribution. When complicated payments and rewards were introduced, there were many quarrels simply because members could not see clearly why one was entitled to so much more than another. Pay arrangements often created not only incentives, but conflicts. In this line, *Pravda* warned in 1925, before Party policy had hardened, that payment might create petty and divisive interests if not well controlled. Without good management, payment for work often led to financial troubles and demoralization of the commune. Inequality undermined the basic social spirit of the commune and sometimes led to sharp differences. It is said that commune directors sometimes lived much better than ordinary members and occupied spacious quarters while others were crowded together. In the mid-1920's, such cases were apparently exceptional but must have increased as communist equality was gradually smothered. Moreover, the opportunity to use position to gain advantages and selfish benefits naturally grew. American Farm Security Administration farms faced the same problem. Administrators knew that equal pay led to laziness and caused the best workers to quit, but most of the men supported it. While they realized that some worked harder or had more important jobs, they feared dissension on the value of any individual man.

From the point of view of the Party and Soviet government, incentive pay should raise productivity. But it could have an undesirable effect: communards might become more interested in withdrawing money and less interested in setting aside profits for investment. Furthermore, if money could be drawn, enough might be accumulated to leave the commune and set up one's own farm. In 1929 a number of the more prosperous families of one commune left, taking with them a good share of commune assets; the president, who was probably planning to follow them into individual farming, had a fortune of over 4000 rubles to his credit.(83)

Apart from such considerations, equality, hatred for privilege, and repudiation of commercial values were emotions which moved the Revolution and long continued dear to many. The commune was equalitarian in large measure not from convenience but because of deeply rooted sentiments—socialist, Sectarian, anarchist, or merely the old belief in the value of human equality. During Soviet times, the Sectarians seem to have been, of all communards, most reluctant to accept unequal pay. But usually the argument was in simple human terms. An agitator for the commune declaimed in 1919, "Our children must be all equal. If some have shoes, then shoes for all. Or if without shoes, then all without shoes. Likewise, the fathers and mothers should be all equal: everybody has a suit or nobody has one. Then nobody will envy anybody, and there will be no quarrels, for quarrels come from envy."(84) Distribution by needs, the communards said, was "Above all praise," a self-evident percept of socialism which needed no justification.(85) When an erring communard brought back from town some candy for his children, others asked, "Are our children worse than yours? Do our children have a balalaika for a belly?"(86)

Equalitarianism was thus strongly fixed in the ethos of the communes—and of other kolkhozes in less degree. It could be rooted out only by the active intervention of the Communist Party and Soviet government over a period of many years.

7 The Subsidized Economy

The economic success of the communes is to be weighed in relation to the help given them by Soviet and Party powers. Such help had several forms: land was assigned; confiscated assets of all kinds were turned over to them; loans were given them; their taxes were reduced; agronomists and others gave help; various minor favors of the bureaucracy eased their way.

Land

Perhaps the chief assistance for the communes was that which cost the Soviet authorities least; namely, land. In the first period, this was chiefly land of former estates, on which Lenin hoped model farms would be established. But the communes came into possession of only a tiny fraction of the estate lands. In the first year after the Revolution, of some 27 million confiscated hectares, communes received only 0.6 per cent or about 160,000 hectares; artels received a trifling 0.03 per cent or 8,000 hectares; state farms, most favored by the Party, got 2.7 per cent or more than four times as much as communes. Bolshevik faith in large-scale agriculture to the contrary, nearly four-fifths was seized by peasants for individual cultivation.(1) In subsequent years most of the remaining fifth was likewise acquired by individual peasants or village communes, but after 1918 the collectives obtained a larger share; ultimately, they came to possess nearly 2 per cent of the entire fund, while the state farms obtained 5 per cent.(2) Most communes founded on estates dated from the first few years, but the total liquidation of pre-Revolutionary large holdings proceeded slowly through the NEP period. One small estate near Moscow was not expropriated until late 1927 and in 1928 was rented to a commune.(3) About 11.5 million hectares of other government land were released by the end of 1927, but even of these, only a tenth went to collective farms, nine-tenths to individual cultivators.(4) Not only in the initial period, when perhaps it had no choice, did the Soviet government allow the peasants to divide large holdings; but long afterwards there was no great effort to keep these lands for socialist farming.

Although the very earliest communes were founded on peasant land, confiscated land became the basis of the commune movement after the Commissariat took control in the spring of 1918. A survey of 1919 showed the following sources of all commune land:(5)

	Estate	Church	Government	Farmstead	Allotment
Communes	74%	12%	4%	3%	7%
Artels	48	10	11	1	30

Estate lands were particularly suited for communes because of their central buildings. Church land in communes and artels was not nec-essarily confiscated, for it includes monastery lands, many of which were turned into collectives by the monks. Farmstead holdings had been, for the most part, separated from the old village commune during the previous decade; their use by communes was probably the result of anti-kulak actions of the Committees of the Poor. Al-lotment land had traditionally belonged to the village commune; that artels owed much more to this source reflects the inclusion in them of more middle peasants enjoying assignment of land.

Just as the proportion of peasants in communes gradually increased, so did the proportion of peasant land. By 1921, it was up to 16 per cent for communes and 36 per cent for artels.(6) By 1924, these proportions had increased much more, to 49 per cent of commune land, 55 per cent of artel and 62 per cent of toz land.(7) By 1929 all forms alike had about two-thirds peasant land. However, this does not mean that peasants voluntarily communized their holdings; although most of the peasant land in artels and tozes was contributed by entrants, that in communes was officially assigned at the expense of the village commune or more prosperous peasants.(8)

Information concerning the amounts of land available to collectives is rather inconsistent, especially in the first years. Accuracy was at first impossible, if only because the land holdings of kolkhozes were not delimited; in 1920 a third of communes and nearly half of artels and tozes were in that condition.(9) However, the figures for area per commune, 1918-20, are interesting; they are given with the corresponding amounts per soul as calculated from commune population figures: (10)

	1918	1919			1920
	Nov.	March	July	Nov.	March
Hectare/commune	84	313	235	71	99
Hectare/person		15	5	1.3	1.9

Unless these data are extremely erroneous, they tell clearly that pro-commune policy in late 1918 and early 1919 gave the communes very large amounts of land in the first part of 1919, probably in anticipation of a big influx of membership. By the end of 1919 policy change had become so effective that the communes had lost most of their land and had only about as much per soul as the unorganized peasants. In total, the communes had 510,000 hectares in July, 1919, but only 115,000 four months later.

During NEP times, there was no clear trend in the size of commune holdings. But with the active collectivization policy, they began to balloon, as shown by the following table showing the average size in hectares: (11)

	1928	1929	1930
Communes	123 Hectares	196 Hectares	505 Hectares
Artels	48	76	413
Tozes	31	64	285

All types of collectives grew greatly during the collectivization drive, but not until 1930 did they become really big farms. The communes tended to expand first, but in 1930 the artels and tozes were catching up.

Figures on land wealth per person in communes, artels, and tozes are somewhat contradictory, but it is clear that the communes were best endowed through the 1920's. Up to 1930, the average commune seems to have had about half again as much land per member as the average artel; only in 1930 did the artels and tozes tend to draw even with communes in this respect as in total land. For example, it is reported that in 1925 communes had 1.9 hectares of plowland per soul; artels had 1.4; and tozes, 1.7. For 1930, the figures *per household* had grown to 7.1; 5.7; and 5.0.(12)

Probably more ample land holdings of communes were evidence of official favor. However, the average size of communes, as of artels, varied greatly from region to region, and communes tended to be more numerous in the peripheral areas of east and south where land was freest and communes were largest—particularly in Siberia. The commune also had more land in part because with more equipment and larger-scale operations it was prepared to plow more per man than individual peasants or even artels. During the years of strife, grain requisitions, and worthless money, cultivation was limited not so much by the availability of land as by the ability and desire to work it; not until 1926 was the area sown to grain restored approximately to the prewar level.(13) During 1924-26, the collective farms, among which the communes were a small minority, actually used only about 70 per cent of the arable land at their disposal.(14) Despite more than average holdings, some communes rented additional land as they became able to work it. But the closer relation of the communes to the government is shown by the fact that artels and tozes rented more non-government land, communes more government, especially sovkhoz land.(15)

In a region of open spaces, as Siberia, the amount of land plowed depended primarily upon the equipment of the farmers. A study of Siberian communes in 1927 showed that those with at least a tractor planted about twice as many hectares per worker as those without machinery.(16) To some extent, also, the communes went out to appropriate virgin lands. It was an old peasant custom to send scouts to look for a new village site; this was easily done when they were organized as a commune.(17) Various leading model communes began romantically by pitching tents on the steppe; the Communist Lighthouse made wheatfields of a sheep ranch. In 1930, 15 per cent of commune land was classed as "new," compared with 6 per cent of artel and the same amount of toz land.(18)

Whether official favor included assigning better lands to communes is not clear. Peasants often thought so, but evidence is lacking. In any case, the surveying and land-assigning agencies were far behind in their work in the 1920's, although fees were charged for these services. In 1925 only about half of communes and artels had definitely assigned land.(19)

Equipment

Generally, the collective farms succeeded to estates in devastated conditions; those in good shape, if not parcelled out by peasants, were taken for state farms. Very few estates became communes until a year or several years after confiscation; by then, their tools and livestock must have been mostly gone and buildings and installations deteriorated. But in 1920 communes had slightly more tools per hectare than individual peasants—that is, substantially more per worker.(20) The gifts to the collectives represented no great affluence. In 1925 the average commune had, from confiscations or old government stores, the following: 4.6 plows, 1.3 drills, 2.2 reapers, .9 winnows, and .6 threshers; artels had about half as much in these categories and tozes, almost nothing from the government. These officially-furnished tools amounted to over a third of the inventory of the communes, a sixth of that of artels.(21) In view of an uneven distribution, many communes and more artels lacked entirely various essential items. In 1930, communes of the Moscow district were definitely better equipped proportionately than artels and tozes with tools except, ironically, old-fashioned wooden plows.(22)

In buildings, the communes were far from rich. Grain often had to be stored in individual households, and collectivized stock was boarded out for lack of barns. In 1925 only 18 per cent of communes were reported to have as many buildings as needed. Crowding may be judged from the average living space, a little under five square meters; however, even this was slightly more than in that for artels and tozes.(23)

Figures on value of means of production were published in connection with the collectivization campaign; they consistently show communes to have had more than artels and much more than tozes. For example, in 1929 the communes were found to have 385 rubles of collectivized means of production (tools, livestock, buildings) per worker; artels had only 201 rubles and tozes, 64 rubles. This was only partially balanced by the uncollectivized means of production, which amounted to 2 rubles in communes, 99 rubles in artels, and 137 rubles in tozes.(24) Much or most of the collectivized means of production in all types was financed by government credits.

Industries

Communes were often lucky enough to acquire small plants or shops, many of them appendages of former estates, such adjuncts as mills (the major type), oil presses, creameries, cheeseries, brick factories, smithies, or repair shops. In the Ukraine in 1925 there were some 60 of these for every hundred communes but only about a fifth as many in artels and tozes.(25) In the Kuban, communes had about three times as many "industries" proportionately as artels. The presence of city workers in communes during the first years, as well as the commune ideology of bringing industry and agriculture together (consecrated in the early model statutes) favored the development of such enterprises. About half of the commune "industries" (according to data of the Kuban) came with estates, about half were built by the communes themselves.(26) The small industries of communes were important in providing employment during the dull season and provided a better utilization of labor. They also furnished services to the peasantry and helped diminish hostility. They may have contributed to commune income, as the brick factory of the Communist Lighthouse, run with hired labor, which sold bricks to projects far and wide.

The communes had many more small semi-industrial establishments than the artels, but they were far from realizing their original hope of uniting industry and agriculture. The evidence implies that the Soviet government took little interest in fostering local, small-scale industry in the communes. Soviet industrialization was strongly biased toward the giant enterprise.

Tractors

It was hoped that the communes would lead in the mechanization of agriculture, and this hope was not entirely unrealized. The backbone of mechanization was the tractor, and tractors were obtainable only by leave of the Soviet government; even during the NEP period they were reserved almost exclusively for state or collective farms. Occasional communes got tractors in the early 1920's, when they were still something of a curiosity. The well-known Communist Lighthouse rented two in 1923, only to give them up as uneconomical because of the excessive cost of gasoline. But many draft animals died in the subsequent drought and in 1924 the price of gasoline was cut by two-thirds, so the commune bought the tractors back. Thereafter they were its mainstay; in 1925 Trotskii marveled that the Lighthouse actually possessed three.(27) Up to this time, however, communes and artels seem to have acquired tractors at an equal rate, an average of one for every 250 to 300 hectares.(28) But in the next few years communes were given preferential treatment; by 1928 there was a tractor per 128 hectares in communes, per 144 in artels and 167 in tozes.(29) In 1929, with an increased number of collectives, half of all communes but only a quarter of all artels and tozes had tractors. In the major grain regions in 1930 the proportion of mechanical power in communes was about three times as high (20 to 30 per cent) as in artels, and four times as high as in tozes. The greater disparity is in large part attributable to the formation of many new artels and tozes which the Soviet government was not prepared to equip, while tractors were still mostly imported from America; also, many of the strongest artels became communes during the collectivization years.

Loans

In the latter part of the communes' history, the most important help to them was financial. During the first period, such aid was liberally proclaimed, but given only in droplets. The first large appropriation was a billion rubles for communes and other agricultural collectives in November, 1918. The amount seems great, but was worth, because of depreciation, only about 9.3 million prewar rubles.(30) The average collective farm received, in terms of gold, 33 rubles in 1919, 17 rubles in 1920, and 3 rubles in 1921.(31) Even this was not a gift but was to be repaid in produce. Short-term loans for seed or fertilizer were due in a year; long-term loans for livestock, buildings, or equipment were due in ten years or less. And the approval of a loan involved submission of detailed plans with much forwarding of papers to tire the patience. In the troubled circumstances, however, any loan must have been very welcome, and long-term loans were equal to gifts.

When the Soviet government was struggling toward financial order in the first years of the NEP period, the collective farms, like many nationalized factories, were cut loose to sink or swim unaided. But as the economy revived, credit was again extended and made increasingly available. In six districts in 1925 loans outstanding already came to 27 rubles per hectare in communes, 22 rubles in artels and 18 rubles in tozes, while individual peasants had received 10 rubles; this was 26 per cent of the collective capital of the communes, 40 per cent of that of the artels.(32) An investigation of 1926-27 showed that communes received about the same per hectare as artels and tozes, but correspondingly more per worker.(33)

In the collectivization period, credits were much increased, and for a time preference for the commune was evident. In 1927-28, in Russian grain regions the communes owed 668 rubles per household, against 312 rubles owed by artels and 167 rubles by tozes.(34) It may be also that communes were given easier terms. In 1929, one received credits for 15 to 25 years, with no interest for 10 years and afterwards interest of 4 per cent on farm buildings and 1 per cent on dwellings.(35) This is remarkable in granting more favorable treatment for the non-productive investment; here, at least, the authorities were definitely helping collective consumption.

Communes in later years were practically not founded without financial assistance; all those organized in 1928 reportedly received loans, while 86 per cent of artels and 82 per cent of tozes had this luck.(36) But, since the communes collectivized more, the loans provided a somewhat smaller share of collective means of production in communes (41 per cent) than in artels (52 per cent), in those founded in 1928. Credits to tozes were even a little more than their collectivized property.(37) Whether or not loans were dispensed with special or undeserved generosity to communes, many peasants seem to have believed this. In 1928, it is stated, numerous artels adopted the commune statute in hopes of qualifying for more material support.(38)

Concessions in Taxation

The Soviet government also sought to foster collective farms by burdening them less heavily than individual peasants, but this aid was less substantial than positive financial help. During the civil war, general requisitioning took the place of taxation and probably lay as heavily on communards as on others. In the first years of the NEP, collectives were taxed like other producers. In 1924, as perhaps the first token of renewed interest in collectivization, there were granted tax reductions of 25 per cent for collective farms and 10 per cent for cooperatives. Yearly agricultural tax laws contained similar provisions until 1928. Then, for the first time, communes were singled out: the reduction was 30 per cent for communes, 25 per cent for artels, and 20 per cent for tozes (with bigger reductions if they were especially poor).(39) In 1930, as the most furious period of collectivization was nearing its end, a new law showed more favor for communes: they were to pay 2 per cent on gross income, while other kolkhozes paid 3 per cent.(40) In March, 1931, changing policy erased special treatment for communes; they and artels were to pay 3 per cent, and tozes 4 per cent.(41) In 1933 and after, all collective farms were again taxed alike.

The collective farms were not alone in receiving concessions under the complicated tax laws. There were exemptions for those without stock, for Red Army men, for those who took up new lands or sheltered orphans, etc.(42) In some ways, it was reported in 1925, the collectives were treated worse than individual peasants, being denied by officials the rights granted them by law. Karpuzi found that, among those he investigated, the communes paid in taxes 2.5 per cent of gross income, artels paid 2.4 per cent, and tozes only 1.5 per cent. This discrepancy he attributed to the greater ease of collecting from the more integrated economies.(43)

But the tax laws are of interest as an objective indicator of policy. Only from 1928 through 1930 did they support the general belief that the commune was the favored "higher" form; and it is remarkable that only four days before Stalin called for a return to moderation in collectivization was the commune given its biggest concession (February 26, 1930). Thus, as the collectivization campaign gathered speed through 1928, 1929, and early 1930, the commune was legally marked as the most desirable form. This is the best indication that for a time the Party thought the commune might be most suitable for collectivizing Soviet agriculture.

Other Helps

In a number of sundry ways, great and small, the Soviet government tried to assist the collectives. The Communist Lighthouse, for example, received a gift of a telephone for its tenth birthday and was awarded prizes from time to time, such as 700 rubles for model cultivation. Doubtless, communes found it easier, for the most part, to obtain scarce goods of all kinds, just as they were able to obtain tractors, and there must have been numberless little bureaucratic assists. But how important these may have been and how much favoritism there was for communes can only be guessed.

As one of the chief arguments for collectives was their potentiality for scientific agriculture, agronomists and other specialists were sent to them. They were also given assistance in procuring blooded livestock to improve herds. Whether or not communes received more than their share of such attention it is hard to say; it was probably extremely uneven, with a few getting most of the cake and the rest getting crumbs or nothing.

That such assistance was meager is indicated by data of Kindeev for 1925. He found that about three-quarters of communes, artels, and tozes had received the visit of an agronomist at least once in the preceding 4 or 5 years; the average number of visits in this period was about 3, roughly the same for all three types. A quarter of the communes had never seen an agronomist, and the average commune saw one less than yearly. During the same period, a third of the communes and artels, and somewhat more tozes, had not been visited by any representative of the cooperative union with which they were supposedly affiliated. (44) By 1928, however, the technical assistance program was much more active; in that year, communes received an average of 11 visits from agronomists, representatives of cooperatives, and local officials; artels enjoyed somewhat fewer such visits, 9, and tozes only 5. (45) In 1930 it was reported that 14 per cent of communes had an agronomist regularly attached, as did 9 per cent of artels and 6 per cent of tozes. (46) Earlier, only a very few, like the Communist Lighthouse, had been so favored.

The Counterbalance

The communes and other collectives owed much to the favor of the government. They received some tools, advice, partial remittance of taxes, generous assignment of land, loans, and other favors. Their way was not made easy but under the circumstances a little was far better than nothing, and without help the hardships would have been much greater. A large fraction of the capital of the communes, and of the collectively owned assets of artels and tozes, was represented by government investment in them.

No doubt many communards believed that, as bearers of the loftiest ideals of communism, they deserved better. Some may have been quite happy to be let alone, but others protested the severance of their close association with the regime in the civil war period. During NEP years before 1925, communes complained time and again that they were treated with indifference and neglect. Local bureaucrats found it easier simply to ignore communes. Complaints became fewer as the Party moved toward collectivization, but real munificence for communes was probably a local vagary. When some poor peasants were persuaded to start a commune in 1929 in the Siberian Barnaul district, the local kolkhoz section leader promised them a tractor, a barn, 80 cows, 5 swine, 18 rams, 500 sheep, seeds, and sundry other gifts. The poor peasants are said to have been giddied at such riches, and the leader earned severe criticism for irresponsible largesse.(47)

Relations with the government were not entirely beneficial. During the civil war, it demanded that communes give the maximum return. Whatever had been on the estates or was handed over from official stores was considered to remain government property, conditionally loaned. Consequently, income from this property was to be spent only on the improvement and expansion of the communal economy, and the commune was to consume only standard rations, delivering its entire surplus to the authorities. So strong was this feeling that it seems, even in the NEP, communes were still expected to turn their grain over to government agencies at low fixed prices, although collective farms, like individual peasants, were supposedly free to sell their produce for whatever they could get. As a result, communards were often so poor that they went around in rags, looking like "people from another world."(48) When the free market for grain was ended during the collectivization drive, the brunt of collections fell as hard upon communes as others. The state grain inspector spared nothing of the model Communist Lighthouse; once he even took away the feed saved for the pigs to be farrowed in the spring on the cogent grounds that non-existent animals ate nothing.(49)

Since at first most property in the communes belonged to the government, some held that the communes themselves owned nothing. An early commune statute said, "The Commune considers nothing its property, but recognizes all as national possession." Another put it, "All lands of the Commune and equipment for working them are property of the Soviet Federal Republic."(50) In practice, this meant that the commune might be regarded as a creature of the government, subject to sometimes arbitrary dispositions of local officials. The morale of communards suffered; even in 1925, when the NEP had gone far to divorce communes from the State, communards were often led to feel that nothing belonged to them.(51) With regard to land, in particular, the communes were unsure of continued possession. Many local authorities charged communes (and other collectives) rent not only for land but also for equipment and livestock, usually at the rate of 5 per cent of its value annually. According to complaints, some authorities took no interest in them except for the rent they could extract; and some kolkhozes lamented that they had to pay more than the landlord charged in the old days.(52) During the NEP, however, some land-rich communes with an eye to gain were able to make a capitalistic profit by renting out small parcels.(53) Not until 1927 were government lands decreed the possession of collective farms using them, with a provison for reversion in case of dissolution; arrears of rents were also forgiven.

The Soviet government and Communist Party had no generous fondness for the commune that would lead them to give much without expecting maximum direct return. However, one must judge in sum that the communes' association with the powers of Soviet society was advantageous, and thanks to government help at least a few communes progressed much more strongly than they could have otherwise. But communes were apparently formed early in 1918, with no official attention. There might well have been a commune movement without official intervention, but it would have been something very different.

The Soviet communes did not die naturally, wasting away from their infirmities, breaking up in disillusionment or bankruptcy despite efforts of a friendly government to bolster them. They were terminated by orders of the Communist Party, which found them no longer suitable. Perhaps if they had been extremely successful, they might have been retained, but the decision against them was a political one over which they had no control. The life allowed them was not long enough to offer an adequate test of their worth, for no generation of born communards had time to grow up and show whether or not the ideal was self-sustaining. But they were not total failures. To some extent they were able to justify hopes—at least, the more modest hopes—laid upon them.

Not all communes had the same goals. Some, no doubt, were formed by stricken peasants for survival through perilous times. For this, the commune probably served, just as artels established in the nineteenth century did, to help destitute peasants onto their feet. Religious or anarchist communes were able to satisfy their aims in brotherly and unselfish living. But in the official Soviet viewpoint, stress lay on the economic factor: more and improved production through collectivization. The better use of labor, equipment, and agricultural technology was the central idea of Lenin and the Party, who cared little for equalitarian consumption. It was also hoped that the commune would improve the lot of its members both by greater productivity and communal services—though the latter received less emphasis with passing years. However, in the eyes of the Party, improvements should be accomplished not so much for what the communes could produce or to raise the standard of living of the communards but mainly to demonstrate by visible example the possibilities of communist or socialist agriculture.

Utilization of Labor

The first advantage of the commune should have been the more rational and productive application of labor. In the early years there was apparently no success in this regard; reports of 1924-25 showed that communes, artels, and tozes alike were quite low in productivity. Later it seems that the utilization of labor in the communes, though poor, became rather better than in artels and tozes; but comparisons are difficult because members of the latter forms divided their time between collective and individual cultivation concerning which no information was given. A survey of 1928, for example, showed communes utilizing 54 per cent to 94 per cent of their potential man-days, while for artels the figures were from 30 per cent to 50 per cent.(1) The chief superiority of the communes was better spread of work throughout the year, thanks to subsidiary enterprises. Communes were able to keep fairly busy in January, while artels did little and tozes practically nothing.(2) Figures of 1930 showed 78 per cent of communes, 58 per cent of artels and 4 per cent of tozes utilizing their labor supply to the extent of more than 75 per cent of its potential.(3)

In considering this high underemployment, it should be remembered that labor was short in the Russian countryside only at planting and harvest time; most of the year there was not nearly enough to do. In 1925 the surplus population was estimated at 43 per cent. It was reckoned that if everyone did a standard job, up to 50 per cent of rural workers were in excess. Actually, about 20 per cent of the male and 10 per cent of the female labor force was idle.(4) Consequently, there was very little pressure to save labor or keep

people busy. Nor were those underemployed in collective farms constrained to leave. Perhaps because of the guaranteed livelihood of
the collective, individual peasants were more inclined to depart to
seek work in the city than the collective farmers.(5)

If the communes kept people at work somewhat more than artels
and tozes, this does not necessarily signify better results. Though
little information appears, there was certainly administrative waste.
It is told of a Siberian commune that 13 of 41 workers stayed in the
offices; of another that the administrative staff took 45 per cent of
the payroll.(6)

It appears, none the less, that either the communes had more
land because they were able to use more, or they were able to make
better use of workers because they had more land. Study of a group
of collectives in 1925 showed that communes got somewhat better
use of horses than artels and tozes and much better than individual
peasants. Planted area in communes was 8.5 hectares per horse; in
artels, 7; in tozes, 7.5; among individual peasants, 3.4.(7) A survey
of the main grain areas in 1930 showed communes to have planted
somewhat more per worker than artels and tozes but usually by a
margin of only 10 to 20 per cent. By this date, however, the Machine Tractor Stations had entered the picture, taking over the mechanical work on collective farms. Among those not yet affiliated
with MTS's, the communes stood out better, planting 20 to 30 per
cent more per worker than artels and tozes.(8) But such differences
may well be ascribed simply to the greater experience of the average commune.

Accounting

In regard to one requisite for efficient management, bookkeeping,
communes were better prepared than artels and tozes, though the
state of all was deplorable. In 1925, half of communes, but a third
of artels and a sixth of tozes were reported to keep accounts.(9)
Data of 1928 on collective farms formed prior to that year show
remarkable improvement: 96 per cent of communes, but only 42
per cent of artels and 60 per cent of tozes, kept accounts of some
sort. Something as sophisticated as double-entry bookkeeping was

practiced in 60 per cent of communes, 22 per cent of artels and 7 per cent of tozes.(10) In 1930, bookkeepers were reported in two-thirds of communes but in less than half of artels and tozes.(11) Again, the difference is largely or entirely explainable by the fact that the average commune was older and somewhat larger.

Hiring of Labor

Having to go outside for labor evinced poor use of manpower. This was clearly a sign, as in Amana and kibbutzim, of some failure of incentives or morale; a community has recourse to paid workers from the outside because its own members work badly or dislike certain jobs or fail to acquire needed skills.

The first commune model statute practically forbade hiring of labor; subsequent models permitted it only for special or emergency requirements (as did artel and toz statutes). However, this was ineffective. In 1924, an investigation of collective farms of seven regions of Russia found that four-fifths of communes and over a third of artels and tozes hired labor.(12) In some communes as much as 30 per cent of gross income went to paying employees. Another report, of 1925, was that three-fifths of communes and about a third of artels and tozes hired labor. But the communes were comparatively much worse offenders than this indicates, for the average commune had 6.6. employees, the artels only 1.5.(13) In 1929, the number of employees per commune had risen to 12 on the average.(14) A Soviet journalist in 1930 spoke of "almost all" communes using hired labor and criticized them for not establishing social services to free women for productive work. In part, communes were to be excused on the ground that, with more activities, they had greater need for specialists, as chefs or kindergarten teachers. But this was not a full explanation. Less than a third of commune employees in 1925 were described as specialists.

Livestock

Since the care of animals is more complicated than the growing of field crops and the penalties of neglect are severer, the raising of livestock was a test of the commune organization.

Evidently they did not pass with high marks. A study in 1920 showed communes to have about as high a worker to horse and cow ratio, as artels and individual peasants had;(15) and this was apparently still true in the Ukraine in 1924.(16) Kindeev in 1927 was very critical of livestock raising in the communes but stated that a third of communes, against a quarter of artels and less than a tenth of tozes kept their stock in satisfactory conditions. The proportion of young animals was the same in all forms, however.(17) Young animals, of course, are much more sensitive to neglect.

Stock raising in the collectives was retarded by the fact that it required big investments. Collective keeping of cows and horses, not to speak of pigs and poultry, also represented a more radical break with tradition than cooperative tilling. Responsibility was harder to maintain. Soviet communes no doubt had the same trouble as the Dukhobors: Who feeds the collective horse? The American Commune had fine wheatfields, but its pigs sickened and died and its hens averaged only one egg a week.(18) But some managed much better—according to Kindeev, in animal husbandry communes presented both the worst and best examples. The unfailing Communist Lighthouse built up a big business in pure-bred incubated Leghorns, which it hoped to export, and was proud of its woolly Merinos and fat English hogs. Among the kolkhozes studied by Gaister in 1928-29, the full commune had by far the highest milk production, a creditable 2,791 liters per cow yearly. Oddly, this commune was low in crop yields.(19)

Field Crops

The cultivation of grain and other field crops was at once more important and easier to organize than the raising of animals, and the communes were more successful in it. But the results were extremely uneven. There were well-run, comparatively efficient communes, and disorganized, shiftless, rundown communes; even small samples showed an enormous spread. Among 23 communes investigated in 1924, gross product per hectare varied from 25 to 155 rubles. In a single region, (the Urals) seven communes showed returns from 25 to 100 rubles. Income per worker in these seven ranged from 92 to 269 rubles; this was roughly correlated with value of means of production, which varied even more.(20) The 25 communes analyzed by Karpuzi showed yields of spring wheat, barley, maize, and beets differing by a factor of ten to one within single districts. Artels and tozes, to be sure, showed similar unevenness.(21)

Taking the good with the bad, the communes usually had higher yields than artels, while artels were ahead of individual peasants. In 1925 a comparison of crops of rye, wheat, oats, and barley in 11 districts showed communes to have the highest yields in 20 of the 36 cases where comparison was possible; artels led in 7, tozes in 2, and individual peasants in 7.(22) A 1927 study by Gosplan of 1,021 kolkhozes in seven regions gave yields of the same crops plus potatoes. In 19 cases where comparison was possible communes showed the best yields; in 11, artels led; and tozes in 3. Peasant yields were usually much below those of the communes but in the same range as the tozes.(23) In the Ukraine in 1927, communes recorded higher yields than individual peasants in all major crops, generally by substantial margins of 25 to 65 per cent. In eight of nine crops, communes were ahead of artels, but by a smaller margin, in no case more than 15 per cent. Toz yields tended to be about midway between artel and individual peasant levels.(24) Figures for grain regions in 1928 and 1929 show commune and artel harvests of winter wheat, spring wheat and oats to have been irregularly superior to the peasant average, usually by 10 to 40 per cent for communes and up to 30 per cent for artels. Only in oats did communes in one region and artels in several drop below the peasant average.(25) To the communes' credit, of course, they did this while farming substantially more land per man. On the other hand, they were the most experienced and best equipped of the collective farms.

Financial Returns

If communes had, as a rule, somewhat higher yields, they must have shown much better results in terms of ruble product per worker. The available information confirms this. In 1924, in six districts where communes' return per hectare was only slightly over the peasant average (87 to 80 rubles), their product per worker was much higher, 204 against 132 rubles; this was despite the backwardness in the communes of the more remunerative branch, livestock raising.(26) Reports of various regions in 1925 and 1926 uniformly show communes to have had average returns per worker higher than artels and much higher, often by 100 per cent or more, than individual peasants.(27) But equipment was responsible to a large extent; Karpuzi, for example, found that the cost of winter grain varied closely with the means of production available, irrespective of type.

The affluent American Commune well showed the effects of equipment. Although its pigs and chickens were neglected and bedraggled, with its many tractors and other machines it claimed to expend from ten to twenty times less labor per hectare than the peasant average and to have a return per worker of close to ten times higher than the peasants, while keeping a genteel eight hour day.

Stability

The effective functioning of the commune required reasonable permanence to gain experience and solidify the loyalty of members; only if people remained steadily with their commune could they develop the necessary skills and attitudes. Likewise stability was some index to the satisfactions found in the communes.

The proportion of communes liquidated year by year from 1924 to 1927 was high, from 22 per cent to 27 per cent; artels and tozes apparently suffered about the same loss.(28) This hardly indicates, however, that the ordinary commune lasted four or five years and then broke up. Many registered liquidations merely took note of long existing situations; many collectives never really got started, and well-established communes do not seem often to have dissolved. But the dissolution of a commune was more serious for its members than that of a less collectivized artel or toz.

With the onset of the collectivization drive, fewer collectives of all types were liquidated. Moreover, as shown by figures for

1928-29, most new kolkhozes were artels or tozes. Communes kept up in numbers by virtue of shifts of other collectives to a "higher" form. Almost no communes lowered themselves to artel or toz status, but 6 per cent of artels and tozes changed form, half of them becoming communes. Naturally, the proportion of liquidated communes was low, only 2.5 per cent, a quarter of the 10 per cent of artels and tozes that succumbed.(29) About twice as many commune members as members of artels and tozes were old hands, that is, had been in the collective since 1918-24.(30)

Liquidated collectives usually had little land—good evidence that they never got well started. In 1924-25, dissolving communes were only about a fifth of the average area.(31) This smallness was a common reason for giving up. Other reasons cited were failure to achieve consolidation of land and lack of competent personnel. It was found in 1924 that there was organizational weakness behind a large majority of commune failures. No communes, but a few artels, stated that they wanted to return to individual farming.(32)

Equally important was the flux of membership. In the prevailing uncertainty of everything, turnover appears to have been extremely high in communes during the first years. There were numerous complaints that communes were used as free boarding houses by the homeless, who would knock pleadingly on the door in the fall but be off to greener pastures in the spring. As late as 1924, turnover in communes was placed at an incredible 123 per cent; that is, the average communard stayed nine or ten months. For artels it was also excessive, 70 per cent; for tozes, 33 per cent.(33) By 1927 the flow had subsided to about 20 per cent for communes and artels, and the last figures, for 1928, are similar.(34) Gaister's study of 13 kolkhozes, including 7 communes, showed communes and artels about equally stable; but stablest of all was the full commune, which had lost only five out of seventeen families in the previous seven years.

Many reasons were given why communards turned their backs on the brotherhood. Some, it seems, simply found collective living, with its petty quarrels and frictions, more than they could stomach. In 1925, a peasant wrote to his local paper how his people fled back to their miserable village from a commune on a former estate which allegedly had a much higher standard of living. The men got along fairly well, but the women would have no more of it. "They ran," he wrote, "like wild animals out of a golden cage back to the woods, to go hungry, to perish, but by themselves." No doubt, as Koniukov put it, many left the commune because they found it tedious and hated to have days laid out in communal doings;(35) but such passionate rejection of togetherness hardly seems characteristic of the Russian peasant. Other causes are more often mentioned. An inquiry in eight immigrant communes in 1926 found reasons given by departers to be mostly material hardships, family reasons, or desire for other work.(36) Motives cited for leaving the American Commune included: unfamiliarity with agriculture; sickness, especially malaria; hard or dull living conditions; lonesomeness of bachelors; dissatisfaction with the food. It may well be that disagreements were minimized by the tact of the departers; Kindeev found disharmonies in three-quarters of communes, half of artels and a third of tozes; quarrels were mostly centered on property questions, and there was more to quarrel about in the communes.

Clearly, many who tried life in the commune did not like it or lacked the gifts of character, far from universal, which capacitate one for life in the big family. In part, high turnover was a by-product of utopianism and the belief that all men must be equally capable of brotherhood. A destitute wanderer would arrive, weep, and beg to be accepted, saying that the commune was the only way to live. A few months later he would move on, wearing his new coat and boots. But when the commune closed its doors, it was betraying its soul.

The Peasant in the Commune

How the peasant found life in the commune depended to a great extent upon his tastes. Some, particularly wives, hated desperately to give up their own home. Others were glad to have no longer to worry about providing for their old age, or taxes, or the calamity it would be if the family cow should die. Some could not stand rubbing shoulders continually with their brethren; others said they liked the commune because it allowed them to get away from their families. There were arguments, gossip, and intrigue in the commune, but philosophic communards said they had always quarreled in the old village anyway. Many petty irritations could be overcome. A man with a sick stomach demanded special food which the commune kitchen was not prepared to furnish him; after discussion, they allowed his wife to cook after hours in the commune kitchen. The father-in-law of a communard became resentful when the commune schedule did not permit passing the customary feastdays together; they had to invite the old man to the commune.(37)

Diversity in productivity was enormous and was reflected in standards of living. There were flourishing model communes, some of which seem to have been islands of prosperity; Western visitors, as the Webbs and others, were much impressed by their nurseries filled with laughter and the dining tables laden with wholesome victtuals. But even model communes suffered shortages of housing. In the Communist Lighthouse, 200 communards were squeezed into a mansion built for 20 at most; in the early days there was one bed per family, and many of the unmarried slept on the floor (a situation which fortified rumors that "All belongs to all" included wives as well as goods).(38) The Siberian Proletarian Way Commune lodged its members where cows and pigs were once at home, and lacked, for some, even such accommodations. Molotov found families living in foul-smelling closets in two communes in 1925. In other respects, too, the best communes were at first very poor. On a rare excursion a party of women from the Communist Lighthouse went into town but felt so humiliated by their bad clothes that they returned in tears.

The commune standard of living was highest in the dining room; this is considered later, as the tendency of communards to consume their produce probably influenced Soviet authorities against the form. In the Communist Lighthouse, men sat separately from women, four to each small table. Potatoes, cucumbers, meat, fish, and other food were brought in bowls for each table; communards dug in for themselves. Soup was served (after 1925) in individual dishes, which aroused the wonder of peasants accustomed to dipping their spoons into the common kettle. The youngsters even got such a delicacy as chocolate, while their elders sipped "fruit tea."(39) Children often had their own dining room in communes and were given, as in the Karl Marx Commune, special food at the expense of the adult diet.(40)

It seems likely, in view of the many rumors, that commune morality tended to be unconventional from the point of view of the Russian peasant. At times, there may have been a sort of commune Puritanism, however, not unlike the sternness of the kibbutzim where display of affection was forbidden though formalized marriages were not considered necessary. Tretiakov claimed of the Communist Lighthouse that cursing was hardly ever heard and drunkenness was almost unknown, except for one wedding feast when the communards consumed a bucket of wine with pangs of conscience. Liquor was banished; to get drunk, communards had to go into town, and the journey was hard enough that they were sober by the time they reached home. In a group of Siberian communes in the early 1920's, on the other hand, drunkenness became a bad problem, particularly when little dictatorships gained power. For example, in the Dawn No. 5 Commune, a man got himself elected president by promising petticoats and kerchiefs to all the women; when those who hated him left, the commune was entirely in his power. Such communes, it is said, became virtual distilleries.(41) A group of students found other enjoyments in commune life in 1927: having received loans and buildings, they used up the former for celebrations and turned the latter into a "rest home."(42)

Social services of the commune undoubtedly gave some satisfaction. A peasant wife entering in 1927 was unhappy to exchange a home for a small room in a communal dormitory but was pleased to have the bath, the communal laundry, and the miracle of hot running water.(43) A leading Ukranian artel in 1925, after considerable debate, decided to switch to commune style, with community eating place, kitchen, bakery, and nursery, to free women from household chores; it must be assumed that they had reason to expect convenience from the change.(44)

However, while appreciating the advantages of cooperative, relatively large-scale production, most peasants probably preferred to have something of their lives to themselves. In the pre-Revolutionary Krinitsa society, the idealistic elders observed with sorrow that the younger generation who should carry on the vision were not entranced with communal living. For the most part, the youth "dream of establishing themselves on their own land, with their separate households, to carry on the major sections of the farm cooperatively, but to manage their personal and family life according to their individual tastes and desires, and so to hedge in their individuality from the infringement of others."(45) In later terms, they preferred artel to commune style.

The Balance

The accomplishments of the communes must be weighed with its advantages and handicaps. The crop yields of communes seem to have been significantly above those of the peasants, but this does not mean that the same resources might not have been used to greater benefit in tozes or loose cooperatives. Certainly, much of the superior production of communes was due simply to material accessories. In Siberian communes it was found that those without machinery had a produce of 193 rubles per worker; those with one tractor or more, 402 rubles.(46) The advance over the peasant level thus seems ascribable more to the machine than to communism. In some places, Kindeev found, collective farms were well served by various Soviet agencies; here and not elsewhere they were distinguished by good yields. The logical conclusion is that the attention of Soviet authorities made the difference.

Considering the theoretical advantages of collective farming and the improved methods and equipment of the communes, a Soviet writer commented that their harvests were not nearly so good as might be expected.(47) Weakness was particularly evident in livestock, which requires closer attention and more organization than field crops. Mismanagement in details was rife; plowing was done, but the chickens were forgotten. There was endless petty waste. Lumber was left lying about, nails stayed where they fell, tools rusted in the rain.(48) What all owned, none cared for.

The fault may have lain as much with the communards as the commune. The human material of the Soviet communes was beyond doubt far behind that of the kibbutzim, which drew many persons of culture and dedication. While many of the very poor of the Russian countryside were doubtless capable and energetic, the abler farmer was more likely to build up his little farm and become a middle peasant or kulak. He who watched his cow and managed his fields with fond attention was not disposed to surrender them; the village drunk, who preferred to lie on the stove with a vodka bottle, might find a good lounging spot in the commune. In Sholokhov's *Virgin Soil Upturned,* the kolkhoz (which was nearly a commune) wanted to draw in the skilled farmers who most despised it. A Party report in the Kuban spoke frankly of communes like poorhouses, filled with lazybones who wanted only to live without working.(49) And even though poor peasants and laborers might be industrious—having to work hard simply to keep alive—they could not be expected to excel in organizational ability and careful respect for property, qualities essential for the successful commune.

For these reasons it is not surprising that communes passed through severe trials. Turnover was inordinately high for years, and stability came only very slowly. But the communes seem gradually to have improved in economy and organization. In part this was because the less successful communes and less well adapted members dropped out; it may be also that communes came to examine applicants with more discrimination. After the first years, moreover, communes came to be the older and more experienced collectives, as larger numbers of artels and tozes were being formed and some more successful artels decided to carry collectivization further, adopting the commune style.

In brief, if the Soviet communes failed to soar high or fulfill the extravagant hopes of 1918, neither did they entirely fail. No one could claim that the commune had proved a social-economic panacea, but, by looking at the most successful examples, the Party was able to claim demonstrations of advantageous collective farming.

9 The Commune as Political Instrument

The Party Fraction

The supreme powers in the Soviet Union, the leaders of the Communist Party, seem to have had in the commune a handy and useful instrument for forwarding their policies, both by example and action. Whereas generally the Party was weak in the countryside, Party control of most communes must have been very strong at all times, if substantial fractions of Party members are proof. Figures for the years 1925-29 show 8 to 18 per cent of commune members were in the Party; artels had only 1 per cent to 7 per cent and tozes 1 per cent to 4 per cent.(1) During these years no trend was evident. Afterwards, however, the mass collectivization drive diluted Party strength in all types of collective farms. In 1929, the communes' Party fraction was still rated at 11.5 per cent, artels' 4.5 per cent and tozes' at 3 per cent. But in 1930, Party members together with Komsomols (Communist Youth) were only 15 per cent commune membership, 6 per cent of artels' and 4 per cent of tozes'. Probably less than half of these were Party members, for data of previous years showed Party members to be only about two-thirds as numerous as Komsomols.(2)

That this was an extraordinary concentration of Party men may be appreciated from the fact that in the mid-1920's a Communist was almost a rarity in the villages; only about 0.2 per cent of the rural population were members. It was apparently due more to low-level enthusiasm than high-level policy; for Communists were urged to enter all types of collectives and cooperatives, not communes in particular. A writer of 1927 called upon Communists to join artels and tozes where they were most needed, but not communes.(3) Locally, Party cells often took the initiative in starting communes, and Komsomol groups would take it upon themselves to put communism into practice. Even when interest in communes was low during the NEP, Party and Komsomol leaders might be locally detailed to communes. But more often the communes complained that those who demonstrated leadership were drafted away from them. In view of the shortage of proven and dedicated talents—and all Party men were supposed to be proved and dedicated—such concentrations in the communes were highly uneconomic unless they were doing very valuable Party work. It can hardly be doubted that the top leadership would have preferred more Party men to give their attention to tozes, artels, and cooperatives rather than to congregate in communes. But Communists were drawn by the name or ideals of the commune.

According to standard Communist procedure, where there were more than three Party members they were supposed to organize a cell in order to exert influence more effectively. Although there is little mention of their activity, one can assume that Party cells were the guiding nuclei, the decision-makers, of many communes. According to reports of 1925, somewhat over a third of communes had Party cells.(4) That this was not higher may reflect a concentration of Communists in a minority of communes; obviously, if they were spread evenly, most communes should have had cells. Religious communes, of course, would have few or none; some other communes may have been virtually Party clubs. The proportion of artels with Party cells was much smaller, 6 or 7 per cent; almost no tozes were so endowed. Until collectivization was well advanced, most Party cells in rural areas were organized on a village, not kolkhoz, basis.

As the Party members were an active and organized group within the commune, and most of the members were surely sympathetic, Party control of governing bodies was naturally very strong. In 1918 it was reported that Communists were 40 per cent to 70 per cent of commune leadership, the proportion rising markedly after the Commissariat began active pro-commune work.(5) In 1927, Communists were reported to be about half of commune directorates, but only about a tenth or less in artels and tozes.(6) The great expansion during collectivization greatly reduced the proportion of Party people in the membership of collective farms, but this was not reflected in the composition of the governing bodies. In 1930, 40 per cent of commune directorates were still Party members, while in artels the percentage had actually risen to 22 per cent.(7) This was possible because the collectives were getting much larger, but it is evident that the Party was taking a firmer hand. Youthful Komsomols were 10 per cent of commune leadership in 1927; in the more conservative artels and tozes they were only 1 per cent or 2 per cent.(8)

Party Control

To some extent, the Party group might manage the commune according to its lights, as Kalinin found a commune in 1925 to be run independently, and badly, by the Party cell.(9) But in communes as elsewhere, Communists were supposed to be guided by instructions from above; those addressed by the Central Committee and other Party organs to Party groups and members in agriculture were legion. Direct control of the Communist cell in collective farms was vested in the district (*raion*) Party Committee. For the most part, this control seems to have been exercised informally, but the Party might intervene formally when it so chose. Party men might be sent to collectives or withdrawn from them; orders were given regarding political and economic work, propaganda, etc.

There were always extensive administrative controls over the communes. At first, while artels were left largely to themselves, communes were flatly put under the land offices, which were to require full accounting from them.(10) Even when the NEP after 1921 brought some separation from the government, the authorities could give or withold their favor in a hundred ways, including authorization to use land. Those charged with the registration of kolkhozes were empowered to cancel the registration, i.e., dissolve the collective, if they were not satisfied. To judge from complaints, these powers were rather freely exercised, but it is not clear that communes were treated much differently from artels. From the beginning of the First Five Year Plan in 1928, reins were pulled tight in all sectors of Soviet life, and this was especially true of the collective farms. They were subjected to a bombardment of orders from both Soviet and Party authorities that was sometimes, if not always, quite overwhelming. For example, in 1930 the president of a commune had his office in the same room as the village soviet. With each daily mail he received about a dozen instructions averaging some ten pages each from all manner of agencies. Some demanded information on plans, crops, activities; some gave categorical commands about deliveries, housing, political work, selection of willow bark, distribution of milk, and similar matters. The harassed president divided them into three piles: a few which could not be ignored; a larger number which should be checked when and if possible; a huge pile of paper for rolling cigarets or kindling the stove.(11) Sometimes Party intervention was received more reverently. A peasant woman reported to a kolkhoz congress, "If our Party organization had not taken a hand, the 'Ear of Grain' Kolkhoz would have fallen apart. It was necessary to change the leadership and to make me, Sopova, the chairman. I am a poor peasant woman, but all the same the Soviet state and Party entrusted me with the leadership of the kolkhoz."

Thus, it is remarkable that Party control of the communes was sometimes weak. This was perhaps to be expected during the first Soviet years, when centralized discipline had yet to be established, but it is none the less surprising that in the December, 1918, Congress of Committees of the Poor, Land Offices, and Communes, resolutions were passed for communes against the wishes of Soviet authorities despite the presence of 364 Party members among the 550 delegates.(12) But even later, communards could resist pressure. In September, 1926, the president of a kolkhoz section in the Kuban was present at an assembly of the Red Orphans Commune when the question arose of changing to individual farming

or to the toz form. He proposed keeping the commune form but
instituting pay for work. The communards assented but later went
ahead and voted to become a toz. The official called representatives of the commune, mostly Party members, to his quarters for
discussion; they then agreed in writing to refrain from making the
change and to consider suggested reforms instead. The vice-
president of the kolkhoz section was afterwards sent to confer again
with the communards, but in the end they had their way and made
the commune into a toz.(13) An incident in 1930 showed similar
independence. A commune assembly was called to approve the
membership of a Party man sponsored by the directorate. But
various members got up to say that during the period of probation
he had shirked hard jobs, found excuses for not working or for
getting easy assignments, and had generally shown himself to be
a poor comrade. Endorsements to the contrary, he was voted
down by acclamation, while four orphans were accepted.(14)

It may only be conjectured how far commune disobedience may
have gone or how common it was. Perhaps communards sometimes simply thought themselves as well qualified as anyone
to judge what was incumbent upon a communist. It may be for
that reason communes were so balky in bowing to repeated suggestions, from 1925 onward, that they use economic incentives and
pay according to labor. The *Agricultural Encyclopedia* in 1951 accused the communes of having failed to pay attention to Party
directives; artels were not so blamed. The directives the communes scorned were those on "economic-organizational strengthening of kolkhozes," freely translatable as the introduction of
payment for work. After 1930, it cannot be doubted, the independent inclinations of communes were less tolerantly viewed by
Stalinist authorities.

Communes in the Civil War

The functions expected of the communes varied from one period
to the next. Only during the civil war, when the Soviets grasped
at any possible help, were the communes given more or less administrative and official functions. In a few cases, as has been

related, large communes were made equivalent to local administrations. More important was the role of many small, voluntary communes, which served as nuclei of reliable supporters for a government as yet feebly organized in the villages. Among the mass of peasants, usually indifferent if not hostile, the communes were listening posts, strongpoints, and administrative stations of a sort; not without reason did the peasants consider "communard" about synonymous with "Communist," or Party member.(15) Communes supplied detachments for convoys and other protective duties, and in the absence of Party men, communards were often drafted for strictly Party work. Perhaps the commonest such activity was helping, gun in hand, to requisition grain from peasants.(16) This, however, was largely taken over in the latter part of 1918 by the Committees of the Poor.

It is impossible to tell the extent of such collaboration of communes with Soviet authorities, and in the prevailing disorder much of it must have been unorganized and unofficial. However, there is ample testimony that anti-Soviet forces in the civil war considered communes virtual Soviet agencies and subjected them to corresponding reprisals. Peasants feared to join communes when White armies were approaching lest as communards they be strung up alongside Communists; the Whites, having overrun a commune, would often execute the leaders, remove what was useful and burn the burnable.(17) Like various other communes, the Communist Lighthouse was a chief target of the anti-Soviet bands of its vicinity. It was often attacked and once captured and thoroughly looted, and many were shot. Consequently, they kept up a military guard until 1926.

Official collaboration of the communes with the Soviet regime seems, withal, to have been rather limited. For the most part, their duties were voluntary, such as might naturally be fulfilledly strong partisans of the regime during a severe struggle. Requisitioning, in particular, was a volunteer activity. In instructions for control of communes by Soviet authorities, emphasis is on the economic facets, chiefly the production and delivery of grain. Political tasks, such as support of the village poor against kulaks, were vaguely defined.

Propaganda and Education

The return of peace and the moderation of Soviet economic policy in the NEP brought a change of emphasis for Party work in the communes. The same Congress of April, 1922, which urged Party members to get into the collective farms made it clear that their activity should no longer be so much in the line of administrative control as of propaganda and economic organization.(18) Hence the communes' assignment became to improve agricultural practices and to advertise these, to furnish services to peasants, to help reduce illiteracy, to carry on political and anti-religious propaganda—in short, to bear the Soviet message by word and example to the dark countryside. Thus, the American Commune repaired machines for peasants, sold them selected seed, and admitted their children gratis to its school. Other typical services included the furnishing of breeding stock, loans of machinery, facilities of grain mills and sawmills. Such services were usually furnished for fees depending upon the economic status of the peasant. *Pravda* criticized as uneconomic the practice of a commune serving peasants gratis in its smithy but praised its taking peasant children freely into the commune nursery.(19)

Although Party instructions that kolkhozes build up relations with the peasants applied to all alike, communes seem to have done more than other forms. Kindeev, in writing of 1925, stated that 66 per cent of communes, 24 per cent of artels and 11 per cent of tozes loaned out equipment. Fewer carried on demonstration work, e.g., plowed one field old style and another according to the latest technique; 20 per cent of communes, 17 per cent of artels, and no tozes carried out such comparisons. Supposedly as a result of their efforts, 24 per cent of communes, 22 per cent of artels, and 12 per cent of tozes were "highly regarded" by neighboring peasants.(20) A study in 1928 showed that 42 per cent of communes, 22 per cent of artels, and 12 per cent of tozes participated in peasant meetings(21); it is not clear whether these were devoted to farming practices or world politics.

The cultural-political work of the communes, at least of the more ideologically motivated, seems to have been varied and extensive. A Kuban commune had the following program in 1924: public lectures on political questions; a reading room with leading Soviet papers; a Marxist discussion club and a dramatic club; preparations for all communist holidays, especially a fine May Day demonstration; donation of grain to the air force; antireligious talks. The latter could not have been required for the communards, 100 per cent atheists.(22)

In 1926 kolkhozes of different types were reported to have cultural facilities in the following percentages:(23)

	School	Club	Library	Reading Room	Lectures	Shows
Communes	42%	37%	50%	37%	47%	41%
Artels	5	10	17	5	17	10
Tozes	12	0	12	0	4	0

The "Shows" charged admission and furnished most of the funds for other cultural activities. Since most of these undoubtedly had a political slant, the real difference of outlook between communes and other kolkhozes is evident. Similarly in 1926 it was reported that half the communes but only a fifth of artels carried on a campaign against illiteracy; three-quarters of communes and one-fifth of artels had lecture programs.(24) With the collectivization campaign, the cultural-political activities of the collectives were spread much thinner by 1929, but the proportions of communes with schools, clubs, libraries and like facilities was several times higher than that of artels. In 1930, nearly half of communes, but only a quarter of artels and tozes claimed "cultural institutions" of some variety.(25) That the communes lent themselves to the propagation of the Party doctrine much better than other collectives is clear. The larger number of Party members in them, however, could account for the difference.

The Commune as a Model

Perhaps the most important function of the commune for the Party was as an example and model for socialism in agriculture—

proof that collective farms could be practical. Not many of them were sufficiently efficient and well-organized to be very useful for this purpose, but the best rendered yeoman service to Soviet agricultural policy. It was to the communes, not to artels or tozes, that foreign visitors were guided to observe the wonders of collective agriculture during the 1920's; it was the communes that provided most material for Soviet writers extolling kolkhozes; it was through the communes that droves of open-eyed peasants were shepherded in the first years of collectivization. Even Kalinin, who was very critical of neglect of economic incentives, in 1924 praised the best communes as even better examples of socialist agriculture than the state farms, and included hard work among their virtues.(26) Soviet economists found the leading communes to give the highest returns; they were the most successful individual kolkhozes, with harvests double the peasant average.(27) A German authority, decidedly unfriendly to collectivization, wrote in 1930, "Astoundingly, one can find among the older communes many distinguished by a good organization of labor and a much higher economic level than is generally the case with collective farms. Of course, such model communes are always the result of long years of working together, which binds and accustoms the members to each other, who mostly were entirely without possessions before their entry."(28) When in 1926 a contest was held among the kolkhozes of the Kuban, the communes, although only about a tenth of the total number, took first place for livestock raising, management, cultural-educational work, and shared first place for field crops. One artel and one toz took prizes of 100 rubles each, and two communes won the same; three communes got 200 ruble prizes; and one took the grand prize of 300 rubles.(29)

Some of the more celebrated communes have appeared frequently on these pages. Though probably all had their share of hardships and setbacks, like the Israeli kibbutzim, they slowly made their way to relative prosperity. For example, a group of guerrillas who had fought under Budenny went out to found the Red Lighthouse on unplowed steppe. At first they lived in tents and mud huts, but when an American visited them in 1929, their assets had grown from near zero to 200,000 rubles, membership had quadrupled to 200, and the huts had given way to fine modern buildings; the visitor was especially impressed by the table they set.(30) The Soviet Sower was similarly begun on bare land by the Komsomol group of a town in the North Caucasus; all the members of the Komsomol joined, but only two adults. They built up a model farm in fairly short order; from dugouts they moved into neat white houses; their dining room, too, was celebrated. They were under the wing of that leading kolkhoz of the Terek district, the Communist Lighthouse, famous for its fine fields, many tractors, and flourishing economy.(31)

A direct way of propagating the message of the commune was to open the gates. The Communist Lighthouse, after it gained fame, had a continual stream of visitors and delegations. In 1929 they were 40 to 50 per week; in the first five months of 1930, that many flooded in daily.(32) One of the Lenin Communes reported that in 1928 it had been viewed by nearly 3,000 people, and by 5,000 in 1929.(33) The Herald Commune, near Moscow, which pioneered in the introduction of American dairy methods, had over 1,200 visitors during the first half of 1928.(34) These peasants, on returning to their villages, were to spread the gospel of collectivization.

But it may well be that the most fateful influence of the model communes was not upon naive peasants who gaped at incubators, modern barns, and nurseries but upon the highest Soviet powers. If the German agricultural attaché in Moscow divined correctly, it was the success of a hundred or so of the best communes which emboldened Soviet leaders in the late 1920's to suppose that, with organization and mechanical equipment, the kolkhozes in general could be brought near their level, and so resolved them to embark upon the totally unprecedented and very dangerous course of mass collectivization,(35) which for a time appeared to be mass communization. If so, the role of the commune in history was pregnant.

Conclusion

The communes were helpful to the Party in creating possible centers for party activity among the peasantry and keeping alive the dream of socialized agriculture during the years when collective farms were little islands in the sea of individual farmers. The communes were the leading lights of socialism in the countryside.

Withal, the Party did not wholeheartedly embrace them. One is rather led to think of a general not entirely happy with a troup of enthusiastic but undisciplined and heady volunteers, whom he cannot put off but whom he does not really want in his regular forces. During the civil war, they were accepted without much gratitude; afterwards they were given little special encouragement and no assignments other than those given "lower" forms of kolkhozes. There may even have been some discrimination against the communes. According to data of 1928, when official policy appeared to be turning toward the commune, the proportion of communes which had representatives in elected Party bodies was not impressive, 25 per cent against 14 per cent of artels and 9 per cent of tozes (although 79 per cent of communes participated in Party meetings, against 35 per cent of artels and 19 per cent of tozes). Since communes had a far larger Party fraction, evidently Party men in them were less likely to be chosen for Party positions than those of other collectives. Even more remarkably, the same source indicates that communes actually took less part in Soviet and cooperative organizations than artels and tozes. In 1928, 25 per cent of communes, 41 per cent of artels, and 52 per cent of tozes were reported having members in Soviet agencies; 26 per cent of communes, 32 per cent of artels and 26 per cent of tozes had members in responsible places with cooperatives.(36) It is too much to deduce from this limited information that the communes were disliked, but they were certainly not regarded as the trusted allies of the authorities one might suppose from their large Party fractions.

Possibly the leaders of the Party did not believe the communes a great asset, at least during the years from 1921 to 1928. They definitely did not after 1930. They may have concluded that the communes' usefulness was outweighed by the fears they aroused in the more solid peasantry, whom the Soviet government was trying to conciliate; that resources might be better spent on less utopian organizations; and that even the political indoctrination would be more effective if carried on by groups which caused less apprehension. That communes were not favored for participation in local Soviet bodies suggests such a calculation, as does their ultimate rejection. In any event, it is striking that the effort was never made to realize fully the revolutionary potential of the communes and to mobilize them for the task of transforming Soviet society. Ultimately, the Soviet government forged itself a political arm in the countryside in the Machine Tractor Stations and their Political Divisions. Far from giving the communes supervisory tasks, the Soviet government took away their machinery and put them, like other collective farms, under the stern jurisdiction of the MTS (which became purely government agencies in 1932). Then the political officers in the MTS were given powers which communes probably had hoped for in vain, to serve as the eyes of the Party and to enforce Party and Soviet decisions in the collectives, from the securing of grain deliveries to the expulsion of kulaks. (37)

Only for a short time in the period of mass collectivization did it appear that the communes might, after all, emerge as leaders of the Soviet countryside. When they failed to do so, they were given a few years to wither away, by decision of a Party that no longer had any use for them.

10 The Commune in Collectivization

The last act of the life of the communes came with the maturation of the Bolshevik Revolution, the forced-draft industrialization of the Five Year Plans, and the mobilization of the entire economy. Ironically, the communes, long the leaders of agricultural collectivization, succumbed when collectivization was made complete.

Evolving Party Policy

Even before Russia had climbed out of the economic abyss of 1920-21 and returned to the level of prewar production, the Party was edging toward a policy of collectivization. In 1924 there were tax concessions for kolkhozes. In February, 1925, *Pravda* decried the progressive differentiation of the peasantry brought about by the economic freedom of the NEP and looked to collectivization as the only remedy. In May of that year, the Congress of Soviets took a firm position in support of collective farming, while stressing "simpler" cooperative associations. Not much came of this talk, and the numbers of kolkhozes of various types, which had not changed greatly since 1923, showed little growth through 1927. In March of that year, the Central Committee of the Party came out more strongly for collectivization. This perhaps marks the real break with NEP attitudes, as it specifically encouraged tozes to move to "higher" forms; however, it urged abolition of the remaining equalitarianism.(1) But there was still indecision. *Pravda* on November 5, 1927, denounced as impractical the Trotskyite proposal to emphasize collective farms over simple cooperatives.

A firmer direction came a few days later from the Party Congress of December, 1927, which at once saw the end of open anti-Stalinism in the Party and for the first time made the formation of kolkhozes the "basic" task of the Party in the countryside. Unlike earlier, weaker edicts, this was effective, for the number of kolkhozes began to accelerate steadily. A year later a new land law gave collective farms preferential rights to land use.(2) The Party Conference of May, 1929, outlined the still modest goals of the First Five Year Plan in collectivization and urged transforming tozes, then by far the most numerous type, into artels and communes.

During this time, Party policy was rather vaguely in favor of the commune. *Pravda* wrote mostly of kolkhozes in general and gave most attention to state farms, but sometimes praised communes. In the field, communes were being pushed: their share of total kolkhoz population increased from 8 per cent in 1928 to 11 per cent in 1929; during this period commune area grew 224 per cent while artel area grew 161 per cent. This was noted by the Central Statistical Board as "qualitative improvement of the composition of the kolkhozes."(3)

All-out collectivization and stronger preference for communes began in late 1929. Stalin spoke on November 7, 1929 of, "The year of the great change," and called for the transformation of the countryside. In November, the Central Committee included dining halls and other symbols in the required improvements of kolkhozes.(4) On December 9, *Pravda* urged attention to collective eating and gave strong support to the communes: plans for equal expansion of all three types should be revised in favor of the commune, for, "The higher the type, the better its economic results"; the artel model statute should be changed to collectivize cows, as the retention of individual livestock distracted the attention of collective farmers. The strongest artel model statute, that of February 6, 1930, by silence on the garden plot and household livestock permitted this interpretation and encouraged the 100 per cent collectivizers.

On January 5, 1930, the Central Committee designated the artel as the "basic" form of kolkhoz but comforted the communards by calling it "transitional to the commune."(5) The following day, the Central Committee asked that the pace of collectivization be radically stepped up from the 20 per cent goal of the Five Year Plan; grain regions in large part should be collectivized by the fall of that year or the spring of the next, less important regions by a year later.(6) This set the wheels moving faster, and the Party proceeded with zest to overfulfill this raised target: 21.6 per cent of peasant households were in collective farms by January 20, 1930, and 55.6 per cent by March 1.(7) This achievement was greatly facilitated by a law of February 1 giving local authorities power to confiscate property of persons judged to be kulaks and expel them from the district. By all accounts, this law was used, and misused, to great effect.

The organizers of kolkhozes overfulfilled their orders not only quantitatively but qualitatively, making de facto or nominal communes instead of the artels described by official policy as "basic." For this there was much encouragement from high quarters. The main feature of *Pravda* during January and February 1930 was the violent anti-kulak campaign, in which anything short of total collectivization appeared as a concession to the class enemy. Exceptionally, the Commissar of Agriculture told workers ("Twenty-Five Thousanders") being sent out to help organize kolkhozes that only draft and commercial stock should be collectivized.(8) But *Pravda* on February 6 called for the collectivization of cows as an anti-kulak measure; the day after, it stressed that the artel statute was only transitional to the commune and subsequently often praised commune ideals. On February 20, *Pravda* denounced the payment of compensation for collectivized livestock and tools as a hindrance to the entry of the poor into the kolkhoz. On February 24, *Izvestiia* chided the Siberians for slowness in collectivizing milch cows. On February 26, the commune received its maximum tax concessions. The Party worker could hardly fail to gather that if it was good to organize artels, it was twice blest to organize communes; and many, if not most, of the new artels were virtual communes, at least in the complete collectivization of livestock. Mass destruction of animals and frenzied opposition of middle peasants were predictable results.

The turnaround came with a suddenness suggestive of a hidden political struggle, as though the losses from violent collectivization gave the upper hand to conservative forces which steadily gathered strength thereafter. Stalin, who had never spoken in favor of communes and as early as 1924 had specifically rejected them as a form of collectivization,(9) gave the word. In an article entitled "Giddiness from Success" published in the most conspicuous spot in the newspapers of March 2, 1930, he changed the tone and emphasis of the collectivization drive and in particular called for a halt to the imposition of communes—just in time, perhaps, to forestall still more serious disorders. The article began with congratulations to the organizers of kolkhozes for their remarkable successes and affirmed that a radical turn had already been achieved in the countryside. But this, Stalin averred, caused some to become overconfident, saying, "We can do anything" and committing abuses. Peasants were driven forcibly into communes, deprived of everything down to the last chicken, and compelled to join communes. Many collectives were established by decree and only on paper. Such deviations, which only aided the enemies of collectivization, must cease. The voluntary principle must be respected and local conditions must be taken into account, the more backward areas being given more time to collectivize. As for the form of collectivization, Stalin wrote that the toz, for reasons not given, had been superseded, but, "The communes represent thus far an isolated phenomenon in the kolkhoz movement. The time is not yet ripe for communes." On the contrary, the artel, in which household plots and some livestock should be exempted from collectivization, was the basic form because it was most suitable for solving the grain problem, which was the main thing. Those who wanted communes before artels were stabilized were trying to run ahead of the masses; this could bring only harm.

At the same time there was published a new model statute for the artel, exempting from collectivization the garden plot, tools needed to cultivate it, and some livestock—one cow, pigs, poultry

—within limits to be established, for each household. The Central Committee quickly followed this up with a formal statement condemning "compulsory collectivization of living quarters, small livestock, poultry, non-commercial milch cows, and, in this connection dizzy jumping over the artel form, which is basic for collectivization, to the commune. They forget that the basic problem of our agriculture is not the 'poultry' problem or the 'cucumber' problem, but the grain problem . . . As a result of these dizzy distortions we find in a number of regions a discrediting of the kolkhoz movement and departure of peasants from half-baked and consequently quite unstable communes and artels." The Central Committee moved to halt the formation of new communes by instructing Party organizations not to permit artels to change to communes without sanction of district authorities.(10) From the beginning of March and for months thereafter, *Pravda* and *Izvestiia* thundered against "distortions" as persistently as they had previously denounced kulaks, though not quite so vehemently. Consequently, more than half of the collective farms formed in the two preceding months (many only on paper) were dissolved, and the proportion of collectivized households fell from just over half to less than a quarter by June, 1930. By less violent procedures, it was brought again over half by mid-1931, and thereafter gradually raised to near-totality.

The Party still hesitated to decide fully against the communes. On March 4, *Pravda* wrote that it was a mistake to try to collectivize peasant dwellings, but the kolkhozes should push on with their own collective building program for schools, homes for the aged and sick, and nurseries for children. That is, apparently, they should become communes as soon as they could provide the proper buildings. On April 2, *Pravda* argued for the extension of collective eating in kolkhozes. But the next day, a more commanding voice, that of Stalin, spoke differently. He even suggested that the best communes be turned into artels. Speaking to kolkhoz representatives, he answered the question whether communes should not be dissolved: "No, there is no need to dissolve them. I speak of real, not paper communes. In the grain regions of the USSR there are a number of splendid communes which deserve help and support. I speak of the old communes, which held out through years of trials and were hardened in the struggle, fully justifying their existence. It is not proper to dissolve them, but it is necessary to turn them into artels." Why it was needful to turn "splendid" communes into artels, Stalin did not explain, but he gave reasons for favoring the artel form: the commune was difficult and required experienced leadership; hasty formation of communes repelled the peasants; only in the future, when artels grew strong, could there be a "mass movement of peasants toward the commune."(11) The implication may be that all collectives together should be first artels, then communes when ready. Following this pronouncement, *Pravda* reversed its position of a few days before and on April 7 warned against residential construction in kolkhozes; neither government nor kolkhoz funds should be invested in consumption facilities.

Apparently still there was indecision. On May 19, *Pravda* wrote that the building of socialism should not be thought complete in the artel, only well begun. The Party Congress of July, 1930, likewise held that the artels, though presently basic, were to be eventually superseded by communes. The change to the "higher form" should come "in accordance with the raising of its technical base, the growth of skilled personnel and the cultural level of kolkhoz members, on the indispensable condition that the peasants themselves accept the corresponding changes in the statute and carry them out themselves." The Congress also called for new model statutes for toz and commune, that for the commune to stress "full collectivization of all means of production without exception, and also the gradual establishment of enterprises for serving the needs of collective farmers (dining room, living quarters, etc.) . . ."(12) There must be caution in collective consumption, but the Party still (Stalin to the contrary) apparently contemplated gradual development of communes, not their reversion to artels. However, the promised new model statutes for toz and commune never appeared.

Early 1931 saw the last pro-commune statements. It was indicative of the change of attitude that communes were now occasionally used as bad examples of inefficiency and mismanagement. However, on January 4, *Pravda* suggested changing artels into communes in regions where mechanization was advanced and urged, while stressing the artel as basic, that "we should not give up the formation of communes." In February, the Central Committee issued apparently its last pro-commune edict: the Party cell in kolkhozes was charged, among its many other tasks, with taking the initiative in the organization of crèches, kindergartens, and collective eating. But the next month the Congress of Soviets made it clear that communes were not to come soon but only when time and conditions were ripe.(13) The word was heard, for communes ceased to increase. They were counted at 7,564 in October, 1930, and 7,600 a year later; in the same time, artels burgeoned from 63,517 to 193,600. Communes shrank to 4,200 in 1932, to 4,000 in 1933, and thereafter were not separately reported.

The very idea of the commune was fading. In all branches of the Soviet economy there was growing emphasis on incentive pay and repudiation of "petty-bourgeois levelling." In various pronouncements Stalin repudiated as non-Marxist the idea that socialism should be equalitarian. The source of equalitarianism, he said, was "the psychology of primitive peasant 'communism'."(14) From 1931 on, many an official pronouncement castigated equalitarian practices in kolkhozes and failure to develop economic incentives. The promise that the commune was to replace the artel one day was gradually forgotten. The *Great Soviet Encyclopedia,* in 1938, still called the commune the "highest" form, for which conditions were not yet ripe. In 1953, as quoted earlier, it found the communes simply impractical.

Communes in the Campaign

Published statistics do not tell, if it be known, how many communes were formed in January and February, 1930. To judge from comments of Stalin and others there must have been many. In the Khopiorsk district of the Lower Volga it was reported that in 1929-30 90 per cent of the peasants were collectivized, almost all of them in communes. In various parts of Siberia in the middle of 1930 the proportion of peasant households in communes was much larger than in artels,(15) and there are similar reports of other regions. Very many of these communes were on paper only, and others owed their existence to the crudest pressure, as was freely admitted later. For example, in a Siberian region, the Executive Committee simply decreed the formation of at least one commune in each district (*raion*); the district committees passed this on to village Party groups, one of which commanded a commune to be established in one week, "with a bloody nose if necessary." Within the week, there stood the commune.(16) Sholokhov, in his novel of collectivization, pictured all cows and chickens being herded into the unprepared collective (formally an artel) willy-nilly, with disastrous results in peasant anger and slaughtered beasts. The promoters of this action were low-ranking enthusiasts for world revolution. Their urgent argument was that the animals must be saved from being butchered by their owners. Naïve or not, this argument appeared in *Pravda* of February 6, 1930.

Not only were communes being spawned wholesale at this time, but older communes were widely used as campaign centers in the collectivization program. When the Party sent out 25,000 (and more) bench workers in the first months of 1930 to give a proletarian backbone to collectivization, they were directed preferentially to communes, although these already had a far larger proportion of Party and Komsomol members than artels and tozes.(17) This is comprehensible only if the "Twenty-Five Thousanders" were to use the communes as bases from which to lead the attack. It was natural that the better communes, long models and propagandizers of collective agriculture, should carry forward their role when general collectivization was the order of the day. As before, they showed peasants around their fields and kitchens; more than before, they themselves organized smaller collectives on every hand. The Ukrainian Achievements of October Commune set up ten artels;(18) the Banner of Communism of the Lower Volga spread its wings over twenty-five communes, artels and tozes, comprising 28,000 hectares.(19) Around the Communist Lighthouse there was built up a "combine," enfolding dozens of small artels, tozes, and communes and covering tens of thousands of hectares. Typical of the work done by the communes was the establishment of a tractor school which trained drivers for kolkhozes from far and wide.(20)

At times the commune was expected not only to help start junior collectives but to expand itself to monstrous proportions. While there were also large artels and tozes, the oversize kolkhozes were mostly communes, at least in name—though such giants could certainly not have functioned as family-style communes in the old manner. In 1929, communes were 26 per cent of all kolkhozes with more than 2,000 hectares of plowland, although only 6 per cent of all kolkhozes.(21) Of the 175 largest kolkhozes in that year, no less than 70 were communes. Even in 1928, the Young Farmer Commune of the Omsk region had 820 persons and 11,000 hectares but was not to remain so small. Authorities wanted to invest a million rubles in it, provide it with 40 tractors and enlarge it to 40,000 hectares for the mass production of seed grain.(22) Also in Siberia, the Krupskaia Commune, once tiny, was swollen to encompass 14 hamlets and 2,260 members on 40,000 hectares.(23) A combination of four communes on the Lower Volga far outstripped these by amassing 300,000 hectares of plowland in 1930.(24) A commune-combine was founded on 14,000 hectares of previously arid land in a great irrigation project in the Caucasus highlands. Here agriculture was to be blended with industry and crafts for advancement into socialism in all spheres.(25)

Commune dreams were grandiose indeed. The Fortress of Communism in the Lower Volga region talked of building a "Socialist Farm City" on the basis of plans prepared by the Agricultural University in Moscow. It would move 60,000 residents of 127 hamlets into a single center and organize all the territory as one farm, with grain supplemented by hogs for a bacon factory, dairying for a big creamery, vegetables for a canning plant, and sunflowers for oil. Farm work would be done by men commuting by auto to encampments in the fields. All would live in apartments with separate rooms for each adult or adjoining rooms for couples; eating and social life would be in communal areas. There would be libraries, club rooms, gymnasium, theater, etc. Children and the aged would be supported free; workers would get food, shelter and education in return for a fixed minimum of labor, and varying wages for work done over this minimum. Children under three would be in a nursery, from three to seven in kindergarten, and over seven in boarding schools.(26) Such was the agro-city dreamed in early 1930, remarkably like that planned more than a generation later.

These outsize communes presumably would take on more or less administrative functions, as apparently did the short-lived big communes of 1918. There was a widespread view that this must happen; as a Samara official said in 1930, "Village soviets in our district are becoming completely superfluous; their role goes over to the kolkhozes."(27) There were anarchist overtones in the argument; some said—and were influential enough to have their views published in *Izvestiia*—that a society organized on a basis of production would not need government organs at all.(28) But the higher authorities declined to accept this notion. Even at the height of the fever, in late January, 1930, Kalinin poured scorn on those who wanted kolkhozes (communes?) to replace soviets.

In the excitement of the day, the commune idea gripped some city folk, just as it had in the early years of the Soviets. Komsomol volunteers, going out to help collectivize, thought it fitting to put all their pay in the hands of a treasurer, who bought meal tickets, gave shoes and clothing to those who needed them, and even sent help to parents.(29) *Pravda* reported on February 25 that workers' communes were springing up in factories to raise productivity by cooperation and sharing of pay; they put all their wages together and divided by the number of mouths in their families. Such groups were cited in Moscow, Leningrad, and Urals industrial plants; one had existed since October, 1929. *Pravda* did not entirely approve their equalitarianism but chided trade union and Party leaders for neglecting them. Twenty-two Komsomols began a Young Workers commune in an automobile factory in May, 1930; by early 1931, a dozen others had sprung up in imitation.(30) Something like a big commune was schemed for all Stalingrad in 1930: collective kitchens should serve as many as half a million persons, preparing meals, and sending them out to "housing combines"; adults would eat and live in apartment blocks for 2,500, and children would stay permanently in nurseries in the same buildings.(31)

Communists in Favor of the Commune

It is not clear who was responsible for such schemes of communization, but Stalin and the Central Committee apparently were not.

A good many in the Party went beyond the official Party doctrine in regard to communes and persisted in attachment to them well after the highest authorities had made it clear that all emphasis was on the artel. Kalinin, the day after Stalin signalled the great change of course with his "Dizziness from Success" pronouncement, placed advocates of total collectivization into two groups, those who feared being accused of rightist deviations or softness toward the kulaks and those, chiefly young communists, who were stirred by sentiments of equality.(32) The first category must have included many faithful readers of *Pravda,* who felt they were doing what was expected of them in herding peasants into communes; the second may have been sufficiently numerous that repeated vague promises of turning artels into communes were largely concessions to placate their zeal.

The argument for communes continued many months after Stalin and the Central Committee had spoken in March, 1930. A writer reasoned in the spring of 1930 that the artel form would leave most of the cows with individual peasants, hence remain incomplete. On the contrary, if all stock were collectivized, it would be possible to scrap peasant barns and use the materials.(33) A journalist of the time contended that it had been a great error to allow private plots in the establishment of a kolkhoz-combine; he claimed the decision, taken "in the study of a non-Party professor" had "nauseated" Party workers and demoralized them. He feared that peasants would spend all their time on their own plots and argued that such concessions were unnecessary, as the communal advantages of collectives were obvious; gardens were not needed to give the women something to do but should be abolished to free them for more productive work.(34) In March, Party chiefs in and around the Communist Lighthouse were discussing whether all the kolkhozes of the district should not be made into communes and then amalgamated; there was no mention of the Party decisions in the debate as recorded by Tretiakov. (He was later purged as a Trotskyite.) The course taken does not appear from the narrative, but it would seem that at least some became communes. In June, it was still possible for a writer in *Pravda* to express concern at the lack of emphasis on the development of artels into communes. He believed that failure to complete collectivization seriously weakened the kolkhozes and urged steady progress toward the total elimination of private property. To be sure, this was refuted at greater length a few days later.(35)

During 1930, the commune was gradually pushed into the background, and only 0.2 per cent of kolkhozes formed in the year following the fall of 1930 were communes. However, the districts which had long had relatively many communes—the North Caucasus, Karelia, Urals, East and West Siberia, Buriat-Mongol, and Far Eastern regions—still in 1931 had over 5 per cent of communes in their vastly increased numbers of kolkhozes.(36) Fondness for the commune still appeared through that year. A book was published titled *Life in the Commune, Book of Documents on Kolkhozes;* this at once equated kolkhozes with communes and consisted largely of glorification of various communes. In 1931, an agricultural specialist still found it possible to write that the commune was more advantageous; where possible, all stock should be collectivized and artels made into communes; "It is necessary to strike at the right-opportunist efforts to forbid the organization of communes where the necessary conditions exist."(37) This was long after such "right-opportunists" as the Central Committee of the Party had forbidden the conversion of artels into communes without special permission and Stalin had suggested that even the best communes be made into artels.

Apparently pro-commune feeling was cherished by some lower-ranking Communists, idealists, all-out revolutionists who were "nauseated" by concessions to property instincts, perhaps the more ideologically-minded journalists, and a good many to whom "commune" meant a step toward the proclaimed goal of "communism." So far as appears, however, no high-ranking leader was associated with it, and it was represented by no open group or faction. There were many references to "Leftist opportunism" as well as "distortions" in collectivization, but the official view was that pro-commune agitation, unlike the anti-collectivization attributed to the kulak class enemy, was mistaken but more or less in good faith. There was some effort to claim that kulaks favored the communes in order to discredit kolkhozes in general, but kulaks were not given implausible credit for the commune movement. "Trotskyite theories of proletarianization of the peasantry" were also blamed, and the belief, credited to Trotsky, that socialism could not be built in a peasant country allegedly meant that peasants had to be proletarianized by pushing them into communes in order to make socialism possible.(38) But Stalin, seldom reluctant to attribute political subversion to those who disagreed with him, merely stated, as in April, 1930, that pro-commune "Leftism" played into the hands of the Rightists and discredited the Party.(39)

Peasants in Favor of the Commune

If some in the Party thought the commune was a good thing, there were peasants to agree. One pro-commune influence was Sectarianism. This must have been important because of the number of Sectarians and the attitudes they often held toward private property. In 1928 Sectarians reportedly objected to piecework pay, claiming to be the best communists and reproaching the so-called communists of the Party for failure to carry out the teachings of Marx. "What kind of communists are you?" they asked, "Just talk and a Party card. We are real communists, we don't want the new system of payment for work." And in a Sectarian commune of the Lower Volga they resisted all efforts of Party agitators to introduce wages.(40) In times of forced collectivization, Sectarian organization in communes was broken up and Sectarian equalitarianism disappeared from Soviet writing, but old attitudes must have remained.

The commune also appealed to some peasant thinking; it was not without reason that Soviet writers called equalitarianism a primitive peasant failing. As *Pravda* wrote on January 15, 1928, free and equal distribution by communal eating or handouts of equal amounts was simple and acceptable to the peasant mind; the accustomed ways had merely been transferred to the new group, the commune, which was a refuge of old usage. As communards of the Communist Lighthouse said when modest moves were made toward accounting, "Tear up the account book and hang the agronomist by his heels!" When in 1930 the peasants of a district were assembled to found the new kolkhoz, one proposal from the floor suggested that it be a commune instead of an artel. "Why bother with shares and norms? Let everything be in common, like in a big family, cup and spoon the same for all. Since we started out this way, let's have full communism, everybody equal. Equal income. For the president and bookkeeper and the whole herd." All speakers supported this idea, but the Party delegate finally convinced them that the commune idea was premature and that they must go first to the artel.(41) This suggests that peasants, not fully convinced of the merits of those sent by the Party to be kolkhoz presidents and accountants, saw in the commune a means of holding down their earnings and perhaps their authority. On the contrary, the Party probably favored the artel as more controllable because it was less permeated with equality. On occasion, peasants also saw the commune as a means of staying out of the kolkhoz consolidations proceeding rapidly at that time. Thus, when it was proposed that various small artels join in a "Giant," the peasants answered that they preferred to change to communes. The local Soviet official, lacking (in 1930) any instructions, vacillated but finally decided to let them go ahead.(42)

In view of the practical difficulties mentioned earlier and the complexities of "labor-days," it is not to be wondered that peasants, once resigned to the inevitability of collectivization, might prefer the simplicity of the commune. Piecework pay was complicated at best, but it had become, by the end of 1930, a veritable jungle of norms, values, classifications, and premiums. The relatively simple operation of plowing had to be graded according to type of equipment, plow and tractor, depth of furrow, and character of the soil; there were no less than 23 ways of working a hectare.(43) It must have required much cogitation for the peasant to understand distribution by "labor-days" and a great effort to appreciate its justice.

The novelist Kataev gave in 1930 what would appear to be a good summary of peasant thoughts in favor of the commune: "Sometimes middle or poor peasants argue for the commune (and consequently against the artel) in a daze of Russian extremism, radicalism of a kind, 'Well, put everything in one pile, if that's the way it's to be . . .' This urge to general equality is very strong, especially in the mind of the most backward, poor peasants, partisan fighters, farm laborers. Here, on the upturned, agitated soil of half-conscious economic aspirations, there easily take root and grow up the seeds of the old dream of brotherhood-equality, seeds drifting, it may be, even from flaming times of *égalité, fraternité,* in any case from booklets and preachings of Populists, legends of migrations and fairy tales of rivers of milk, from partisan dreams of 1919."(44) Resignation, aspirations of the poorest classes to equality, civil war memories and revolutionary enthusiasm, the general turmoil, Populist-anarchist agitation, and Sectarian visions of heaven on earth, all scrambled together, were the stuff of commune-fancies.

Persistent Equalitarianism

Whether or not many peasants really wanted communes, there was stubborn attachment to equalitarian practices in the collectives, as shown by repeated injunctions against them. In August, 1930, the Central Committee castigated division by eaters, collective consumption, use of kolkhoz income for nonworkers, failure to pay the prescribed five per cent of gross income on property contributions, equal division of fodder, and the furnishing of an "existence-minimum" without charge.(45) The great majority of kolkhozes still distributed by eater, according to the Commissar of Agriculture. In October, collectives were reproached not only for dividing harvests equally, but also for giving out industrial goods by need instead of according to work.(46) In March, 1931, the Congress of Soviets similarly berated collective farms for equalitarian distribution, which encouraged laziness, and demanded piecework pay.

But still the evil would not die. In March, 1931, *Pravda* admitted that many of the poorer peasants still held out for equal sharing. Friends of the commune must have continued active, for in February, 1932, the Central Committee condemned "attempts artificially to hasten the transition from the artel form to the commune."(47) A month later, the Central Committee struck at the "collectivization of cows and small stock, that in the grossest manner infringes repeated instructions."(48) In mid-1933 there were more rebukes for artels that consumed their grain in collective eating.(49) Thereafter, the problem received less attention. But as late as 1938, the authorities complained that many artels spent most of their funds on collective or administrative expenses, paying out little or nothing on "labor-days." In all cases, they were ordered, 60 per cent to 70 per cent of income should be paid according to "labor-days" earned.(50) In September of that year, *Pravda* charged that in 77 of 187 kolkhozes of Riazan no money at all was paid for "labor-days."(51) By 1938, the old commune was hardly more than a fading memory.

Impracticality of the Commune

If there was ideological fondness for the commune in the Party and a fraction of the peasants were favorably disposed, one may well wonder why the Party turned away from pro-commune policies of 1928 and 1929 and discontinued the use of the commune form along with the artel as a vehicle of collectivization. Artels might at least have been invited to graduate to the "higher" stage as soon as they felt ready. Such was the well understood policy which observers of 1929 and early 1930 expected to continue. Instead, it was decided, presumably at the end of February, 1930, to limit collectivization to artels, permitting individual gardens and some household livestock and mostly excluding collective consumption; in following months, artels were more and more discouraged from changing to communes. This decision is fairly comprehensible on two practical grounds: the commune was too costly for mass collectivization; and it hindered the program by alarming a large section of the peasantry, especially middle peasants who were indispensable for the success of the collectives.

The commune was impractical or too costly in a number of ways. One was needed for buildings and facilities. While it was fairly easy to establish communes on confiscated estates, these were soon occupied often beyond capacity. Increase of membership then meant diverting scarce resources to new and unproductive construction; many a commune had to reject members for lack of room. Even in the American Commune, which was relatively wealthy, bachelors couldn't bring in brides for there were no private rooms. Eating halls, nurseries, and other services required large expenditures and space; these might be made for a few communes but

were out of the question when the peasantry was being collectivized en masse. Full collectivization of livestock implied barns,
poultry houses, storage space for feed, and generally heavy investments without which collectivization could be, and was, fear-
fully destructive. The state might think of luring the peasant into
the commune with agricultural machinery, great constructions, and
modernization. This was suggested in 1930,(52) but this was not
feasible then or for many years afterwards.

Stalin, as quoted, stressed the need of the commune for another
scarce resource, trained and dedicated personnel. The commune,
which he called "the university of socialist methods of economy,
not the elementary school," was more difficult and demanding in
administrative skill than the artel; the Soviet state could ill afford
to use its limited cadres in this way. The collectivization of field
cultures and management of men and machines was difficult
enough; collectivizing all animals and even all households compounded the opportunities for mismanagement, muddle, and corruption. In the judgment of the Webbs, the chief drawback of the
commune was just this need for higher character and better management.(53)

Increase of size also strained the commune form. The average
kolkhoz of all forms grew in the years of collectivization; the average commune swelled from a reasonable 19 households in 1928,
to 28 in 1929, and 71 in 1930. The smaller the group, the more
readily could commune solidarity and family type relations be
preserved, the more effectively could social pressure stimulate work
and control consumption. The larger the communes, the more they
turned to distribution by labor, though still calling themselves communes.(54) In 1928 in the Central Black Earth region, it was found
that few of the poorest communes distributed by work performed,
but all those with resources over 63,000 rubles did so.(55) Communal services were also harder to organize for bigger groups.
When the Lenin Commune grew to 269 families, it had to go over
to mixed artel-commune form, despite devotion to the principles of
the commune, simply because outlying households lived too far
away to trek to the dining hall(56)

Increase in size would have caused difficulties enough even if
membership could have been carefully selected, but this was im-

possible in the collectivization drive. Instructive is the story of the Ukrainian Achievements of October Commune. A model in 1930, it doubled in size and was a wreck in 1932. While the economy was getting bigger and more complex, it had taken in many new, untrained, and doubtless unsuitable members; it almost fell to pieces before deciding to revert to artel form with the sacrifice of cherished services.(57) Communes had many sad experiences with members interested only in consumption and not in work. One complained in 1928 that it had spent 40,000 rubles on the support of a large number of peasants who wintered in it with their cattle; when spring blossomed, they left without paying board. The commune decided to accept applicants only in the summer.(58)

Moreover, during the collectivization campaign the question of willingness became acute. The full commune could work only if its members wanted it to succeed; membership must be truly voluntary. This would be hard to assure when peasants were being pushed into collectives. The dissident in the artel might lower morale and productivity but was subject to economic compulsion; in the full commune, he could work disaster. Of the Krupskaia Commune it is said that a group of former Kolchak adherents entered in a body, wasted as much as they could, and then left a sadly weakened commune behind.(59) Consequently, some communes tried to remain exclusive and raised obstacles to entry, such as high contributions. Others cooperated with the Party and were swamped, so that they had to cease to be communes. Large-scale communal arrangements having proved impractical, the communes that remained in the spring of 1931 were almost all of less than 50 households.(60)

Of course, these difficulties might have been overcome if the Party had been willing to allow communes to remain small and to proceed gradually to collectivization. But the Party wanted big collectives, not little ones, and it wanted them quickly.

Peasant Dislike for the Commune

A no less forceful reason for not using the commune in collectivization was peasant dislike for the form. Though by no means unanimous, this was widespread from the beginning. Soon after the Revolution, it is said that many peasants raised the cry, "Long live the Soviets, down with communes!" to express gratitude at having received land and fear of losing it.(61) Lenin in 1919 said the word "commune" sometimes became an anti-communist slogan. The first communes were admittedly strange islands in the mass of uncomprehending and often hostile peasantry. For many or most peasants, the commune was an alien world and the communards people of another sphere. In the Tula district, the young men of a Lenin Commune were eager for marriage and were encouraged to romance by the collective, which needed more hands. But peasants adamantly refused to let communards woo their daughters. They said that communards were not their own masters, they had no money, could give their wives nothing, and were always quarreling.(62) One may surmise that they felt a girl going into the commune was socially and morally lost.

Such attitudes were not extremely important for the Party when communes were few, but they became critical in 1930. The prevalence of communes in a given region was said to be an important brake on the peasants' acceptance of collectivization; certainly, the implantation of communes raised distrust.(63) When, after Stalin's "Dizziness from Success" article, withdrawals were permitted, most of them were in regions where many communes had been imposed.(64)

Of course, fondness for property repelled many from the commune. It is axiomatic that the more a peasant had to sacrifice, the less likely he would be to enter a commune. Although it seems, surprisingly enough, that a small proportion of middle peasants did become communards, it was generally taken for granted that they would not; and the poorer the peasant, the more likely to accept the commune. But other reasons for peasant antagonism require more discussion.

One was that the very name of "commune" was strange to their ears. *Pravda* considered this to be the reason that, in 1919, there were only 6 communes to 52 artels in the Orlov district, although many artels were managed as communes. Peasants simply did not want to call their associations communes.(65) In time, the term must have lost some of its strange foreign sound, but the traditional "artel" no doubt continued to be much more acceptable.

More important was the fact that the artel, with its individual household, was much closer to common tradition. When the village commune had periodically redivided the land, the peasants kept their own homes and garden plots in nearly full ownership. There was precedent for cooperative plowing and other joint working, but collective housekeeping was quite exceptional, except in so far as the big family under serfdom had been a collective. A large commune must have been incomprehensible. Much as the peasant, especially if prosperous, might dislike the artel, it would not appear so monstrous if he kept his own house, cow, small livestock, and garden.

But there was a deeper and more emotional repugnance, an underlying fear of the radicalism, irreligion, and strange life of the commune. Peasants dreaded many things they heard about in communes, from plural marriage to being buried without prayers. About a new Caucasian commune they asked: Will they drive us to work? Will there be holidays? Will everybody dress alike? Will there be communists and non-Party or all equal? Can we marry?(66) Women visitors to other communes wanted especially to know whether all lived in the same room, whether children were snatched away from their mothers, whether communards ate fodder-cakes for bread, whether in the commune everybody belonged to everyone else.(67) Anti-commune tales included: all entering the commune would be stamped with the seal of the Anti-Christ; all would sleep rolled together under a hundred-meter blanket; men would shave their beards and women cut their hair (contrary to the Bible); everyone would take turns sleeping with everyone else.(68) Religious hesitations were not without foundation; atheist lectures were a regular commune activity. Though there were religious communes and tolerant communes, young communists would cry, "You can't have God in the commune," and older peasants refused to renounce God.(69) One commune was so harassed by religious peasants that it packed up and moved from the Ukraine to Siberia.(70)

Women were most determined in their opposition to kolkozes in

general and to communes in particular, although they were promised more in them than their husbands. In 1919, *Pravda* reported
that feminine antipathy was the chief brake on the formation of
communes. Men might decide on a commune, but they had a hard
time either convincing their womenfolk or dragging them in by
male authority.(71) If they did go into the commune or artel, they
usually held back from active participation. This continued through
the whole period of collectivization. The riotous rebellion against
the collective pictured by Sholokhov was a mob of furious women
tearing open the granaries and beating the Communist chairman
nearly to death; it was women who raised an outraged protest
against the collectivizing activities of the Communist Lighthouse.
Especially the women, *Pravda* reported on January 15, 1930, objected to collectivization of household livestock; the men usually
didn't make much fuss about horses and equipment. As late as
1934, the Central Executive Committee spoke of "Hopes of the
enemies of the Soviet Union to wreck the kolkhozes, taking advantage of the backwardness of peasant women."

If the commune, depending upon its facilities, freed women
from chores, it required of them much more readjustment than it
did of men; and they often were dissatisfied. Many quarrels arose
from the community kitchen and dining hall. Women did not like
cooking for those outside their family, doing impersonal menial
jobs, caring for others' children, and the like; they engaged in all
manner of recriminations and dodged the work. Tretiakov, a re-
porter very sympathetic to the commune, found that women disliked the communal kitchen as much as the nursery and had to be
rotated very often. When freed of domestic duties, they fell into
boredom, felt lost, and passed their time bickering and gossiping.
Perhaps, like some women in the kibbutzim, they felt they had lost
their role in life.

The Threat to the Family

The crux of feeling against the commune was its threat to the family, or at least the family as the peasants knew it. Family and community are natural opponents; to resolve the antithesis, communal

societies resort either to celibacy, as in the monastery, or to freer relations between the sexes and the generations. The close union of the larger group inevitably loosens bonds between husband and wife, and between parents and children. The patriarchal family is particularly incompatible with the socialist commune, which releases woman from dependence on man and consequently weakens the code by which she was restricted. Hence the main anticommune themes were that women were dishonored and mothers lost their children.

Again and again, in all parts of Russia, there appeared the story of the eighty-meter or hundred-meter blanket, under which all the communards were rumored to bundle together. The Communist Lighthouse made a special point of showing visitors the individual bedrooms. It was also told that in the commune children were beaten and went naked, while men and women were matched by height.(72) Such is the leitmotif of anti-collectivist whisperings in Sholokhov: "You give up your wife to the others, and you go yourself to the whores," and, "It will start with the kolkhoz, but it will go on to the commune, to the complete abolition of property. Not only your oxen, but your children will be taken away to be brought up by the State. Everything in common, children, wives, cups and spoons." Women would be socialized, the rumor went; elsewhere they had already been socialized, with the Communists being first to use them. When an artel hired two women cooks and a laundress, the village wives spread the tale that they had been communized and now couldn't marry honorably; the women quit their jobs in shame.(73)

Mothers were particularly fearful of bringing their children into the commune. At the Communist Lighthouse visiting mothers wanted to know if the children weren't thin and pale; they believed that children were taken away from their mothers as soon as born. Even communards were very distrustful of the nursery and the "specialists" brought in to manage it. Women going through the Fortress of Communism inquired, "Is it true you put all your babies in wagons and send them where you never see them again?"(74) Others objected less naïvely, "Nowadays the children won't listen to their parents; there'll be even less obedience in the commune."(75)

The eighty-meter blanket may have been mythical, but the peasants had reason to suspect, if they did not in fact know, that communes often deviated from old moral standards. Communism meant free love, as was well known; the Russian encyclopedia of 1895 had defined it squarely as, "Social order without private property, with general sexual cohabitation instead of marriage." This went well beyond the *Communist Manifesto,* which called laws, morality, and religion, "bourgeois prejudices, covering up so many bourgeois interests." Madame Kollontai, the trumpet of feminism after the Revolution, proclaimed liberation from these bourgeois prejudices; the individual household would be replaced by the collective, society would take over the care of children, and marriage would cease to be a slavery to become, "the free and honest union of men and women who are lovers and comrades."(76) The idea of comradely marriage, as interpreted by young enthusiasts, led easily to the theory that sexual relations were no more important than (in Lenin's phrase) "drinking a glass of water." Lenin, to be sure, found this "completely un-Marxist and, moreover, anti-social";(77) but the revolutionary, anti-religious mood of the Revolution was strongly conducive to slackening of restraints. Early Soviet laws on marriage, an observer wrote, "led to a great degradation of the family. This was especially noticeable in the villages, where patriarchal customs had hitherto existed. These customs were in opposition to the new, individualistic and very loose ideas concerning the family and marriage; the resulting chaos was in accordance with the view of legislators, who hoped to destroy the family at one blow."(78) If there was a degradation of the family in the village, where Party influence was feeble for many years, some communes must have been shocking.

Not only Bolsheviks, but Sectarians, it may be recalled, tended toward unconventional morals. Orthodox priests before the Revolution talked darkly of unmentionable scandals in Sectarian rites, just as later opponents of collectivization gossiped of sins in the communes. The orgies of the Khlysty (a rather communistic sect) were most famous; allegedly they were climaxed by general promiscuity and always featured complete communism of women.(79) Other Sectarians were less notorious, but rejection of Orthodox sacraments often included rejection of marriage formalities. Some Old Believers said, "Better to have ten natural children than one wedded husband," or, "Have a child every week if you like, only don't marry in church."(80) Even among those less extreme, as the Dukhobors, women smoked and drank, considered themselves equal to their husbands, and had no great respect for matrimony. Since the Bolsheviks agreed with many or most Sectarians in their disapproval of money, scorn for Orthodoxy as a tool of the rich, praise of brotherhood and equality, and favor of a higher status for women, peasants were likely to find their suspicions of the Soviet commune confirmed by the impression that it was another form of the various short-lived Sects, which fill Russian history.

Revolutionary freedom in family relations was to be expected in the commune. In 1919, young communards said, "Down with humdrum routine, down with official marriage, weddings, Christmas, tulle curtains, carpets."(81) The urban youth commune held that, "Sexual relationships (love) should not be restricted. We must approach them consciously and seriously."(82) Quite apart from ideology, it is clear that the commune fostered a different sort of family from that to which the peasants were accustomed. The economic independence of women in itself meant a loss of masculine authority and erosion of old ways. This was true also of the artel, in which women were supposed to be paid individually for their work; but the commune was incomparably worse.

Soviet writers were silent regarding the marital customs of the communes, which were not a normal topic of Soviet publicity. There were reports of debauchery or of liaisons between commune chairmen and feminine comrades, but these were represented merely as lapses. However, the Kuban Congress of Soviets in 1926 found that, "Unhealthful and abnormal phenomena in the life of members of kolkhozes, especially communes" required steps "to undertake the study of the life of members of kolkhozes, especially communes, to terminate the at times abnormal and depraved phenomena which now take place."(83) Those to whom these instructions were addressed must have understood what abnormalities were involved.

For such reasons, stressing the commune in collectivization must cause trouble. First the Party might logically have tried to get all peasants into tozes; then the tozes might have been gradually made into artels without the losses of life and property that artel-collectivization actually cost. Finally, artels might have been made into communes, if and when this seemed desirable and practical. The Party proceeded very differently: for a time, it favored communes, or something close to them; as soon as they appeared unfeasible, the aim was lowered to the artel, and there it remained.

11 The Extinction
of the Commune

Upon receiving, in January and February, 1930, mounting reports of massive resistance to collectivization and wholesale slaughter of livestock by the peasantry, the Soviet leadership decided to make the artel with limited household production the "basic" form of collective farm. This was understandable prudence. Full communes required much unproductive investment, good leadership, selected membership, and willing cooperation; and they frightened many or most peasants. But, having decided on the artel, the Party could well have kept such communes as were reasonably successful as models and showcases of the new order. At the same time, the best artels might have been permitted, if not encouraged, to build barns and collectivize all stock, and to establish collective eating and such services as they were able. For such changes toward the commune there were well-established economic and ideological arguments.

Alternatively, if the communes were a serious liability in causing peasants to fear collectives of any kind, a comprehensible policy would have been to demote them immediately to artels. The peasants, like everyone else in 1930, continued to believe that the artel was only a stepping-stone toward the commune. Though they no doubt appreciated the concession of being allowed to keep their own household, with cow and chickens, this appeared as a mere reprieve; they remained convinced that they were on the road to a commune as soon as they stepped into the artel.

The Last Years

Neither of these obvious courses was followed. The commune was still called the form of the future, but that future became ever more distant and hazy. The communes were kept for a few years in declining numbers but were increasingly ignored and forgotten. The final curtain fell only slowly and after the battle of collectivization had been won. In 1932 and 1933, the communes still constituted about 2 per cent of kolkhozes; how long they managed to carry on after that is obscure. Mention of them in the press grew rarer, though they were occasionally cited as examples in 1933. Among 100 kolkhozes of the Moscow district praised in 1933, 4 were communes in name, though all had "labor-day" payment.(1) In February, 1933, a congress of kolkhoz workers had about 10 per cent representatives of communes; but their speeches dwelt on feats of production and dekulakization, not collective consumption.(2) It is not even possible to say to what extent commune-type services continued in kolkhozes, for these, too, disappeared from statistics.

The fate of the communes was largely consummated in 1932 and 1933, the last years for which any data about them seem to have been published. In 1933, the remaining political utility of the communes was undermined by the establishment of "Political Divisions" in Machine Tractor Stations, the Central Committee's instruments for controlling all collective farms. More directly, the communes were denatured by having to permit individual production. In May, 1932, a decree allowing free sale of household produce made the garden plots more profitable. By a decree of June, 1933, all members of communes should have the right to own a cow, small livestock, and poultry; they should be assisted in obtaining such livestock; and the commune must provide members with feed according to "labor-days" worked.(3) In February,

1934, *Pravda* called for the development of individual as well as collective stockraising to overcome the effects of the slaughterings; and in May, communes were permitted to transfer as much as one-third of the collective herds to private ownership.(4) These measures were opposed to much that Soviet economists had written about the advantages of collectivizing stock. As late as July, 1930, authorities were urging collective farms to devote their resources to full collectivization of livestock; in February, 1934, they were castigating leaders who failed to loan kolkhoz horses to members to cultivate their individual plots, saying that such practices undermined incentives.(5) The change can only have been dictated by the state of Soviet agriculture in the wake of collectivization; it suffices to note that in 1933-34 total livestock herds had fallen to about half of the 1928 level.

Private livestock and gardens deprived collective eating of much of its rationale, but some commune services could have continued. Legally, however, the commune seems to have been terminated by the adoption of the new Stalinist artel model statute in February, 1935. At first, model statutes had been only models, suggested forms which kolkhozes had to follow only in a general way to qualify for registration. But in the time of mass collectivization the model statute was turned into legislation, and changes in administration of the collectives were made simply by amending the model. For example, in September, 1933, the provision was inserted that collective farmers must receive a monetary advance of 20 per cent to 30 per cent on their accumulated "labor-days".(6) The artel model statute of 1935 differed from its predecessors in that it was made specifically obligatory for all kolkhozes in its official wording, with only insignificant, officially sanctioned modifications to suit local conditions; other deviations were made unlawful.(7) In this statute, various provisions other than those for household gardens, livestock, and progressive piece-work pay were incompatible with the old idea of the commune. Most important, only small amounts were allowed to be used for social benefits, so the collective was virtually prohibited from furnishing much in the way of services to its members.(8) Accordingly, the commune was illegal. In July, 1935, land patents were issued to artels only, and in 1936 the right of kolkhoz members to own livestock and cultivate a garden plot was solemnized in the Soviet Constitution.

Withal, the last communes were slow to surrender. The Webbs in 1935 found the American Commune still going strong with no apparent intention of becoming an artel; on the contrary, it impressed them as a commune.(9) Later specific mention of communes does not appear, but as late as 1939 the agricultural tax law still mentioned artels, communes, and tozes.(10) The law of March, 1941, mentioned artels and tozes only, suggesting that the toz outlived the commune, and subsequent laws speak only of "kolkhozes."

Thus the commune quietly dropped into limbo. Nor has there been in the Soviet Union any revival of that title. In 1953, the Central Committee pronounced the artel to be, "The only correct form for the whole period of socialism."(11) In 1959, Khrushchev, speaking to Polish farmers, wrote an epigraph for the Soviet commune: "Soon after the civil war, we began setting up not agricultural artels but communes. There were people who reasoned, 'Since we are fighting for communism, let us set up communes.' Apparently many people at this time had a poor understanding of what communism is and how communism is to be built.

"We organized communes, although material and political conditions—I mean the consciousness of the peasant masses—were lacking at the time. The result was that everyone wanted to live well and yet work as little as possible for the common good. 'Work when you feel like it, receive as you need', as they say. Nothing came of many of these communes. The Party adopted the path pointed out by V. I. Lenin. It began organizing the peasants into cooperatives, in agricultural artels, where people work collectively and receive according to their work."(12)

The Commune as a Discordant Element

The reason suggested by Khrushchev for eliminating the communes—that they had poor labor discipline—was certainly not the only one and very likely not the most important. Administrative convenience was possibly one motive. During the 1930's the collective farms were more and more minutely regulated in all their activities; administrators would find it easier to have them all, so far as possible, operating under the same set of rules. The taint of Sectarianism which lingered about many communes was a black mark against them. Stalin's personal lack of enthusiasm for the idea also figured. His published works show not a single favorable mention of communes in general; and several times, from 1924 through 1934, he expressed scorn. His Georgian origin possibly influenced him; communes were rare in Transcaucasia. Political motives must be suspected, also, though never publicized. The communes were a reminder of the Marxian promise that the coercive government would wither away after a post-revolutionary transitional time; as such, they were inconvenient when Stalin was busy strengthening state coerciveness. Quite possibly, Stalin disliked communes as refuges of Leftist tendencies hostile to his Party supremacy. Of course, communes could be purged, but belief that economic relations shape mentality would dictate abolition of these institutions of ultra-leftism. The *Agricultural Encyclopedia* of 1951 attributed "anti-government tendencies" to the communes; however, it specified resistance to economic incentives and low marketing rather than more sinister opposition. Withal, the commune tradition of discussion and equality was in itself enough to make it suspect in the era of Stalinism.

The broad and obvious reason for doing away with communes was that they were a profoundly discordant note in an increasingly conformist and regimented social structure. At that time, literature was being squeezed into the patterns of "Socialist Realism"; painting, music, and architecture were being shaped to a uniform grandioseness, with decreasing leeway for individualism. There was more and more talk of the possiblility of foreign attack and the need for military preparedness. Old Bolsheviks were being purged and replaced by Party bureaucrats. The commune carried the flare and zest of the Revolution; old enthusiasms were giving way to the graphs of the Five Year Plan. The commune revelled in the anti-conventional, anti-family spirit of early Soviet days; in the general tightening of the 1930's divorce was rendered very difficult, and parents were made responsible for their children. When all emphasis was on conformity and production, the commune no longer fitted.

Nor did the commune fit into the official Marxist-Leninist philosophy of the Soviet state. The commune was not part of the agrarian program of Marx and Engels or their followers. The ultimate communism of the communist historical scheme was a state of abundant production, with a highly advanced technology; it was not to rest on brotherly inspiration in backwardness. For them, communism of consumption in poverty was "primitive" or "communism of the monastery." The anarchist Prince Kropotkin and the Bolshevik Stalin agreed that this peasant-family communism was essentially nostalgic and backward-looking. As Marx explained and as Soviet writers stressed, the social product should be divided according to work, until there should be abundance for all and work should be a pleasure.

In theory, the Party never liked the commune. Even in the throes of civil war, an old Communist called a bunch of eager communards together to give them a lecture on historical materialism, the orderly sequence of economic systems, and the need for patience. A sign of the depth of the Party's dislike for the commune idea was the silence with which urban communes were buried. Probably composed in large part of idealistic youths, these might well have been greeted with enthusiasm and given at least moral support; instead, even in 1918 and 1930 they were almost ignored and apparently neither Stalin nor Lenin ever mentioned them in published works. How numerous they were one can only guess from the accounts of foreign journalists; little can be said except that they were common enough to attract the attention of visitors. However, for the reader of *Pravda,* they were virtually non-existent.

For the Party philosophy, the idealistic commune ethos was incomprehensible. This can be sensed from an account of an exemplary commune in 1927: the poor peasants founding it received almost no assistance, but by working day and night and denying themselves such luxuries as soap and tobacco, they slowly built up the farm; they did without spoons to buy clover seed; all was done without anyone's owning a shred of property.

Admirably as they seem to have carried out the Party's purposes of collectivization and improvement of agriculture through self-sacrifice, the Party paid little attention to their efforts.(13)

It was possible, though not reasonable, shortly after the Revolution to believe that the new society of abundance was around the corner; that the communes could be harbingers of a dawning communism. Although the Soviet economy progressed fairly rapidly after 1922, it became more and more evident that the awaited communism as a total way of life was a long, long way in the future. Hence the reminders of that future, the communes, became embarrassingly anomalous in Marxist philosophy.

In 1918 there was something of a debate within the Party between those who considered the state farm a more progressive form than the commune, because the former was nationally owned, and those who found the commune more advanced, because it had communistic sharing. In 1930 the same topic rose again, but now there was only one side to the argument. Communistic sharing had become either unimportant, or a detriment to production; socialism was not a question of division of income but of working for society as a whole. Only national property, not cooperative property, could be called fully socialistic; collective farms would graduate to socialism when they became state farms. Some even contended that collective farms, including communes, represented collective capitalism, for they could serve for gain and accumulation of capital, albeit collective.(14)

The banishment of the commune thus represented a reaffirmation of the basic Marxist outlook and the dialectic which treats society as unitary. Soviet society had to grow through its socialist stage as a whole and as a whole should in due time begin the transition to pure communism, the Marxist technological utopia. To try to skip far ahead of the times in a little community of brotherhood and equality was futile, if not harmful.

However, the significance of political theory alone should not be exaggerated. Lenin, who was rather pragmatic by temper, was apparently ready to accept communes if they worked. Theoretical justification could have been found at any time if they had proved useful. But the communes were, practically as well as theoretically, out of harmony with the developing Soviet state.

"Petty-Bourgeois Equalitarianism"

"In the period of the victory of collectivization, equalitarian payment of labor became a basic evil hindering the normal development of production in the commune," wrote a Stalinist.(15) Stalin himself spoke of equalitarianism as the mortal sin of the commune. In 1934, he told the Party Congress that the artel form was best because it "correctly joins the personal consumption interests of the collective farmers with their collective interests," while in the commune personal interests were swallowed up "for the sake of petty-bourgeois equalitarianism." This, he said, explained the small number of communes, which, in order to continue to exist, began giving up collective living, paying by "labor-days", and permitting individual ownership of limited livestock; that is, became de facto artels. (Stalin failed to mention the many decrees which had helped convince communes of the correctness of this course.) The commune would become necessary in the advancement of the future, but the present commune was based on poverty and backwardness; thence came its equalitarianism. Moreover, "Equalitarianism in distribution and personal life is petty-bourgeois foolishness, worthy of some primitive and ascetic sect, but not of a socialist society organized in Marxist fashion, for it is impossible to demand that all should have identical needs and tastes . . ." Stalin then reiterated the Marxist doctrine of pay in socialism and condemned equalitarianism in general as "utopian-socialist."(16) This has remained the official position. For example, the 1959 *History of the Communist Party of the Soviet Union* stated flatly that "Equalitarian distribution is incompatible with socialism." Although they yielded in many ways to the leveling spirit of the early Revolution the Bolsheviks, like Marx, were never equalitarian in outlook.

Not all communists agreed; some argued that material incentives were not needed in the Russia of 1930. In urban communes in Moscow, they maintained that surrender of pay by no means decreased industriousness; those who contributed most felt most responsible for the common weal.(17) But official policy was less idealistic. In the 1930's the use of economic incentives increased in all spheres of Soviet life, with more and more wage differentials, bonuses, piecework, and progressive piecework pay to stimulate effort and acquisition of skills for a mechanized economy. How the demand for a production stimulated by material rewards struck the spirit of the commune is best reported of the city youth commune, visited by Mehnert. In the early 1920's, the young people of both sexes were idealistically endeavoring to put communist equality into practice; they pooled all earnings for general expenses, shared clothing, and even debated whether it were not excessively selfish to have a private sweetheart. In 1932, some of the same youths were still living in the same building, but now they called it a "collective." Each paid a definite amount for room and board and had a separate bedroom. An ex-communard explained, "Isn't it really a contradiction, when we in the Soviet Union are trying by every means, even with piece rates and premiums, to increase production, and at the same time are living in communes, where everyone has to throw what he has earned into the common pot?"

A contradiction it was, and not to be tolerated in Stalinist times. It could be attacked by introducing a wage system into communes, but the effectiveness of this was limited by commune traditions. And the very name of commune was the symbol of equalitarianism. The name, too, had to go.

Introversion of the Commune

Just as the commune ideal did not fit Soviet theory, the commune reality tended to draw apart. At first there were efforts to integrate the communes into a unified movement, but they were markedly unsuccessful; despite instructions for union, all commune leagues came to nothing. Even in 1919 communes were attacked for self-sufficiency, as "the typical self-regarding organization, which exists for its own sake and does not work and produce for society."(18) It was easier to avoid participation in Soviet life in a commune than out of it. In the first years, some intellectuals, small traders and the like "holed-up" in communes as shelters from the political and social storms.(19) Isolation must have increased when the NEP brought a commercial society uncongenial to the communes. Kalinin in 1925 found the communes to suffer from a kind of sectarianism; they became, he wrote, like communist monasteries, losing touch with the people and cutting themselves off from the market. This he considered even more harmful than equalitarianism in lowering the productivity of labor.

There were various manifestations of the isolationism of the commune. They tended to grow crops for their consumption, hence produced much less industrial crops than artels and tozes. Some communes, to avoid buying and selling, had their own craft shops to make shoes, clothing, and the like.(20) Possibly the larger number of subsidiary enterprises in communes, compared with artels, owed something to this urge for self-sufficiency. Some communes, like old-time monopolistic artels, raised entry duties as a barrier and kept silent about their income and property lest they have many applicants. One commune even kept so much to itself that surrounding peasants didn't even know it was a commune.(21) Of the Communist Lighthouse Tretiakov recorded that the spirit of communal particularity rose as feeling for individual property declined, and instead of thinking of the general welfare the communards would envy the successes of other kolkhozes and gloat over their discomfitures. Sometimes new members were admitted only if married to communards. This had to be overcome, Tretiakov thought, by merger in the "combine." Success gave feelings of collective snobbery; the model Lenin Commune felt considerable scorn for the backward and ignorant peasants around them.(22)

A practical result of commune separateness was a tendency to hold members close, hindering their migration to the factories, as required by industrialization. One can also guess that it exacerbated conflicts of management when the MTS took over mechanical work in the collective farms after 1930.

A tendency to separatism is a common trait of the commune form. Perhaps the higher the feeling of community and corporate morale, the more the group feels its distinctiveness, especially if the outside world rejects its values. The kibbutzim, despite strong identification with Jewish nationalism, dreamed of being self-sufficient; this was relinquished only under pressure of need for commodities not produceable in them. Even utopian societies, in theory desirous of converting humanity by example, tend to isolate themselves, as though to guard from the degrading contamination of the backward world or in resentment of the failure of the others to understand. As Soviet values diverged from those of the communes, there must have risen the urge to save revolutionary purity by shutting themselves away. This would of course smack of political opposition, not to be tolerated.

The Commune as Consumer

Predisposed to live apart, the commune likewise was inclined to consume its produce. Humans are likely to be free in using what is everybody's to use; some may even have an extra helping lest they fail to receive their share. If there is no accounting, individual frugality can be encouraged only by ascetic idealism. The relaxed pace and amenities of the Amana community, the preference for enjoyment over toil, is said to have brought the system to grief. Long ago, Owen's New Harmony struck visitors more for abundant entertainment than strenuous labor; where the work schedule was sloppy, recreation was admirably organized.

Soviet communes quite humanly tried to give themselves a good life. Kalinin found in 1924 that a commune, despite a loss of 20,000 rubles from a bad harvest, had indulged in new overcoats worth 24,000 rubles, "much above the peasant standard." In another commune he found the stock was suffering neglect, but the kitchen was excellent and tendencies to consumption were obvious.(23) Of approximately 50 communes in the Kuban in 1923-24, 14 had theaters and 15 had clubs, though only 9 had reading rooms.(24) It may be that the "cultural work" of the commune, generally much ahead of that of the artel, was not entirely given either to improvement or politics. The most popular "cultural work among the masses" carried on by the American Commune was the American-style dance every Saturday until Sunday dawn.(25) The "indivisible fund," according to Tretiakov, was too often used for dining room or clubhouse instead of the purchase of machinery.(26) Those entering communes expected such things as homes for the retired; a commune founded in 1929 built accommodations for the children and for the aged before it brought in its first crops.(27) Like the workers of Amana with easy chairs beside workbenches and the peons of Mexican ejidos who turned prosperity into leisure, the communards often relaxed as the economy improved. Even the noted Communist Lighthouse, like others, began to shorten the workday as soon as hardships eased.(28)

The Soviet authorities wanted the collective farms to sell as much as possible to the government to feed the cities and, through exports, help finance the industrialization of the country; the proceeds of sales the collectives should invest, so far as possible, in further raising production. But communes were decidedly prone to consume their own produce; there is ample testimony that, whatever other hardships there may have been to life in the commune, lack of nourishment was not one of them. In the Proletarian Will Commune, cows waded knee-deep in manure and gave only cupfuls of milk, but the communards were fat and rosy.(29) A Tver report for 1925 stated that although communards had less cash income than individual peasants, since they did not work out, they ate "incomparably" better, having an abundance of poultry, milk all year, and meat almost all the time.(30) Although there were complaints of monotonous cuisine, the American Commune had an abundance of meat, tea, butter, and milk. These two items, meat and milk, are most often mentioned as gracing commune tables; the Red Lighthouse Commune had meat daily and all the milk its members could drink.(31) That abundance of these foods was impressive is clear from the per capita consumption by the rural population in 1926 of about .01 lb. of meat and .75 lb. of milk daily.(32) In that same year, Karpuzi found that the communes he investigated used an average of fourteen times as much meat and twice as much milk as the average for the peasants of the country.(33) The Soviet Sower Komsomol commune was famous for good victuals, even over the Communist Lighthouse, which had grandly hired a professional cook from Moscow. In 1930 another commune provided two cups of milk, two eggs and porridge for breakfast, and meat, soup, milk, and grits for lunch and dinner, with all the bread one wanted. Members, it is said, all took bread away from the table, often to discard it.(34)

Communes were not entirely consumption-minded. Instances were cited from time to time of communes which nobly put the personal interests of their members in second place to the needs of production, built barns when housing was atrocious, and the like. Concretely, budget figures of the Banner of Labor in the Ukraine show that in 1922 it spent 70 rubles on clothing and culture, but 2,250 rubles on equipment. In following years with larger returns it increased consumption only moderately, while investing more; in 1925, it spent 9,715 rubles for equipment, 1,000 rubles for clothing, 550 rubles for "personal needs" and "culture."(35) Figures for larger numbers of communes in later years show them investing a much larger share of net income than artels and tozes, but this would mean little if communes simply consumed their produce instead of marketing it.

It is evident, in any event, that opportunities for consumption and even waste were wider in the commune than in the artel. The commune, in a sense, was organized for consumption; an agitator spoke of the advantages of "commune living or artel production."(36) The *Great Soviet Encyclopedia* in 1938 was probably quite correct in speaking of increased consumption and reduced marketing of grain as a serious fault of communes.

The Commune as Marketer of Grain

The communes tended to eat up their produce, and this was concretely shown by their marketing less than they might have for the cities—a most grievous fault from the point of view of the Soviet government. "The artel is the basic form of kolkhoz because it is the most suitable for solving the grain problem," said Stalin, and this was repeatedly echoed. It was ample reason to reject the commune.

It was claimed that communes of the first period performed well enough, delivering their surpluses to the government just as the state farms did. Later, some communes probably did well, as the American Commune, which was credited with marketing 52 per cent of its produce in 1927 and 63 per cent in 1928,(37) as against 10 per cent to 20 per cent usual for individual middle peasants. But generally communes seem to have reduced marketing in the NEP when they were more or less left to themselves. In 1925, Kindeev reported, communes marketed only about the same proportion as peasants, slightly more in some districts, slightly less in others. This shortcoming, attributed to a lack of attention to industrial crops and "consumption-mindedness,"(38) was very remarkable when it is recalled that commune production per man was much higher than that of individual cultivators. It could only mean that communes, not obliged to sell, or urged to sell at low government prices, preferred to eat. It also meant that, from the point of view of the national grain supply, the communes did worse than the kulaks. Other writers made similar complaints, but there is little concrete information. Figures for various districts for 1926 and 1927 show communes marketing a slightly lower proportion of grain than artels;(39) the differences, which are irregular, would not be significant except, again, as commune production was higher per man. In the Kuban in both 1926 and 1927 the communes' marketed percentage of field crops was a few points below that of artels and tozes.(40) Gaister's study covered only a small sample in 1928-29, but it is worth noting that the marketing percentage for 7 communes was 47 per cent; for 4 artels, 57 per cent.(41) The communes' performance apparently had improved since 1925, but they were still behind the artels, so far as can be judged, despite more equipment and more production per worker. The least that can be said is that Soviet authorities must have expected more.

Data from the period after 1931 are not available to determine whether the communes were still able to withhold more of their produce than artels, but it seems that commune structure or traditions were not favorable to the state grain collections. The actual amounts of grain the communes failed to market might not weigh seriously in the national balance, but it meant that the Soviet government could not regard communes with great favor. One of the chief uses of the commune had been as a model of socialism when collective farms were few. When collectivization was complete, the Party could not be expected to hold as a model a commune remiss in the prime duty, the delivery of grain to the state.

In sum, the Soviet powers did not lack reasons to reject the commune unless they were determined to go through with integral communization. Politically and philosophically the commune had always, except for a brief period, been an outsider in the Soviet system; when Stalinist conformity became the rule, it was no longer tolerated. Its usefulness came to an end when the mass of peasants was collectivized and direct party controls were established in the countryside. It was repugnant to most peasants and a political liability. Perhaps most important, it was an economic failure from the point of view of the state, since it tended to defeat the main purpose of collectivization, the procurement of maximum amounts of grain from the peasants.

12 Conclusion

The aim of an early transition to full communism was given up and the communes were brought to an end in the Soviet Union a generation ago. What seemed in 1930 a temporary retreat has become permanent. Will there again be communes in Russia? It is possible that the name, brilliant in the traditions of radicalism, will someday be revived. But it is unlikely that there will again be anything like the old communes. New communes, if they come, will be very different. There is discussion in the Soviet Union of the transition from socialism to communism; but it does not seem to be contemplated that small, or even the enlarged artels, will be converted to communes as they often were in the 1920's. Rather, all are to be melted into society together, into what might be called a single huge commune (although the term has gone out of fashion). Then all productive property will be national property, the distinction between artel and state farm being erased. The artel, then, is not to develop toward a commune but toward a state farm, while the latter is gradually to be brought to general communism.(1)

In 1934, Stalin spoke of the eventual rebirth of the commune in Marxist terms: "The future agricultural commune will arise when there is on the fields and in the barns of the artel an abundance of grain, cattle, poultry, vegetables, and all manner of other products, when the artels have mechanized laundries, modern dining service, mechanical bakeries, etc. When is this to be? Of course, not soon . . . the process of transformation of the artel into the future commune . . . must proceed gradually, in such measure as *all* collective farmers become convinced of the necessity of such transformation."(2)

How Stalin expected this future commune to stand in relation to the rest of society he did not explain, but the idea is clear that technological advance should bring communism gradually and generally. The vision remains much as Stalin painted it but ripened and enlarged by intervening decades. Now it is the agricultural town, or *agrogorod*, an urban-rural community of several thousands, with workers' apartments, community central heating, communal restaurants, laundries, nurseries, boarding schools, theaters, and clubs. Workers, transported to fields twenty kilometers around, will till with the most advanced machinery, while livestock loll in automated barns. To this utopia, the transition can be only gradual, as mechanized labor becomes more productive and more services can be offered at less cost or gratis.(3) Aims for kolkhozes were formulated in the Party program adopted in November, 1961: they should improve community services and raise production to make individual gardening and livestock-keeping unnecessary; but then, instead of turning into communes, they should join their neighboring collectives in more and more common endeavors, and kolkhoz property should gradually be made equivalent to state property, and the kolkhozes should merge into the great society entering communism.

Consequently, the old commune cannot be regarded as a long-term goal from which the Soviet Union had reluctantly to turn aside until better times should permit its restoration. Rather, the commune was part of the birth pangs and childhood of the Soviet system, inherently bound up with its origins but cast off as it matured.

The Russian Revolution was more an outburst of primitive feelings than a Bolshevik-Marxist creation. It did not come, as Marx held social revolution should come, as the explosive breakdown of an over-developed capitalist society but in an underdeveloped, predominantly peasant country with a small, though concentrated industry. Red agitators did not carry the inflammatory message to a large proletariat, schooled and organized in trade unions, but to workers who were little removed from peasants—who often returned to the village for summer work—to an impoverished and land-hungry peasantry, to soldiers and sailors who had been dragged away from the fields to bleed for causes they did not understand. The tightly organized Marxist revolutionary party provided the leadership and ideology which prevailed in the Revolution's contest for power, but the "dark people" furnished its explosive forces: hatred of the oppressive and alien bureaucracy, resentment of a privileged and haughty but weak and outworn aristocracy, and a fierce demand for "Brotherhood and Equality." These were the feelings of Sectarianism, of anarchism, and of the Left Socialist-Revolutionaries. They were the passions on which the Bolsheviks rode to victory, the moral indignation and sense of outrage without which the Revolution would never have been made, passions which were a revolt against mercenary values and the extremes of unjustifiable inequality. They were basically the sentiments of the communes, but not of true Bolsheviks.

The communes stood for the primitive drives of the Revolution. As such, they continued to draw support from those both within and without the Party, more concerned with emotional brotherhood than Marxist schemes of socialist evolution. But they gradually lost their fire as the Revolution ceased to be revolutionary, and as Soviet society was stabilized and slowly formed to the patterns desired by Bolshevik leadership. By the time the Party was ready to undertake the collectivization of agriculture, the old commune had lost much of its meaning, but it probably could have survived and might even have grown somewhat in numbers, as long as the mass of peasants remained unorganized. When collectivization was made general, the commune, though a symbol of collective agriculture, became by its very nature a discordant element no longer useful, and was discarded.

The communes were essentially anarchistic, to the extent that the Revolution itself had been anarchistic in genesis. The only party wholeheartedly to favor and argue for the communes was the anarchists'; anarchists helped make the Revolution but soon found that they did not have a place in the Soviet order, either. Communes existed for over fifteen years within the Soviet realm, never quite fitting. They might have gone on existing on the margins of Soviet society, but after 1930 dissent and separateness were increasingly eliminated, and the Stalinist order had no room for the deviation which they represented.

None the less, it is not inconceivable that history might have turned out differently. The fully ordered society is an engineer's daydream of potential efficiency and productivity, and Bolshevism is filled with a strong engineering urge to remodel society for maximum controlled effectiveness. The revolution which starts by nationalizing industry can logically continue to the dissolution of the family and at each step find arguments of economic and social gain.

Poverty is not an argument against collectivism, but for it. The greater the need, the more there is to gain from joining all as closely as possible. Pioneers facing a hostile wilderness band together, "All for one and one for all," of necessity, just as in emergencies towns are fed from community soup kitchens. Wealth permits the luxuries of individualism, privacy, and freedom from control, the waste of each for himself.

The machine likewise reinforces the collective. The larger the scale on which an operation is performed, the more advantageous, often the more necessary, its mechanization. It is likely to be expensive or impossible to mechanize the peasant patch or the family kitchen. But the savings promised by mechanized collectivism are impressive in housekeeping as well as in the field or factory. Consequently, pressures for collectivizing may be greatest where there is a keen if not exaggerated awareness of possible gains, a leadership which is prepared to cut through resistance, and poverty which requires that limited resources be used as effectively as possible. This was, of course, the situation in the Soviet Union, where the leadership was perhaps overly impressed with the potential benefits of doing things on a large scale and had little hesitation in attacking old institutions.

Marx insisted, as did the Soviet leaders, that communist distribution could not come until there should be abundance enough for society to supply all needs generously. It is not clear just how such open-handed distribution could be managed in practice, as human needs are extraordinarily elastic. But the total collectivization of the commune did not necessarily imply total equality and general sharing. Ethical, not economic reasons prevented the commune from charging for many or most of its services. Members could be required to pay for meals, housing, and child care. Needs of the sick and aged could be put on the basis of insurance. A scheme suggested in 1930 and probably instituted to a degree in some communes was to furnish an "existence-minimum" without specific charge, for which all able-bodied members should perform a certain minimum of work, for the rest paying wages and charging economic prices. In practice, such arrangements would not be easy to administer, but should not be impossible.

Consequently, it was not necessary for communes to be excessively equalitarian. If the Soviet government had embarked upon communization, the communes would doubtless have used material incentives and payment of labor; they would have been based less upon "brotherhood and equality" than upon economic and political calculation. They would have been larger than the communes familiar in the 1920's, and different in their close ties to the Soviet state. But they would have been essentially communes due in their high degree of integration of life, in collectivization of all production and in most consumption.

There were moves in that direction in 1918, when a few huge communes sought to bring thousands into unified revolutionary communities. The extravagant schemes of giant communes in 1930, which were to mechanize and organize all aspects of life for the quick building of a new society bespoke similar ambitions. Outwardly, the fuzzy blueprints of 1918 and 1930 looked much like the prospectus of the agrogorod of 1975, but there was a fundamental difference: the agrogorod is to be achieved slowly through technological advancement, a by-product of high industrialization. The big communes of the days of commune fever were themselves to make possible high productivity and application of technology by organizing the life and work of their members.

The primitive little commune was doubtless doomed, but one

may wonder whether the Soviet leadership might have followed up the tentative steps of 1918 or 1930 and moved decisively toward the big, futuristic, mobilizing commune, with its fully subordinated and regimented economy, collective consumption and the prospect of greater economic and political control. It can hardly be doubted that Soviet leaders were aware of the potentialities, but they did not strongly attempt to realize them.

Perhaps it was psychologically and politically impossible for them to do so. Lenin and Stalin and probably all leading Bolsheviks shrank from the deeper radicalism and profounder upheaval which full communization would have meant. Lenin was averse by philosophy; the leader who a few weeks before the Revolution suggested that private bank accounts and security holdings would be unaffected by nationalization and who after the Revolution thought former owners might remain in communes on their estates was no full-blown anarchist. But he was willing to see communes succeed. As he said in 1919, "If the communes show in practice that they really improve the peasants' life, then, no doubt, the authority of the Communists and the Communist Party will rise."(4) However, in the midst of grave troubles he was not disposed to take on the additional burdens of a further cataclysmic transformation after the storm Russia had suffered. The communes could not by themselves convert the mass of peasants, and Lenin did nothing to impose them. Instead, he turned sharply away from a commune outlook to economic moderation, although he permitted communes to continue to exist in the looser Soviet society of the NEP years.

Under Stalin, there was an all-round deepening and intensification of the Revolution, and it might well have seemed, in late 1929 or early 1930, that commune ideology was to be the basis of Soviet policy. It is not impossible that, under more favorable circumstances, Stalin might have decided that full communization promised gains in economic and political control that were worth the trouble and risks. Perhaps were such intentions in the first wild months of 1930. But difficulties proved too great. By March, the heavy-fisted policy of mass collectivization had brought Russian agriculture to the brink of chaos. As the Party congress expressed it in 1930, forcible and extreme collectivization "would have *threatened* a breakdown of the collectivization of agriculture, *undermining* the very *basis* of the Soviet Government, the union of the working class with the peasantry."(5) In other words, peasant antagonism was too menacing. Stalin was not prepared or not able to force the mass of the people into the commune mould, and he signalled the retreat. This at first seemed to involve merely tactical concessions, that peasants should no longer be driven but only gently pushed into collectives, and that individual households should be permitted to retain garden plots and some livestock. But it became a turning point in the history of the Soviets, as Stalinism thereupon began to move away from radicalism.

With the rejection of the commune, the Revolution halted. The extremism of the First Five Year Plan was muted. There came a turn away from revolutionary ideals, from glorious innovation to traditional ways, from internationalism to nationalism—a broad trend which continued through the 1930's. Whether the personality of Stalin or the maturation and consolidation of the Soviet state was the greater cause, there were growing pragmatism and tough-mindedness, less sentiment and idealism, more hard-boiled autocracy. Stalinism rejected not only the primitiveness and anarchism of the peasant commune, but its odor of insurrection and the world communist movement. Although loosely organized groups could be called communes and artels could be collective as anthills, as some pre-Revolutionary artels seem to have been, Stalin preferred the designation that came from the Russian past to the one from French socialism. He nationalized the Revolution, declaring its independence of world revolution by his doctrine of "Socialism in one country." He rehabilitated Russian history, making half-heroes of formerly execrated old Tsars. Once no term had been worse than "Tsarist general," but such men as Suvorov, winner of victories for Express Catherine, and Kutuzov, who harried Napoleon, were now exalted. The popular and national in culture found higher esteem; the classics were lauded while Futurism and Proletarian Culture were forgotten. Like the best of conservatives, Stalin stressed the family and the urge to make money. He finally made a peace of sorts with the Orthodox Church. In brief, he instituted a thoroughly revolutionary program of forced industrialization and made quite an omelet collectivizing agriculture (as he once expressed it); having done so, he turned to old-fashioned methods of authority.

Stalinism thus meant the death of the communes; and, the economic philosophy of the Soviet Union having remained about where Stalin left it, they have remained buried with scant mention in the histories. But a strange fact has slightly rescued them from oblivion in the Soviet land: in 1958 the Communist Party of China brought its huge rural population into "People's Communes" with a dispatch that Stalin might have envied. These People's Communes (the name in Chinese has no relation to the word for "communist") were very different from the ordinary Soviet communes of the 1920's, but were remarkably like the abortive big communes with which Soviet authorities experimented briefly in 1918 and 1930. They were official government bodies of many thousands of members, designed primarily for the mobilization of labor. But they were essentially communes in equalitarianism, collective consumption, and a degree of collectivism perhaps unique in history.

Since the times of their founding, the Soviet press has rarely mentioned the People's Communes. But there have been occasional indirect attacks upon them by reference to the unsuccessful Soviet experience. Such was the 1959 pronouncement of Khrushchev, quoted in the previous chapter (p. 224). As though to keep the door closed to the Chinese deviation, similar statements have since appeared from time to time. For example, an article of *Pravda* of December 1, 1961, stated: "We all recall how, when the collectivization drive was in full swing, hotheads among theoreticians and practical workers tried forcibly to implant 'communes' with equalitarian distribution and so to hasten the transition of the village to communism. If the Party had not rejected these utopian exercises, we would have undermined the realization of Lenin's cooperative plan and broken its basic principle, the principle of material incentives with the joining of personal and social interests."

In China, conditions were more favorable to the implantation communes than in Russia: greater poverty of the peasant masses, who had less to lose; more prospective gains from mobilizing labor for mass projects; and stronger party control in the countryside.(6) In spite of this, the Chinese People's Communes seem to have failed and in the disruption of agriculture to have caused a grave economic setback after 1958. Consequently, by 1962 they had in effect been largely dismantled.(7) The Russians no doubt warned the Chinese comrades that they would not succeed. In any event, whatever the failure and whatever the cost, the Chinese have stubbornly maintained the thesis of the People's Communes as a badge of their militancy. Thus, at ceremonies in Moscow marking the anniversary of the Chinese People's Republic on October 1, 1962, while Soviet speakers talked of Marxism-Leninism, the Chinese Ambassador stressed, just as previous years, the "Three Red Banners" of the "General Line of the Party," the "Great Leap Forward," and the "People's Communes." None of these, of course, means anything at all to ordinary Russians. It is curious that the commune idea, once upheld as the way of the future in Russia, has come into a strange new role as a point of divergence between the more restrained Russian and more voluntaristic Chinese versions of Marxism.

Bibliographical Note

There is remarkably little material in English concerning the Soviet communes. For background on Soviet agriculture in general, there might be cited such works as Leonard Hubbard's *The Economics of Soviet Agriculture* (London, 1939), or Lazar Volin's *A Survey of Soviet Russian Agriculture,* (U.S.D.A., Monograph No. 5, 1951); most complete is Naum Jasny's *The Socialized Agriculture of the USSR* (Stanford, Cal., 1949), which has a brief treatment of the communes. Visitors to the Soviet Union gave some descriptions of individual communes; notably, Sidney and Beatrice Webb, in *Soviet Communism, a New Civilization* (London, 1944).

Soviet discussion of communes was fairly extensive until official policy turned away from them after 1930. The most informative writers are K. Kindeev and I. A. Koniukov, their chief works on the subject being, respectively, *Kollektivnye khoziaistva* (Collective Farms) and *Kollektivnoe zemledelie* (Collective Agriculture), both published in Moscow in 1927. Many other sources are useful, as cited in the text, and a rather surprising amount of statistical information (of doubtful exactness) can be found in numerous official publications. The better writers seem to show a reasonable objectivity, which was not difficult to achieve during the 1920's when Soviet society was relatively tolerant of diverse opinions and the Party view of communes was not yet clearly fixed. After 1928, as the Party moved toward general collectivization, material grew increasingly abundant and less reliable.

The New York Public Library contains the largest number of the works used in this study. The libraries of Columbia, Harvard and Princeton Universities also gave valuable and much appreciated assistance.

Notes

Chapter 1

[1] *Pravda,* May 1 and July 1, 1919; March 18, 1920.
[2] V. I. Lenin, *Sochineniia* (Works, 4th ed., Moscow, 1950), Vol. 27, p. 226. This edition of Lenin's works was used throughout and is henceforth cited as "Lenin."
[3] Kii (pseudonym), *Sel'skaia kommuna* (The Village Commune, pamphlet, Petrograd, 1918).

Chapter 2

[1] For Russian views, cf. S. S. Maslov, *Trudovyia zemledel'cheskiia arteli* (Working Agricultural Artels, Yaroslavl, 1918), pp. 124ff.; M. I. Tugan-Baranovskii, *Obshchestvenno-ekonomicheskie idealy nashego vremeni* (Social-Economic Ideals of Our Time, S. Peterburg, 1913), p. 110.
[2] Charles Gide, *Communist and Cooperative Colonies* (trans. Ernest F. Row, London, 1930), p. 152.
[3] Henrik F. Infield, *Cooperative Communities at Work* (New York, 1945), pp. 37-43.
[4] Gide, *op. cit.,* pp. 158ff.
[5] Maslov, *op. cit.*
[6] Wm. Bradford, *Of Plymouth Plantation* (ed. S. E. Morison, New York, 1952), pp. 120-21.
[7] For details, see E. T. Craig, *History of Ralahine and Cooperative Farming* (London, 1882).
[8] Jean-Paul Koch, *Quelques Experiences Collectivistes* (Brussels, 1947), p. 197.

[9] K. Kindeev, *Kollektivnye khoziaistva* (Collective Farms, Moscow, 1927), p. 12.

[10] Eyler N. Simpson, *The Ejido: Mexico's Way Out* (Chapel Hill, N.C., 1937), pp. 317ff.

[11] Henrik F. Infield and Koka Freier, *People in Ejidos* (New York, 1954), p. 130.

[12] Pietro Scotti, *Communismi Non Marxisti* (Genova, 1954).

[13] Karl Kautsky, *Vorlaeufer des Neueren Sozialismus* (Berlin, 1947), Vol. 1, p. 149.

[14] L. E. Deets, *The Hutterites: A Study in Social Cohesion* (Gettysburg, Pa., 1939), p. 22.

[15] These communities have been frequently discussed. For example, in Maslov, op. cit.; Infield, *Utopia and Experiment* (New York, 1955); Robert Liefmann, *Die kommunistischen Gemeinden in Nordamerika* (Jena, 1922).

[16] See Deets, *op. cit.;* Ivan A. Vallier, *Production Imperatives in Communal Systems* (Ph.D. dissertation, Harvard University, 1959); Bert Kaplan and Thomas A. Plaut, *Personality in a Communal Society* (Lawrence, Kansas, 1956); Joseph W. Eaton, "The Mental Health of the Hutterites," in *Scientific American,* Dec., 1953; *idem, Exploring Tomorrow's Agriculture* (New York, 1943); Infield, *Cooperative Communities at Work.*

[17] See Melford E. Spiro, *Kibbutz: Venture in Utopia* (Cambridge, Mass., 1956); Murray Weingarten, *Life in a Kibbutz* (New York, 1955); Joseph Baratz, *The Story of Dagania* (Tel Aviv, 1937).

[18] Francis H. E. Palmer, *Russian Life in Town and Country* (New York, London, 1901), pp. 146-47.

[19] I. A. Koniukov, *Ocherki o pervykh etapakh razvitiia kollektivnogo zemledeliia* (Sketches of the First Stages of the Development of Collective Agriculture, Moscow, 1949), p. 87; A. Kaz, "Evreiskie kolkhozy v Belorusii" (Jewish Colective Farms in Belorussia), *Na agrarnom fronte,* No. 5, May, 1928.

[20] Gideon Baratz, *et al., A New Way of Life: The Collective Settlements of Israel* (London, 1942); Spiro, *op. cit.;* Edwin Samuel, *Handbook of the Jewish Communal Villages in Palestine* (Jerusalem, 1945).

[21] Infield, *Utopia and Experiment,* p. 144.

[22] Spiro, *op. cit.,* p. 17.

[23] Vallier, *op. cit.,* p. 204.

[24] Infield, *Cooperative Living in Palestine,* (London,1946) p. 26.

[25] Spiro, *op. cit.,* p. 207.

[26] *Ibid.,* p. 252.

[27] Weingarten, *op. cit.,* p. 164; Vallier, *op. cit.,* p. 7.

[28] I. A. Koniukov, *Kollektivnoe zemledelie* (Collective Agriculture, Moscow, 1927), p. 77.

[29] G. Vasilevskii, *Krinitsa* (S. Peterburg, 1908), p. 71.

Chapter 3

1 F. Engels, *Landmarks of Scientific Socialism, "Anti-Duehring"* (trans. Austin Lewis, Chicago, 1907), p. 238.
2 Engels, *Letter to Bebel,* January 23, 1886.
3 *Ibid.*
4 Karl Marx, *Selected Works* (New York, 1942), Vol. 2, p. 565.
5 Engels, "Beschreibung der in neuerer Zeit entstandenen und noch bestehenden kommunistischen Ansiedlungen," in Marx-Engels, *Werke* (Berlin, 1958-   ), Vol. 2, pp. 353ff.
6 Karl Kautsky, *Die Sozialisierung der Landwirtshaft* (Berlin, 1919), p. 63; *idem, Die Agrarfrage* (Stuttgart, 1899), pp. 339ff.
7 Lenin, *op. cit.,* Vol. 13, pp. 327-28.
8 A. Faresov, *Narodniki i marksisty* (Populists and Marxists, S. Peterburg, 1899), p. 3.
9 Lenin, *op. cit.,* Vol. 6, p. 374.
10 *KPSS v rezoliutsiakh i resheniakh s"ezdov, konferentsii i plenumov Ts K* (The CPSU in Resolutions and Decisions of Congresses, Conferences, and Plenums of the Central Committee, 7th ed., Moscow, 1953), Vol. I, pp. 80-81. A standard compilation of Party documents hereafter referred to as *KPSS v rezoliutsiakh.*
11 Lenin, *op. cit.,* Vol. 13, pp. 195ff.
12 *Ibid.,* Vol. 25, p. 465.
13 *Ibid.,* pp. 440-41.
14 *Ibid.,* Vol. 24, p. 62.
15 *Ibid.,* Vol. 28, p. 122.
16 *Ibid.,* Vol. 24, pp. 62-65; Vol. 27, pp. 102ff.
17 Palmer, *Russian Life in Town and Country,* p. 173.
18 G. T. Robinson, *Rural Russia Under the Old Regime* (New York, 1949); A. A. Karelin, *Obshchinnoe vladenie v Rossii* (Communal Possession in Russia, S. Peterburg, 1893); Sir Donald M. Wallace, *Russia* (London, New York, 1912), p. 140; Naum Jasny, *The Socialized Agriculture of the USSR* (Stanford, 1949), p. 135.
19 A. Kochegarov (pseudonym for Karelin), *Zemel'naia programma anarkhistov-kommunistov* (The Land Program of the Anarchist-Communists, London, 1912); Oliver H. Radkey, *The Agrarian Foes of Bolshevism* (New York, 1958), p. 11.
20 Karelin, *op. cit.,* p. 165; N. G. Chernyshevskii, *Izbrannye ekonomicheskie proizvedeniia* (Selected Economic Works, Moscow, 1948), Vol. 1, pp. 159, 190.
21 Robinson, *op. cit.,* p. 71.
22 Otto Schiller, *Die Landwirtschaft der Sowjetunion, 1917-1953* (Tuebingen, 1954), p. 14; Leonard E. Hubbard, *The Economics of Soviet Agriculture* (London, 1939), p. 74.

[23] *Ten Years of Soviet Power* (Central Statistical Board, Moscow, 1928), p. 120.

[24] A. Agranovskii, *Kommuna, sovkhoz, kombinat* (Commune, Sovkhoz, Combine, Moscow, Leningrad, 1930), p. 81.

[25] Sergei Tretiakov, *Feld-Herren* (trans. from Russian, Berlin, 1931), p. 135.

[26] Georg Staehr, *Ueber Ursprung, Geschichte, Wesen und Bedeutung des russischen Artels* (2 Vols., Dorpat, 1890-91), Vol. 1, p. 28.

[27] Paul Apostol, *L'Artele et la Cooperation en Russie* (Paris, 1899), p. 23; "Artel," in *Entsiklopedicheskii slovar' Brokgausa* (Brockhaus Encyclopedic Dictionary, S. Peterburg, 1890-1904); Palmer, *op. cit.*, pp. 101, 220.

[28] I. V. Maiorov, *Trudovoe tovarishchestvo* (Laboring Fellowship, S. Peterburg, 1907), p. 25.

[29] Stepniak (pseudonym for Kravchinskii), *The Russian Peasantry, their Agrarian Condition, Social Life and Religion* (London, 1905), p. 636; Wallace, *op. cit.*, p. 95.

[30] Apostol, *op. cit.;* Ernest Lavigne, *Introduction a l'Histoire du Nihilisme Russe* (Paris, 1880), p. 132.

[31] Stepniak, *op. cit.*, pp. 635-36.

[32] Chernyshevskii, *op. cit.*, p. 202.

[33] Palmer, *op. cit.*, pp. 52, 96.

[34] Chernyshevskii, *op. cit.*, pp. 203, 206; Staehr, *op. cit.*, Vol. 2, pp. 182-83.

[35] Karelin, *op. cit.*, pp. 206-07, 210; Kochegarov (Karelin), *op. cit.*, pp. 42-43.

[36] A. Kh. Mitrofanov, *Kolkhoznoe dvizhenie, ego proshloe sovremmenye zadachi i znachenie* (The Kolkhoz Movement, Its Past, Present Tasks, and Significance, Moscow, 1929), p. 15; Schiller, *op. cit.*, p. 23.

[37] As quoted by Robinson, *op. cit.*, p. 125.

[38] W. G. Simkhovitsch, *Die Feldgemeinschaft in Russland* (Jena, 1898), p. 156; Maslov, *Trudovyia zemledel'cheskiia arteli,* p. 165.

[39] Mitrofanov, *op. cit.*, p. 17; Schiller, *op. cit.*, p. 23.

[40] Maslov, *op. cit.*, pp. 182ff., 206; Faresov, *op. cit.*, p. 14.

[41] Schiller, *op. cit.*, p. 20.

[42] Karelin, *op. cit.*, p. 182.

[43] I. A. Koniukov, *Trudovye zemledel'cheskie arteli l kommuny* (Laboring Agricultural Artels and Communes, Moscow, 1925), p. 9.

[44] Kochegarov (Karelin), *op. cit.*, pp. 43-44.

[45] Wallace, *op. cit.*, p. 92.

[46] Chernyshevskii, *op. cit.*, pp. 209-11.

[47] Ludwig Kulczycki, *Geschichte der russischen Revolution* (trans. from Polish, A. Schapiro-Neurath, 3 Vols., Gotha, 1910-1914), Vol. 1, pp. 379-81.

[48] Vasilevskii, *Krinitsa*, p. 11.

[49] Kulczycki, *op. cit.*, Vol. 2, pp. 181-82.

[50] Wallace, *op. cit.*, pp. 144, 612.

51 Kulczycki, *op. cit.*, Vol. 2, pp. 72ff., 102-03.
52 Vasilevskii, *op. cit.*, p. 13.
53 Lavigne, *op. cit.*, pp. 252-53.
54 Faresov, *op. cit.*, p. 56.
55 I. A. Rykov, and N. N. Khmelev (eds.), *Sel'sko-khoziaistvennye kollektivy moskovskoi gubernii* (Agricultural Collectives of the Moscow Gubernia, Moscow, 1926), p. 3.
56 Vasilevskii, *op. cit.*, pp. 80, 104.
57 Ivan Kataev, *Dvizhenie ianvar' i febral' 1930 goda na Kubani* (The Movement, January and February 1930 in the Kuban, Moscow, 1932), p. 198.
58 Engels, "On Social Conditions in Russia," in Marx, *Selected Works*, Vol. 2, p. 682.
59 Marx and Engels, *Selected Correspondence* (Moscow, 1956), p. 526.
60 Kautsky, *Die Agrarfrage*, pp. 332-33.
61 Kulczycki, *op. cit.*, Vol. 2, pp. 341-42, Vol. 3, p. 16; A. Volgin (pseudonym for Plekhanov), *Obosnovanie narodnichestva v trudakh g-na Vorontsova* (The Basis of Populism in the Works of Mr. Vorontsov, S. Peterburg, 1896).
62 Lenin, *op. cit.*, Vol. 13, pp. 389-90.
63 *Deviatyi vserossiskii s"ezd sovetov* (Ninth All-Russian Congress of Soviets, Stenographic Record, Moscow, 1921), p. 101.
64 James H. Billington, *Mikhailovsky and Russian Populism* (Oxford, 1958); Kulczycki, *op. cit.*, Vol. 2, p. 310; Koniukov, *Kollektivnoe zemledelle*, p. 5.
65 Tugan-Baranovskii, *Natsionalizatsiia zemli* (The Nationalization of Land, S. Peterburg, 1906), pp. 136-38; I. V. Maiorov, *Trudovoe tovarishchestvo*, pp. 18ff.; Oliver H. Radkey, *op. cit.*, pp. 27-28.
66 Viktor Chernov, *Proletariat, trudovoe krest'ianstvo i revoliutsiia* (The Proletariat, Toiling Peasantry and Revolution, Petrograd, 1918), p. 56.
67 E. A. Morokhovets, *Agrarnye programmy rossiiskikh politicheskykh partii v 1917 g.* (The Agrarian Programs of Russian Political Parties in 1917, Leningrad, 1927), p. 109.
68 Lenin, *op. cit.*, Vol. 27, p. 485.
69 *Pravda*, August 10, 1918.
70 Il'ia Maiorov, *Zemlia i khleb* (Land and Bread, Berlin, 1920), pp. 8, 34, 51-54.
71 Novomirskii (pseudonym), *Manifest anarkhistov-kommunistov* (Manifesto of the Anarchist-Communists, no place [Petrograd?], no date [1917?]), p. 14.
72 P. Kropotkin, *Khleb i volia* (Bread and Freedom, S. Peterburg, 1906), p. 201.
73 Novomirskii, *op. cit.*, p. 27; Kulczycki, *op. cit.*, Vol. 2, p. 124; Kochegarov (Karelin), *op. cit.*, *passim*.
74 D. Fedotoff-White, *The Growth of the Red Army* (Princeton, 1944), p. 25.

[75] Anatolii Gorelik, *Anarkhisty v rossiskoi revoliutsii* (Anarchists in the Russian Revolution, Buenos Aires, 1922), p. 13.

[76] Leonard Schapiro, *The Origin of the Communist Autocracy* (London, 1955), pp. 183-84.

[77] *Vos'moi vserossiiskii s"ezd sovetov, stenograficheskii otchet* (Eighth All-Russian Congress of Soviets, Stenographic Record, Moscow, 1921), p. 204.

[78] Gorelik, *op. cit.,* pp. 13, 34-35.

[79] A. A. Bitsenko, *K voprosam teorii istorii kollektivizatsii sel'skogo khoziaistva v SSSR* (On Questions of the Theory of the History of Collectivization of Agriculture in the USSR, Moscow, 1929), p. 25.

[80] K. Petrus, *Religious Communes in the USSR* (mimeographed, New York, August, 1953), p. 32.

[81] A. Kochegarov (Karelin), *K voprosu o kommunizme* (On the Question of Communism, no place [Petrograd?], no date [1917?]).

[82] Kropotkin, *op. cit.,* Tugan-Baranovskii, *Obshchestivennye ekonomicheskie idealy nashego vremeni.*

[83] Novomirskii, *op. cit.,* pp. 14-18.

[84] Karl Kautsky, *Communism in Central Europe in the Time of the Reformation* (trans. from German, London, 1897).

[85] N. Tsanki, *La Russie Sectaire* (Paris, 1888), p. 130; V. D. Bonch-Bruevich, *Iz mira sektantov, sbornik statei* (From the World of the Sectarians: Collection of Articles, Moscow, 1922), p. 25.

[86] S. P. Mel'gunov, *iz istorii religiozno-obshchestvennykh dvizhenii v Rossii XIX v.* (From the History of the Religious-Social Movements in Russia of the 19th Century, Moscow, 1919), p. 159.

[87] I. Iuzov (pseudonym for I. I. Kablits), *Russkie dissidenty, starovery i dukhovnye khristiane* (Russian Dissenters, Old Believers and Spiritual Christians, S. Peterburg, 1881), p. 109.

[88] Frederick C. Conybeare, *Russian Dissenters* (Cambridge, Mass., 1921), pp. 215-19; Tsanki, *op. cit.,* p. 33.

[89] *Ibid.,* p. 162.

[90] Stepniak, *op. cit.,* p. 490.

[91] Conybeare, *op. cit.,* p. 225.

[92] Fülop-Miller, *The Mind and Face of Bolshevism* (trans. from the German, New York, 1928), p. 107.

[93] V. D. Bonch-Bruevich, *Izbrannye sochineniia* (Selected Works, Moscow, 1959), Vol. 1, pp. 15, 32-33, 163.

[94] Tsanki, *op. cit.,* p. 193; Bonch-Bruevich, *Znachenie sektantsva dlia sovremmenoi Rossii* (The Significance of Sectarianism for Modern Russia, Geneva, 1902), pp. 306-08; Kochegarov (Karelin), *Zemel'naia programma anarkhistov-kommunistov,* p. 45.

[95] Stepniak, *The Russian Peasant,* p. 511; Iuzov, *op. cit.,* p. 131.

[96] Conybeare, *op. cit.,* p. 269; Maslov, *op. cit.,* p. 114; Bonch-Bruevich, *Dukhobortsy v kanadskikh preriiakh* (Dukhobors in the Canadian Prairies, Petrograd, 1918).

[97] See Tsanki, Iuzov, Bonch-Bruevich, *et al., op. cit.*

[98] Conybeare, *op. cit.,* p. 221; Tsanki, *op. cit.,* pp. 209ff.; Stepniak, *op. cit.,* p. 582.

[99] Tsanki, *op. cit.,* pp. 21ff., 162.

[100] F. M. Putintsev, *Sektantsvo i antireligioznaia propaganda* (Sectarianism and Anti-religious Propaganda, Moscow, 1928), p. 5.

[101] Vasilevskii, *op. cit.,* pp. 122ff.

[102] Fülop-Miller, *op. cit.,* pp. 123.

[103] Lenin, *op. cit.,* Vol. 4, p. 223.

[104] Fülop-Miller, *op. cit.,* pp. 102, 126.

[105] F. M. Putintsev, *Politicheskaia rol' sektantsva* (Political Role of Sectarianism, Moscow, 1928), p. 73.

[106] Koniukov, *Kollektivnoe zemledelie,* p. 69.

[107] Koniukov, *Ocherki,* p. 32; Putintsev, *Politicheskaia rol' i taktika sekt* (Political Role and Tactics of the Sects, Moscow, 1935), p. 472.

[108] Petrus, *op. cit.*

[109] L. F. Boros, *Reise durch Hundert Kollektivwirtschaften* (Moscow, 1934), p. 53.

[110] Koniukov, *Ocherki,* p. 87.

[111] Bonch-Bruevich, *Iz mira sektantov,* pp. 140ff.

[112] Putintsev, *Politicheskaia rol' sektantstva,* pp. 255.

[113] Karl Borders, *Village Life Under the Soviets* (New York, 1927), p. 58.

[114] Fedor Belov, *The History of a Soviet Collective Farm* (New York, 1955), p. 7.

[115] Tretiakov, *op. cit.,* p. 39.

[116] Petrus, *op. cit.*

[117] Kataev, *op. cit.,* pp. 124ff.

[118] Putintsev, *op. cit.,* p. 246.

[119] Bonch-Bruevich, *Iz mira sektantov,* p. 142.

[120] M. Sumatokhin, *Davaite zhit' kommunoi!* (Let's Live in a Commune, Kharkhov, 1919), p. 7.

[121] S. P. Sereda, *Osnovnye zadachi sotsialisticheskogo zemledelia* (Basic Tasks of Socialist Agriculture, pamphlet, Moscow, 1920), p. 13.

[122] I. A. Kirillov, *Ocherki zemleustroistva za tri goda revoliutsii* (Sketches of Land Reform through Three Years of the Revolution, Petrograd, 1922), p. 191; Bitsenko, *op. cit.,* p. 24.

[123] Wallace, *op. cit.,* pp. 98-99, 110-11, 530ff.; Robinson, *op. cit.*

Chapter 4

[1] *Pravda,* April 3, 1919.

[2] A. Bolgov, compiler, "K istorii provedeniia v zhizn' leninskogo dekreta o zemle" (On the History of the Application of Lenin's Decree on Land), *Krasnyi arkhiv,* Vol. 4-5, No. 89-90 (1938), p. 72.

[3] Klaus Mehnert, *Youth in Soviet Russia* (New York, 1933), pp. 249ff.

[4] *Pravda,* July 26; August 6, 10, 11, 1918.

[5] S. S. Kislianskii, *Komu vygodna kommuna i kto ee boitsia* (Who Gains by the Commune and Who Fears It, pamphlet, Moscow, 1921), p. 5.

[6] A. F. Chmyga, *Ocherki po istorii kolkhoznogo dvizheniia na Ukraine* (Sketches in the History of the Kolkhoz Movement in the Ukraine, Moscow, 1959), p. 211.

[7] T. Zelenov, compiler, "K istorii osnovaniia sel'skogo-khoziaistvennykh kommun i artelei v SSSR" (On the History of the Formation of Agricultural Communes and Artels in the USSR), *Krasnyi arkhiv*, Vol. 4, No. 101 (1940), p. 122.

[8] N. D. Kazantsev, *Voprosy kolkhoznogo i zemel'nogo prava* (Questions of Kolkhoz and Land Law, Moscow, 1951), p. 235; *Pravda*, July 13, 1918.

[9] *Agrarnaia politika sovetskoi vlasti* (1917-1918 gg.) *dokumenty i materialy* (The Agrarian Policy of the Soviet State, 1917-1918, Documents and Materials, Moscow, 1954), p. 403. Hereafter referred to as *Agrarnaia politika*.

[10] *Pravda*, November 1, 1918.

[11] *Agrarnaia politika*, p. 127.

[12] *Ibid.*, p. 407.

[13] *Izvestiia*, October 9, 1918.

[14] *Ibid.*, p. 415.

[15] Koniukov, *Kollektivnoe zemledelie*, p. 38.

[16] Hubbard, *The Economics of Soviet Agriculture*, p. 77.

[17] *Pravda*, October 16, 1918.

[18] Mitrofanov, *Kolkhoznoe dvizhenie*, p. 28.

[19] Bolgov, *op. cit.*, p. 101; A. A. Bitsenko, *Khrestomatiia spravochnik po istorii kollektivnogo zemledeliia v SSSR za gody 1918-1924* (Reader-Guide to the History of Collective Agriculture in the USSR, 1918-1924, Moscow, 1925), p. 214.

[20] *Pravda*, December 12, 18, 22, 1918; *Agrarnaia politika*, p. 417.

[21] V. N. Meshcheriakov, *Derevenskaia bednota i put' k sotsializmu* (*o sel'skykh kommunakh*) (The Village Poor and the Road to Socialism [on Agricultural Communes], pamphlet, Petrograd, 1918).

[22] Kii, *Sel'skaia kommuna*, pp. 13-14.

[23] *Izvestiia*, December 13, 1918.

[24] Koniukov, *Ocherki*, pp. 50-51; T. Shepeleva, compiler, "Sotsialisticheskie formy sel'skogo khoziaistva, 1918-1919 g." (Socialist Forms of Agriculture in 1918-1919), *Krasnyi arkhiv*, Vol. 5, No. 96 (1939), p. 8.

[25] Koniukov, *Kollektivnoe zemledelia*, p. 38; Mitrofanov, *op. cit.*, pp. 46-47.

[26] P. Ia. Dyshler, *Pochemu i kak nado ustraivat' sel'sko-khoziaistvennye kommuny* (Why and How One Must Form Agricultural Communes, Petrograd, 1919), p. 25.

[27] Sumatokhin, *Davaite zhit' kommunoi!* p. 15.

[28] Meshcheriakov, *op. cit.*, p. 10.

[29] *Komitety bednoty Belorussii* (Committees of the Poor of Belorussia, Collection of Documents, Minsk, 1958), p. 386.

[30] *Pravda,* December 18, 1918.

[31] Ia. Zhigur, *Organizatsiia kommunisticheskikh khoziaistv v zemledelii* (The Organization of Communist Farms, Moscow, 1918, pamphlet), pp. 30-34.

[32] *Agrarnaia politika,* p. 480.

[33] Bitsenko, *K voprosam teorii istorii kollektivizatsii,* pp. 58-59; *Agrarnaia politika,* p. 480.

[34] *Ibid.,* p. 310.

[35] *Shestoi vserosiiskii chrezvychainyi s"ezd sovetov, stenograficheskii otchet* (Sixth All-Russian Extraordinary Congress of Soviets, Stenographic Record, Moscow, 1919), p. 86ff.

[36] *Istoriia kolkhoznogo prava* (History of Kolkhoz Law, 2 Vols., Moscow, 1959), Vol. 1, p. 17.

[37] Koniukov, *Kollektivnoe zemledelie,* p. 33.

[38] *Sbornik dokumentov po zemel'nomu zakondatel'stvu SSSR i RFSR 1917-1954* (Collection of Documents on the Agrarian Legislation of the USSR and RSFSR, 1917-1954, Moscow, 1954), p. 38.

[39] Lenin, *op. cit.,* Vol. 28, pp. 314-25.

[40] *Pravda,* December 28, 1918.

[41] *Vos'moi s"ezd rossiiskoi kommunisticheskoi partii, 18-23 marta, 1919 g.* (Eighth Congress of the Russian Communist Party, 18-23 March, 1919, Moscow, 1919), pp. 202ff.

[42] Zhigur, *op. cit.,* pp. 15-16; V. P. Miliutin, *Agrarnaia politika SSSR* (The Agrarian Policy of the USSR, Moscow, 1926), pp. 52-53.

[43] Kirillov, *Ocherki zemleustrolstva,* p. 56.

[44] Dyshler, *op. cit.,* p. 26.

[45] Shepeleva, *op. cit.,* p. 11.

[46] Lenin, *op. cit.,* Vol. 30, pp. 89, 126, 176-82.

[47] *Ibid.,* Vol. 31, p. 313.

[48] *Pravda,* February 19, 1921.

[49] Lenin, *op. cit.,* Vol. 33, p. 425.

[50] *Pravda,* August 10, 1921.

[51] Mitrofanov, *op. cit.,* p. 8.

[52] *Pravda,* September 5, 1920.

[53] Kindeev, *Kollektivnye khoziaistva,* p. 161.

[54] *Agrarnaia politika v resheniiakh s"ezdov i konferentsii RKP(b) s 1917 do 1925 g.* (The Agrarian Policy in Decisions of Congresses and Conferences of the RCP(b) from 1917 through 1925, Moscow, 1926), p. 58.

[55] Lenin, *op. cit.,* Vol. 33, p. 431.

[56] *Pravda,* March 5, 1925.

[57] A. G. Goikhbarg, *Obobshchestvlenie sel'skogo khoziaistva* (The Collectivization of Agriculture, pamphlet, Moscow, 1919), p. 24.

[58] *Sel'sko-khoziaistvennaia kooperatsiia, sbornik dekretov, tsirkuliarov i ustavov* (Agricultural Cooperation, Collection of Decrees, Circulars and Statutes, Moscow, 1924), pp. 40-41.

[59] *Pravda,* February 27, 1925.

[60] E. Kviring, "Kollektivnye khoziaistva" (Collective Farms) *Na agrarnom fronte*, No. 4, April 1925, p. 26; *Pravda*, July 2, 1927.

[61] *Pravda*, May 22, 1921.

[62] Chmyga, *op. cit.*, pp. 70-71, 206-07.

[63] *Pravda*, July 22, 1925.

[64] *Ibid.*, November 14, 1925.

[65] *Direktivy KPSS i sovetskogo pravitel'stva po khoziaistvennym voprosam* (Directives of the CPSU and the Soviet Government on Economic Matters, 2 Vols., Moscow, 1957), Vol. 1, p. 327.

[66] Koniukov, *Kollektivnoe zemledelie*, p. 220.

[67] *Direktivy KPSS, loc. cit.*

[68] M. I. Kalinin, *Stat'i i rechi, 1919-1935* (Articles and Speeches, 1919-1935, Moscow, 1936), p. 228.

Chapter 5

[1] E. Lutskii, "Borba vokrug dekreta O Zemle" (The Struggle over the Decree On Land), *Voprosy istorii*, No. 10, October, 1947, p. 17.

[2] S. S. Maslov, "Kollektivno-zemledel'cheskoe dvizhenie v sovremennoi Rossii" (The Collective-Agriculture Movement in Contemporary Russia), *Sovremenniia zapiski* (Paris), Vol. X (1922), p. 202.

[3] Zelenov, *op. cit.*, in *Krasnyi arkhiv*, Vol. 4, No. 101 (1940), p. 126.

[4] Maslov, *op. cit.*, p. 206.

[5] M. A. Kraev, *Pobeda kolkhoznogo stroia v SSSR* (Victory of the Kolkhoz Form in the USSR, Moscow, 1954), p. 195.

[6] Zelenov, *op. cit.*, p. 126.

[7] *Ibid.*, p. 123.

[8] Kazantsev, *Voprosy kolkhoznogo i zemel'nogo prava*, p. 242.

[9] *Ibid.*, p. 231.

[10] Bolgov, *op. cit.*, in *Krasnyi arkhiv*, Vol. 4-5, No. 89-90 (1938), p. 95.

[11] *Agrarnaia politika*, pp. 483-85.

[12] *Ibid.*, p. 413.

[13] *Komitety bednoty Belorussii*, p. 412.

[14] Chmyga, *Ocherki po istorii kolkhoznogo dvizheniia*, pp. 79-80; Kazantsev, *op. cit.*, p. 223.

[15] Lenin, *op. cit.*, Vol. 30, p. 176.

[16] I. Budovnits, *Vesna, 1930* (Spring, 1930, Leningrad, 1930), p. 15.

[17] Bitsenko, *K voprosam istorii*, p. 35.

[18] I. V. Stalin, *Sochineniia* (Works, 13 Vols., Moscow, 1949), Vol. 4, p. 256.

[19] A. Agranovskii, *Ot stol'btsov do Bukhary* (From the Pillars to Bukhara, Moscow, Leningrad, 1930), p. 64.

[20] Koniukov, *Kollektivnoe zemledelie*, p. 87.

[21] Kazantsev, *op. cit.*, p. 249.

[22] *Ibid.*, p. 230.

[23] *Kollektivizatsiia sel'skogo khoziaistva na Kubani, sbornik dokumentov i*

materialov (Collectivization of Agriculture in the Kuban: Collection of Documents and Materials, Krasnodar, 1959), pp. 44-46.

24 Tretiakov, *Feld-Herren*, p. 91.

25 *Kollektivizatsiia sel'skogo khoziaistva na Kubani*, pp. 30-35.

26 Zelenov, *loc. cit.*

27 N. D. Kazantsev, *Kolkhoznoe pravo* (Kolkhoz Law, Moscow, 1955), p. 30.

28 Zelenov, *op. cit.*, p. 136.

29 B., *Zadachi sotsial'noi revoliutsii* (Tasks of the Social Revolution, published by the Brotherhood of Free Communers of the Federation of Anarchist-Communists, no place [Petrograd?], no date [1917?]), p. 6.

30 Lenin, *op. cit.*, Vol. 28, p. 319.

31 *Kak zhivetsia v kommune, kniga dokumentov o kolkhozakh* (Life in the Commune: A Book of Documents on Kolkhozes, Moscow, Leningrad, 1931), p. 18.

32 Kraev, *Pobeda kolkhoznogo stroia v SSSR*, p. 207.

33 A. L. Strong, *The Soviets Conquer Wheat* (New York, 1931), p. 121; Chmyga, *op. cit.*, p. 92.

34 Koniukov, *op. cit.*, p. 94.

35 Chmyga, *op. cit.*, p. 91.

36 *Izvestiia*, November 13, 1925; S. Khalturin, *Dostoinaia imeni Lenina* (Worthy of the Name of Lenin, Voronezh, 1930), pp. 7ff.

37 P. Ia. Tadeush, *Amerikanskaia kommuna 'Seiatel'* (The American 'Seattle' Commune, Moscow, Leningrad, 1930); Webb and Webb, *Soviet Communism: A New Civilization* (London, 1944), pp. 213-14.

38 Lenin, *op. cit.*, Vol. 29, p. 18.

39 *Kollektivizatsiia sel'skogo khoziaistva na Kubani*, p. 97.

40 Chmyga, *op. cit.*, p. 106.

41 *Kollektivizatsiia sel'skogo khoziaistva na Kubani*, p. 110.

42 *Pravda*, December 5, 1925.

43 Tretiakov, *op. cit.*, pp. 91-92.

44 *Kollektivizatsiia sel'skogo khoziaistva na Kubani*, p. 157.

45 *Ibid.*, p. 105.

46 P'ianykh, *Odna iz mnogikh, kommuna 'Zavet Il'icha'* (One of Many: The 'Lenin's Legacy' Commune, Voronezh, 1930), pp. 3-9.

47 A. A. Bitsenko, *Sel'sko-khoziaistvennye kommuny* (Agricultural Communes, Moscow, 1924), pp. 121ff.

48 G. R. Glezer and P. A. Kalashnikov, *Kolkhozy nizhnego povolzh'ia* (Collective Farms of the Lower Volga Region, Moscow, 1929), p. 20.

49 *Pravda*, December 20, 1918.

50 *Pravda*, February 22, 23, 1921.

51 Miliutin, *Agrarnaia politika SSSR*, p. 177.

52 *Pravda*, June 24, 1926.

53 I. A. Rykov and N. N. Khmelev, *Sel'sko-khoziaistvennye kollektivy moskovskoi gubernii*, p. 21.

54 N. S. Vlasov, *et al.*, *Kolkhozy zernovykh raionov, severnogo Kavkaza,*

Sibiri, Povolzh'ia i Ukrainy (Kolkhozy of the Grain Regions, North Caucasus, Siberia, Volga Area and Ukraine, Moscow, 1930), p. 83.

[55] Kindeev, *Kollektivnye khoziaistva*, pp. 20-21.

[56] *Pravda*, June 1, 1919.

[57] Chmyga, *op. cit.,* p. 207; Koniukov, *Ocherki*, p. 113.

[58] A. Gaister, *Materialy issledovaniia. Protsess kollektivizatsii* (Investigation Materials: The Collectivization Process, Moscow, 1931), p. 3.

[59] Koniukov, *Kollektivnoe zemledelie*, p. 9.

[60] Kindeev, *op. cit.*, p. 19.

[61] Koniukov, *Ocherki*, p. 112; Glezer and Kalashnikov, *op. cit.*, p. 47; P. Kulikov, "Kontol'nye tsifry po kolkhozam na 1928/9 g." (Control Figures for Kolkhozy for 1928-29), *Na agrarnom Fronte*, December, 1928, p. 20.

[62] *Kolkhozy SSSR, statisticheskii spravochnik* (Kolkhozy of the USSR: Statistical Guide, Moscow, 1929), p. 33. This statistical handbook is hereafter referred to as *Kolkhozy SSSR*.

[63] Zelenov, *op. cit.*, p. 123.

[64] *Sel'sko-khoziaistvennaia kooperatsiia v usloviakh novoi ekonomicheskoi politiki* (Agricultural Cooperation in Conditions of the New Economic Policy, Moscow, 1923), p. 33.

[65] D. A. Karpuzi and N. L. Meshcheriakov, director and editor, *Opyt issledovaniia kollektivnogo zemledeliia* (An Essay in Investigation of Collective Agriculture: Account Analysis of 66 Collective Farms of Different Agricultural Regions of the USSR, Moscow, 1928), p. 22.

[66] Rykov and Khmelev, *op. cit.*, p. 25.

[67] *Sdvigi v sel'skom khoziaistve SSSR mezhdu XV i XVI partiinnym s"ezdami* (Shifts in Agriculture of the USSR between the XV and XVI Party Congresses, Gosplan, Moscow, 1930), pp. 22, 30. Hereafter referred to as *Sdvigi*.

[68] Kindeev, *op. cit.*, pp. 11, 16: *Sotsialisticheskoe stroitel'stvo SSSR, statisticheskii ezhegodnik 1935* (Socialist Construction of the USSR: Statistical Yearbook, 1935, Gosplan, Moscow, 1935), p. 162.

[69] Kindeev, *op. cit.*, p. 11.

[70] *Sdvigi*, p. 28.

[71] Kindeev, *op. cit.*, pp. 72, 75.

[72] *Narodnoe i gosudarstvennoe khoziaistvo SSSR k seredine 1922-1923 g.* (The National and Governmental Economy of the USSR to the Middle of 1922-1923. Peoples' Commissariat of Finances. Moscow, 1923), p. 56.

[73] Figures for the following months: 1926, June; 1927, October; 1928 and 1929, June; 1930, May. Sources are as follows: 1926, *Pravda*, July 2, 1927; 1927, *Kolkhozy SSSR*, p. 15; 1928-30, *Kolkhozy v 1930 g.* (Kolkhozy in 1930, Moscow, 1931), p. 15.

[74] Kindeev, *op. cit.*, p. 34.

[75] *Ibid.*, p. 22.

[76] Rykov and Khmelev, *op. cit.*, p. 17.

[77] *Kolkhozy SSSR*, p. 39.
[78] Vlasov *et al., op. cit.*, p. 46.
[79] Kindeev, *op. cit.*, pp. 35, 37; E. P. Terletskii, *Kolkhozy SSSR* (Moscow, 1929), p. 42.

Chapter 6

[1] *Agrarnaia politika*, pp. 400-03.
[2] *Ibid.*, pp. 403-05.
[3] *Ibid.*, pp. 433-41.
[4] *Ibid.*, p. 462.
[5] *Pravda*, May 22, 1921; Koniukov, *Kollektivnoe zemledelie*, p. 9.
[6] *Sel'sko-khoziaistvennaia kooperatsiia, sbornik dekretov, tsirkuliarov i ustavov*, pp. 114-22.
[7] *Ibid.*, pp. 123-41.
[8] *Ustav sel'sko-khoziaistvennoi kommuny* (Statute of the Agricultural Commune, 4th ed., pamphlet, Moscow, 1926).
[9] *Pravila vnutrennego rasporiadka sel'sko-khoziaistvennoi kommuny* (Internal Rules of the Agricultural Commune, pamphlet, Moscow, 1926).
[10] Pamphlet editions of Statutes and Internal Rules for communes, artels, and tozes appear to have been published regularly throughout the 1920's. For the commune, 1926, 1928 (8th ed.) and 1930 statute pamphlets were consulted; for the artel, those of 1926, 1928 (9th ed.), and 1930 (14th and 15th eds.).
[11] N. D. Kazantsev, *Kolkhoznoe pravo* (Moscow, 1950), pp. 62ff.
[12] *Vos'moi s"ezd rossiiskoi kommunisticheskoi partii*, p. 209.
[13] Chmyga, *Ocherki po istorii kolkhoznogo dvizheniia na Ukraine*, p. 151.
[14] *Pravda*, July 12, 1930.
[15] Bitsenko, *Khrestomatiia*, p. 56.
[16] Chmyga, *op. cit.*, p. 87.
[17] Koniukov, *Kollektivnoe zemledelie*, pp. 174-75.
[18] Kazantsev, *Voprosy kolkhoznogo i zemel'nogo prava*, pp. 261-62.
[19] Koniukov, *Kollektivnoe zemledelie*, p. 174.
[20] Chmyga, *op. cit.*, p. 182.
[21] Lancelot Lawton, *An Economic History of Soviet Russia* (London, 1932), Vol. 2, p. 464.
[22] Kazantsev, *op. cit.*, p. 261.
[23] Strong, *The Soviets Conquer Wheat*, p. 127.
[24] Tadeush, *Amerikanskaia kommuna 'Seiatel'*, p. 74.
[25] Koniukov, *Kollektivnoe zemledelie*, pp. 142-43.
[26] Wallace, *Russia*, p. 41.
[27] Koniukov, *Kollektivnoe zemledelie*, p. 175.
[28] Gaister, *Materialy issledovaniia*, p. 279.
[29] Tretiakov, *Feld-Herren*, p. 183.
[30] Kindeev, *Kollektivnye khoziaistva*, pp. 60-61.

[31] K. G. Lugovskii, *Kolkhoznoe dvizhenie na perelome* (The Kolkhoz Movement at the Turning Point, Moscow, 1929), p. 158; Tadeush, *op. cit.*, p. 19.

[32] Terletskii, *Kolkhozy SSSR*, p. 90.

[33] Kindeev, *op. cit.*, p. 58.

[34] Karpuzi and Meshcheriakov, *Opyt issledovaniia*, p. 38.

[35] D. A. Karpuzi, "Sotsial'naia priroda kollektivnogo zemledeliia" (The Social Nature of Collective Agriculture), *Puti sel'skogo khoziaistva*, August, 1927, p. 31.

[36] *Sdvigi*, p. 34.

[37] V. P. Nifontov, *Zhivotnovodstvo SSSR v tsifrakh* (Stockraising in the USSR in Figures, Moscow, Leningrad, 1932), p. 91.

[38] Kindeev, *op. cit.*, p. 92.

[39] Terletskii, *op. cit.*, p. 90.

[40] Kindeev, *op. cit.*, p. 158.

[41] *Kolkhozy v 1930 g.*, p. 247.

[42] Otto Auhagen, *Das Schicksalswende des russlanddeutschen Bauerntums in den Jahren 1927-1930* (Leipzig, 1942), p. 36.

[43] P. Lezhnev-Finkovskii, *Sovkhozy i kolkhozy* (Moscow, 1928), p. 187.

[44] *Izvestiia*, November 13, 1925.

[45] Strong, *op. cit.*, pp. 37, 123.

[46] Tretiakov, *Feld-Herren*, pp. 155-56, 257-62.

[47] *Sdvigi*, p. 47.

[48] F. Panferov, "Chto takoe kommunizm?" (What is Communism?) *Oktiabr'*, January, 1960, pp. 105-07.

[49] Mehnert, *Youth in Soviet Russia*, p. 172.

[50] Chmyga, *op. cit.*, p. 168.

[51] Tretiakov, *op. cit.*, pp. 96-97.

[52] Chmyga, *op. cit.*, pp. 171-72.

[53] Strong, *op. cit.*, p. 224.

[54] Agranovskii, *Kommuna, sovkhoz, kombinat*, p. 142.

[55] Mehnert, *op. cit.*, p. 167.

[56] N. Demianov, "K istorii trudodna" (On the History of the Labor-Day), *Problemy ekonomiki*, June, 1940, pp. 199-204.

[57] Hubbard, *The Economics of Soviet Agriculture*, p. 179.

[58] M. A. Kraev, "Organizatsionno-khoziaistvennoe upravelenie kolkhozov i borba za plan" (The Organizational-Economic Direction of the Kolkhozy and the Struggle for the Plan), *Planovoe khoziaistvo*, January, 1934, p. 159.

[59] Also described by Trotskii, in *Pravda*, December 5, 1925.

[60] *Pravda*, March 4, 1925.

[61] Chmyga, *op. cit.*, pp. 171-72.

[62] K. Kindeev, "Organizatsiia truda i raspredelenie v kolkhozakh," (Organization of Labor and Distribution in Kolkhozy), *Planovoe khoziaistvo*, July-August, 1930, p. 106.

[63] Lezhnev-Finkovskii, *Sovkhozy i kolkhozy*, p. 198.

[64] *Pravda*, August 25, 1925.
[65] Kindeev, *Kollektivnye khoziaistva*, p. 86.
[66] S. N. Prokopovicz, *Russlands Volkswirtschaft unter den Sowjets* (Zurich, 1944), p. 84.
[67] *Izvestiia*, November 13, 1925.
[68] Lezhnev-Finkovskii, *op. cit.*, p. 190.
[69] Strong, *op. cit.*, p. 224.
[70] Khalturin, *Dostoinaia imeni Lenina*, pp. 18-19.
[71] *Kak zhivetsia v. kommune*, p. 16.
[72] "Russia's Collective Farms," *Living Age*, Vol. 339, No. 4370 (November, 1930), pp. 257-58.
[73] Boros, *Reise durch hundert Kollektivwirtschaften*, p. 162.
[74] Koniukov, *Ocherki*, p. 170.
[75] Kindeev, *op. cit.*, p. 83.
[76] Terletskii, *Kolkhozy SSSR*, pp. 44-45.
[77] *Kolkhozy nakanune XVI s"ezda VKP(b)* (Kolkhozy on the Eve of the XVI Congress of the All-Union Communist Party, Moscow, 1930), p. 114.
[78] *Pravda*, October 7, 1930.
[79] Chmyga, *op. cit.*, p. 161.
[80] Tretiakov, *Feld-Herren*, p. 215.
[81] Chmyga, *op. cit.*, p. 169.
[82] Kindeev, "Praktika stroitel'stva kolkhozov v RSFSR" (The Experience of Building Kolkhozy in the RSFSR), *Ekonomicheskoe obozrenie*, May 1928, p. 112.
[83] Vlasov *et al.*, *Kolkhozy zernovykh raionov*, pp. 21-22.
[84] Sumatokhin, *Davaite zhit' kommunoi*, p. 13.
[85] Bitsenko, *K voprosam teorii istorii kollektivizatsii*, p. 112.
[86] P'ianykh, *Odna iz mnogikh*, p. 33.

Chapter 7

[1] *Agrarnaia politika*, p. 506.
[2] *O Zemle, sbornik statei o proshlom i budushchem zemel'nogo-khoziaistvennogo stroitel'stva. Vypusk I* (On Land; Collection of Articles on the Past and Future of Agrarian Reconstruction. Issue I., Moscow, 1921), pp. 8-9.
[3] *Pravda*, October 4, 1928.
[4] *Ibid.*, February 22, 1928.
[5] P. A. Mesiatsev, *Zemel'naia i sel'sko-khoziaistvennaia politika v Rossii* (Land and Agricultural Policy in Russia, Moscow, 1922), p. 151.
[6] Lugovskii, *Kolkhoznoe dvizhenie na perelome*, pp. 7-8.
[7] S. I. Sdobnov, *Vozniknovenie i razvitie kolkhoznoi sobstvennosti v. SSSR* (Origin and Development of Kolkhoz Property in the USSR, Moscow, 1956), p. 39.
[8] Lugovskii, *op. cit.*, p. 11.

9 Koniukov, *Trudovye zemledel'cheskie arteli i kommuny, p. 65.*

10 N. Skrypnev, *Pervye shagi sotsialisticheskogo pereustroistva sel'skogo khoziaistva v. 1918-1920 gg.* (First Steps in the Socialist Reconstruction of Agriculture in 1918-1920, Moscow, 1951), p. 46.

11 *Apercu Statistique sur l'Argriculture en URSS pour la Periode 1928-1931* (Moscow, Leningrad, 1932).

12 *Kolkhozy v 1930 g.,* p. 15.

13 *Ten Years of Soviet Power, 1917-1927,* p. 118.

14 *Ibid.,* p. 165.

15 Koniukov, *Kollektivnoe zemledelie,* p. 135.

16 Kindeev, *op. cit.,* in *Ekonomicheskoe obozrenie,* May, 1928, p. 92.

17 Strong, *The Soviets Conquer Wheat,* p. 195.

18 *Kolkhozy nakanune XVI s"ezda VKP(b),* p. 111.

19 Kindeev, *op. cit.,* pp. 91-92.

20 Skrypnev, *op. cit.,* p. 51.

21 Kindeev, *Kollektivnye khoziaistva,* pp. 53-54; Sdobnov, *op. cit.,* p. 48.

22 *Kolkhozy moskovskoi oblasti* (Kolkhozes of the Moscow Oblast, Moscow, 1930?), table 4.

23 Kindeev, *op. cit.,* pp. 99-100.

24 N. Mikhailov, "Nekotorye cherty postroeniia kollektivnykh form sel'-skgo khoziaistva" (Some Features of the Building of Collective Forms of Agriculture), *Ekonomicheskoe obozrenie,* July 1929, p. 154.

25 Kindeev, *op. cit.,* p. 162.

26 *Ibid.,* p. 172.

27 Tretiakov, *Feld-Herren,* pp. 75, 108; *Pravda,* December 5, 1962.

28 Kindeev, *op. eit.,* p. 114.

29 *Sdvigi,* p. 110.

30 Prokopovicz, *Russlands Landwirtschaft,* p. 83.

31 Bitsenko, *K voprosam istorii teorii,* p. 50.

32 Kindeev, *op. cit.,* pp. 140f.

33 Terlctskii, *Kolkhozy SSSR,* p. 114.

34 Vlasov *et al., Kolkhozy zernovykh raionov,* p. 70.

35 Auhagen, *Das Schicksalwende des russlanddeutschen Bauerntums,* p. 38.

36 Lugovskii, *Kolkhoznoe dvihenie na perelome,* p. 155.

37 A. Gaister, "Dostizheniia i trudnosti kolkhoznogo stroitel'stva" (Achievements and Difficulties of Kolkhoz Formation), *Na agrarnom fronte,* December, 1928, p. 12.

38 Terletskii, *op. cit.,* p. 11.

39 *Ibid.,* p. 111.

40 *Pravda,* February 26, 1930.

41 *Ibid.,* March 31, 1931.

42 *Istoriia kolkhoznogo prava,* Vol. 1, p. 203.

43 Karpuzi and Meshcheriakov, *Opyt issledovaniia,* p. 69.

44 Kindeev, *op. cit.,* p. 161.

45 Mikhailov, *op. cit.,* in *Ekonomicheskoe obozrenie,* July, 1929.

46 *Kolkhozy v 1930 g.,* p. 247.

[47] Agranovskii, *Kommuna, sovkhoz, kombinat,* p. 132.
[48] Bitsenko, *op. cit.,* p. 50; Kislianskii, *Komu vygodna kommuna i kto boitsia ee,* p. 14.
[49] Tretiakov, *Feld-Herren,* p. 147.
[50] Kazantsev, *Voprosy kolkhoznogo i zemel'nogo prava,* pp. 242-44.
[51] *Izvestiia,* November 13, 1925.
[52] Kindeev, *op. cit.,* pp. 8, 42.
[53] Karpuzi and Mescheriakov, *op. cit.,* p. 42.

Chapter 8

[1] Mitrofanov, *Kolkhoznoe dvizhenie, ego proshloe, sovremennye zadachi i znachenie,* p. 95.
[2] *Pravda,* February 9, 1930.
[3] *Kolkhozy v 1930 g.,* p. 170.
[4] "The Five Year Plan and the Regulation of the Labour Market in the USSR," *International Labour Review,* Vol. 27 (March, 1933), pp. 352-53; Palmer, *Russian Life in Town and Country,* p. 245.
[5] *International Labour Review, loc. cit.,* p. 359.
[6] Agranovskii, *Kommuna, sovkhoz, kombinat,* p. 148.
[7] Kindeev, *Kollektivnye khoziaistva,* p. 105.
[8] *Sdvigi,* p. 59.
[9] Kindeev, *op. cit.,* p. 74.
[10] Gaister, *op. cit.,* in *Na agrarnom fronte,* December, 1928, pp. 13-15.
[11] *Kolkhozy v 1930 g.,* p. 247.
[12] Kindeev, *op. cit.,* pp. 79-80.
[13] Karpuzi, *op. cit.,* in *Puti sel'skogo khoziaistva,* August, 1927, p. 25.
[14] *Sdvigi,* p. 126.
[15] *Sel'sko-khoziaistvennaia kooperatsia v usloviakh novoi ekonomicheskoi politiki,* p.
[16] Chmyga, *Ocherki po istorii kolkhoznogo dvizheniia na Ukraine,* p. 133.
[17] Kindeev, *op. cit.,* pp. 58, 107, 111.
[18] Tadeush, *Amerikanskaia kommuna 'Seiatel',* p. 59.
[19] Gaister, *Materialy issledovaniia,* p. 208.
[20] Kindeev, *op. cit.,* pp. 147-49.
[21] Karpuzi and Meshcheriakov, *Opyt issledovaniia,* pp. 450ff.
[22] Kindeev, *op. cit.,* p. 126.
[23] *Kontrol'nye tsifry narodnogo khoziaistva SSSR na 1927/1928 god* (Control Figures of the National Economy of the USSR for the 1927-1928 Year, Gosplan, Moscow, 1928).
[24] Terletskii, *Kolkhozy SSSR,* p. 73.
[25] *Sdvigi,* p. 141.
[26] Kindeev, *op. cit.,* p. 145.
[27] *Pravda,* June 14, 1928; Terletskii, *op. cit.,* p. 85; Karpuzi and Meshcheriakov, *op. cit.,* pp. 201, 425, 539, 549, 63.
[28] Bitsenko, *K voprosam istorii teorii,* pp. 5, 6, 70-72.

[29] *Kolkhozy SSSR*, p. 33.
[30] Mikhailov, *op cit.*, in *Ekonomicheskoe obozrenie*, July, 1929, p. 159.
[31] Terletskii, *op. cit.*, p. 41.
[32] Kindeev, *op. cit.*, p. 15.
[33] *Ibid.*, p. 82.
[34] Terletskii, *op. cit.*, p. 35.
[35] Koniukov, *Kollektivnoe zemledelie*, pp. 150, 169.
[36] Kindeev, *op. cit.*, p. 156.
[37] *Kak zhivetsia v kommune*, pp. 21-22.
[38] Tretiakov, *Feld-Herren*, pp. 95, 152.
[39] *Ibid.*, pp. 71, 113, 156.
[40] Bitsenko, *op. cit.*, p. 29.
[41] Lezhnev-Finkovskii, *Sovkhozy i kolkhozy*, p. 191-83.
[42] *Pravda*, January 7, 1928.
[43] *Kak zhivetsia v kommune*, p. 19.
[44] F. Dubkhovetskii, *Na putiakh k kommunizmu* (On the Roads to Communism, Kiev, 1951), pp. 31ff.
[45] Vasilevskii, *Krinitsa*, p. 56.
[46] Kindeev, *op. cit.*, in *Ekonomicheskoe obozrenie*, May, 1928, p. 92.
[47] Agranovskii, *Kommuna, sovkhoz, kombinat*, p. 145.
[48] *Kak zhivetsia v kommune*, p. 28.
[49] *Kollektivizatsiia sel'sko-khoziaistva na Kubani*, p. 96.

Chapter 9

[1] For figures, see Chmyga, Kindeev, Koniukov, Terletskii, *et al.*
[2] *Kolkhozy v 1930 g.*, p. 224.
[3] Mitrofanov, *Kolkhoznoe dvizhenie, ego proshloe, sovremennye zadachi i znachenie*, p. 127.
[4] Kindeev, *Kollektivnye khoziaistva*, p. 157.
[5] Kazantsev, *Voprosy kolkhoznogo i zemel'nogo prava*, p. 227.
[6] *Kolkhozy SSSR*, p. 41.
[7] *Kolkhozy v 1930 g.*, p. 236.
[8] *Kolkhozy SSSR*, p. 41.
[9] *Izvestiia*, November 13, 1925.
[10] *Agrarnaia politika*, p. 405.
[11] Budovnits, *Vesna 1930*, pp. 51ff.; also T. Levichev, *Sel'sovet litsom k kolkhozam* (The Village Soviet Facing the Kolkhozy, Moscow, Leningrad, 1930).
[12] *Agrarnaia politika*, pp. 17-18.
[13] *Kollektivizatsiia sel'skogo khoziaistva na Kubani*, pp. 157-58.
[14] A. Lebedev, ed., *Kak zhivut i rabotaiut kolkhozy* (How the Kolkhozes Live and Work, Moscow, 1930), p. 51.
[15] *Pravda*, June 23, 1919.
[16] Panferov, *op. cit.* in *Oktiabr'*, January, 1960, p. 104.
[17] Bolgov, *op. cit.* in *Krasnyi arkhiv*, Vol. 4-5, No. 89-90, p. 82.

18 *KPSS v rezoliutsiakh* (7th ed., Moscow, 1953), Vol. 1, p. 619.

19 *Pravda*, August 24, 1921.

20 Kindeev, *op. cit.*, pp. 166-70.

21 Mikhailov, *op. cit.* in *Ekonomicheskoe obozrenie*, July, 1929, p. 162.

22 *Kollektivizatsiia sel'skogo khoziaistva na Kubani*, pp. 96-98.

23 Kindeev, *op. cit.*, pp. 157-58.

24 Lezhnev-Finovskii, *op. cit.*, p. 177.

25 *Kolkhozy v 1930 g.*, p. 247.

26 Kalinin, *Stat'i i rechi*, p. 126.

27 Ia. P. Nikulikhin, *Kolkhoznoe dvizhenie na novom pod'eme* (The Kolkhoz Movement in a New Surge, Moscow, 1931), pp. 76, 101.

28 Otto Schiller, *Die Kollektivbewegung in der Sowjetunion*, Band 8, N.F., Osteuropa Forschungen (Berlin, 1931), p. 82.

29 *Kollektivozatsiia sel'skogo khoziaistva na Kubani*, p. 158.

30 Negley Farson, *Seeing Red: Today in Russia* (London, 1930), pp. 146-55.

31 Tretiakov, *Feld-Herren*, p. 133.

32 *Ibid.*, pp. 189-93.

33 Khalturin, *Dostoinaia imeni Lenina*.

34 *Pravda*, October 4, 1928.

35 Auhagen, *Das Schicksalswende des russlanddeutschen Bauerntums*, p. 102.

36 Mikhailov, *op. cit.* in *Ekonomicheskoe obozrenie*, July, 1929, p. 162.

37 *KPSS v rezoliutsiakh* (1953 ed.), Vol. 2, pp. 733ff.

Chapter 10

1 Kazantsev, *Kolkhoznoe pravo* (1950 ed.), p. 51.

2 *Ibid.*, p. 53.

3 *Kolkhozy RSFSR* (Central Statistical Bureau, Moscow, 1930), p. 12.

4 *Direktivy VKP(b) po khoziaistvennym voprosam* (Directives of the All-Union Communist Party on Economic Matters, Moscow, 1931), pp. 620-21.

5 *KPSS v rezoliutsiakh*, Vol. 1, p. 546.

6 *Pravda*, January 6, 1930.

7 *Izvestiia*, March 9, 1930.

8 *Pravda*, January 24, 1930.

9 Stalin, *Sochineniia*, Vol. 6, p. 217.

10 *Direktivy VKP(b) po khoziaistvennym voprosam*, p. 679.

11 Stalin, *Voprosy leninizma* (Question of Leninism, 11th ed., Moscow, 1952), p. 351.

12 *Direktivy KPSS i Sovetskogo Pravitel'stva po khoziaistvennym voprosam* (Directives of the CPSU and Soviet Government on Economic Questions, 2 Vols., Moscow, 1957), Vol. 2, p. 211.

13 *Ibid.*, p. 263.

[14] Stalin, *Sochineniia*, Vol. 13, p. 118.
[15] Nikulikhin, *Kolkhoznoe dvizhenie na novom pod'eme*, p. 159.
[16] Agranovskii, *Kommuna, sovkhoz, kombinat*, p. 120.
[17] *Kolkhozy v 1930 g.*, p. 224.
[18] Dubkhovetskii, *Na putiakh k kommunizmu*, p. 34.
[19] *Krupnye kolkhozy RSFSR, spravochnik* (Big Kolkhozes of the RSFSR, Guidebook, Moscow, 1929), p. 19.
[20] Tretiakov, *Feld-Herren*.
[21] *Krupnye kolkhozy RSFSR, spravochnik*, pp. 63ff.
[22] *Pravda*, November 24, 1928.
[23] Strong, *The Soviets Conquer Wheat*, p. 206.
[24] *Ibid.*, p. 25.
[25] Agranovskii, *op. cit.*, pp. 5ff.
[26] Strong, *op. cit.*, p. 142.
[27] Levichev, *Sel'sovet litsom k kolkhozam*, p. 11.
[28] *Izvestiia*, September 11, 1929; January 22, 30, 1930.
[29] Strong, *op. cit.*, p. 150.
[30] Mehnert, *Youth in Soviet Russia*, p. 179.
[31] Strong, *op. cit.*, p. 147.
[32] *Pravda*, March 3, 1930.
[33] Budovnits, *Vesna 1930*, p. 48.
[34] Agranovskii, *op. cit.*, pp. 56ff.
[35] *Pravda*, June 2, 6, 1930.
[36] *Kolkhozy vesnoi 1931 goda* (The Kolkhozes in the Spring of 1931, Moscow, Leningrad, 1931), p. 10.
[37] Nikulikhin, *op. cit.*, p. 161.
[38] Nikulikhin, "Osnovnye voprosy kolkhoznogo dvizheniia" (Basic Question of the Kolkhoz Movement), *Bol'shevik*, No. 30, November, 1930, p. 24; *Pravda*, January 4, 1931.
[39] Stalin, *Sochineniia*, Vol. 13, pp. 217-18.
[40] Putintsev, *Politicheskaia rol' i taktika sekt*, p. 392.
[41] Kataev, *Dvizhenie, ianvar' i febral' 1930 goda na Kubani*, p. 198.
[42] *Ibid.*, p. 70.
[43] *Kolkhoznoe kooperativnoe zakondatel'stvo* (Kolkhoz Cooperative Legislation, Moscow, 1931), pp. 100ff.
[44] Kataev, *op. cit.*, pp. 198-99.
[45] V. F. Shustov, "Raspredelenie dokhodov i urozhaia v kolkhozakh" (Distribution of Income and Harvest in Kolkhozy), *Na fronte kollektivizatsii*, No. 18-19, August, 1930, p. 19.
[46] *Kolkhoznoe kooperativnoe zabondatel'stvo*, p. 129.
[47] *Direktivy KPSS* (1953), Vol. 2, pp. 341-42.
[48] *Kollektivizatsiia sel'skogo khoziaistva, vazhneishie resheniia kommunisticheskoi partii i sovetskogo pravitel'stva* (Collectivization of Agriculture: Most Important Decisions of the Communist Party and Soviet Government, 1927-1935, Moscow, 1957), p. 410.
[49] *Pervyi vsesoiuznyi s"ezd kolkhoznikov-udarnikov peredovykh kolkhozov*

(First All-Union Congress of Kolkhoz-Shock Workers of Leading Kolkhozy, Moscow, Leningrad, 1933), p. 94.

50 *Direktivy KPSS* (1953), Vol. 2, pp. 535, 538.

51 *Pravda,* September 1, 1938.

52 Agranovskii, *Kommuna, sovkhoz, kombinat,* p. 60.

53 Webb and Webb, *Soviet Communism,* pp. 185-86.

54 Bitsenko, *K voprosam teorii istorii kollektivizatsii,* p. 112.

55 I. Vareikis, "Zadachi organizatsii i ukrepleniia kolkhozov" (Tasks of Organization and Strengthening Kolkhozes), *Bol'shevik,* No. 10, May 31, 1930, p. 112.

56 Berta Lask, *Kollektivdorf und Sowjetgut* (Berlin, 1932), p. 157.

57 Dubkhovetskii, *Na putiakh k kommunizmu,* p. 37.

58 Nikulikhin, *Kolkhoznoe dvizhenie na novom pod'eme,* p. 214.

59 Strong, *op. cit.,* p. 214.

60 *Kolkhozy vesnoi 1930 goda,* p. 179.

61 V. P. Miliutin, *Sotsializm i sel' skoe khoziaistvo* (Socialism and Agriculture, Moscow, 1919), p. 50.

62 Kindeev, *Kollektivnye khoziaistva,* p. 171.

63 Nikulikhin, *op. cit.,* p. 214; I. Altaiskii, "K voprosu ob unichtozhenii klassovykh razlichii mezhdu proletariatom i krest'ianstvom" (On the Question of Obliteration of Class Differences Between the Proletariat and Peasantry), *Na agrarnom fronte,* July-August, 1932, p. 48.

64 Nikulikhin, *op. cit.,* p. 195.

65 *Pravda,* June 1, 1919.

66 Agranovskii, *op. cit.,* pp. 25-27.

67 Khalturin, *Dostoinaia imeni Lenina,* p. 20; Tretiakov, *op. cit.,* p. 20.

68 Budovnits, *Vesna 1930,* p. 40.

69 Strong, *op. cit.,* p. 198.

70 Lask, *op. cit.,* p. 154.

71 *Pravda,* June 1, 1919.

72 Putintsev, *Politicheskaia rol' i taktika sekt,* p. 374.

73 B. I. Baratov, *Kolkhoz 'Krasnaia Zor'ka'* (The 'Red Dawn' Kolkhoz, Moscow, 1930), p. 17.

74 Strong, *op. cit.,* p. 126.

75 Auhagen, *Das Schicksalwende des russlanddeutschen Bauerntums,* p. 70.

76 Alexandra Kollontai, *Communism and the Family* (trans. from Russian, New York, 1920?), pp. 7ff.

77 Clara Zetkin, *Errinnerungen an Lenin* (Berlin, 1957), pp. 72-73.

78 P. Malevsky-Malevitch, *Russia-USSR: A Complete Handbook* (New York, 1933), pp. 236-37.

79 Fülop-Miller, *The Mind and Face of Bolshevism,* p. 117.

80 Stepniak, *The Russian Peasantry,* p. 480; Iuzov (Kablits), *Russkie dissidenty,* p. 105.

81 Panferov, *op.cit.* in *Oktiabr',* January, 1960, p. 103.

82 Mehnert, *Youth in Russia,* p. 173.

83 *Kollektivizatsiia sel'skogo khoziaistva na Kubani,* pp. 152-53.

Chapter 11

[1] *100 Kolkhozy moskovskoi oblasti* (100 Kolkhozes of the Moscow District, Moscow, 1935).

[2] *Pervyi vsesoiuznyi s"ezd kolkhoznikov* (First All-Union Congress of Kolkhoz Workers, Moscow, Leningrad, 1933).

[3] *Istoriia kolkhoznogo prava*, Vol. 1, pp. 127, 132.

[4] *Ibid.*, p. 407.

[5] *Pravda*, July 12, 1930.

[6] *Istoriia kolkhoznogo prava*, Vol. 1, p. 375.

[7] Kazantsev, *Kolkhoznoe pravo* (1950 ed.), pp. 88-95.

[8] *Direktivy KPSS i Sovetskogo Pravitel'stva po khoziaistvennym voprosam* (1957), Vol. 2, pp. 451-62.

[9] Webb and Webb, *Soviet Communism*, pp. 213-14.

[10] *Istoriia kolkhoznogo prava*, Vol. 2, p. 118.

[11] *KPSS v rezoliutsiakh*, Vol. 2, p. 1157.

[12] *Pravda*, July 21, 1959.

[13] *Ibid.*, February 13, 1927.

[14] Nikulikhin, *Kolkhoznoe dvizhenie na novom pod'eme*, p. 123.

[15] Kazantsev, *Voprosy kolkhoznogo i zemel'nogo prava*, p. 257.

[16] John Maynard, *Collective Farming in the USSR* (London, 1931), p. 10.

[17] Mehnert, *Youth in Russia*, p. 184.

[18] Miliutin, *Sotsializm i sel'skoe khoziaistvo*, p. 52.

[19] Kindeev, *Kollektivnye khoziaistva*, p. 41.

[20] Rykov and Khmelev, *Sel'sko-khoziaistvennye kollektivy moskovskoi gubernii*, pp. 75-76.

[21] Agranovskii, *Ot stol'btsov do Bukhary*, p. 280.

[22] A. Williams-Ellis, "Life in a Communal Farm in Russia," *Spectator*, Vol. 144, March 29, 1930, p. 520.

[23] *Izvestiia*, November 13, 1925.

[24] *Kollektivizatsiia sel'sko-khoziaistva na Kubani*, p. 108.

[25] Tadeush, *Amerikanskaia kommuna "Seiatel'"*, p. 81.

[26] Tretiakov, *Feld-Herren*, p. 272.

[27] *New York Times*, February 22, 1931, Sec. III, p. 3.

[28] *Pravda*, July 2, 1927.

[29] Panferov, *op. cit.* in *Oktiabr'*, January, 1960, p. 106.

[30] Kindeev, *op. cit.*, p. 152.

[31] Farson, *Seeing Red: Today in Russia*, pp. 146-55.

[32] *Statisticheskii spravochnik SSSR 1927* (Statistical Guide of the USSR, Central Statistical Board, Moscow, 1927).

[33] Karpuzi and Meshcheriakov, *Opyt issledovaniia*, pp. 188, 411.

[34] *Kak zhivetsia v kommune*, p. 27.

[35] Chmyga, *Ocherki po istorii kolkhoznogo dvizheniia na Ukraine*, p. 191.

[36] Shiriaev, *Kak organizovat' kommunu ili artel'* (How to Organize a Commune or Artel, pamphlet, Moscow, 1921), p. 3.

[37] Tadeush, *op. cit.,* p. 67.

[38] Kindeev, *op. cit.,* pp. 152-53.

[39] I. Volodkovich and P. Kulinov, "K voprosu o razvitii kollektivizatsii v derevne" (On the Question of the Development of Collectivization in the Village), *Na agrarnom fronte,* January, 1927, p. 41; P. Kulikov, "Kontrol'nye tsifry po kolkhozam na 1928/29 g." (Control Figures for Kolkhozy for 1928-1929), *Na agrarnom fronte,* December 1928, p. 28.

[40] *Kollektivizatsiia sel'sko-khoziaistva na Kubani,* pp. 192-94.

[41] Gaister, *Materialy issledovaniia,* pp. 28-29.

Chapter 12

[1] A. Pashkov, "O perspektivakh slivaniia dvukh form sotsialisticheskoi sobstvennosti" (On the Prospects of Fusion of the Two Forms of Socialist Property), *Voprosy ekonomiki,* May, 1960, p. 41.

[2] Stalin, *Voprosy leninizma,* pp. 505-06.

[3] A. Obraztsov, "Zavtra kolkhoznogo sela" (The Future of the Kolkhoz Village), *Nauka i zhizn',* September 1960.

[4] Lenin, *op. cit.,* Vol, p. 176.

[5] *KPSS v rezoliutsiakh* (1953 ed.), Vol. 2, p. 597.

[6] See Richard Hughes, *The Chinese Communes* (Chester Springs, Pa., 1960).

[7] *Far Eastern Economic Review,* Vol. 37, No. 13. (September 27, 1962), p. 586.

Index

Adventists, 72, 74

Agrogorod, 237, 240

Amana Community: 18-19, 28; size of villages, 21

Anabaptists: in Germany, 17; advocacy of communism, 66

Anarchism: argument for equality, 62-65; in Revolution, 60-61, 238-239

Anarchist communes, 53, 61-62, 74; in France, 13

Anarchists, 6, 52, 81, 88, 111; advocacy of full communism, 60; in Kiev commune, 53

Artels: administration, 136; area, 160-161; collectivization in, 140-141; compared with communes and tozes, 7, 118; designated as "basic," 198-200; economic incentives, 133; equipment, 162; favored in division of estates, 104; land, 158-159; living space, 163; membership, 123-124; numbers, 119-120; origin of term, 46; size, 122

Artels, pre-Revolutionary: in agriculture, 50-51; organization, 46-48; origins, 47-49; use of term, 46

Bakunin, Mikhail, 59, 72

Baptists, 68, 74

Baptist-Stundists, division, 68

Bolshevik Party: agrarian program in 1917, 38 39; see also Lenin, Communist Party

Bonch-Bruevich, V. D., 75, 77

Bookkeeping in communes, 155, 173-174

Bukharin, N. I., 100, 117

Buriats, 49, 121

Cabet, Etienne, Icarian Society, 12

Campanella, Tommaso, *The City of The Sun,* 12

Chaikovskii Friends, 53

Chernyshevskii, N. G., view of village commune, 52

Child care: in communes, 31, 143-144; in Hutterite Brotherhoods, 19; in kibbutzim, 23, 26

Christian communism, 16-17

Collective farms. See kolkhozes

Collective consumption, 141-143, 215, 239

Committees of the Poor, 93, 106, 159, 189; foreshadowed, 38

72
74
75
76
77
79
81
83
85
88